CAMBRIDGE
Global English

Teacher's Resource

Annie Altamirano,
Caroline Linse and Elly Schottman

University Printing House, Cambridge CB2 8BS, United Kingdom

Cambridge University Press is part of the University of Cambridge.

It furthers the University's mission by disseminating knowledge in the pursuit of education, learning and research at the highest international levels of excellence.

www.cambridge.org
Information on this title: www.cambridge.org/9781107664968

© Cambridge University Press 2014

This publication is in copyright. Subject to statutory exception and to the provisions of relevant collective licensing agreements, no reproduction of any part may take place without the written permission of Cambridge University Press.

First published 2014

Printed in India by Replika Press Pvt. Ltd

A catalogue record for this publication is available from the British Library

ISBN 978-1-107-66496-8 Teacher's Resource

Cambridge University Press has no responsibility for the persistence or accuracy of URLs for external or third-party internet websites referred to in this publication, and does not guarantee that any content on such websites is, or will remain, accurate or appropriate.

Contents

Map of the Learner's Book	4
Introduction	6
How to use *Cambridge Global English*	7
Framework correlations	11
Unit 1 Look in a book	19
Unit 2 Good neighbours	32
Unit 3 Ready, steady, go!	44
Unit 4 The big sky	55
Unit 5 Let's count and measure	66
Unit 6 Bugs: Fact and fiction	78
Unit 7 Our green earth	89
Unit 8 Home, sweet home	100
Unit 9 Inside and outside cities	112
Photocopiable activities	124
Photocopiable word lists	144

Map of the Learner's Book

page	Unit	Words and expressions	Use of English	Reading/Writing
6–19	1 Look in a book	Books and parts of a book Classroom objects Numbers 1–15 Clothes and personal possessions *What is it about?* *How do you spell …?* *How do you say ___ in English?*	Singular/plural nouns *There is/are* … Present simple Possessive pronouns (*mine, yours*) Genitive 's *have got* + noun *like* + *ing* *Which one?* / *the ___ one*	Poems/songs Information text Write personal information Write about your school Write an original song verse Use a capital letter and full stop
20–33	2 Good neighbours	People and places in the community Extended family Places in the world Jobs Shops Ordinal numbers *Left, right* *A lot of*	Present continuous Question forms Present simple 3rd person endings: *-s, -es* Irregular plurals Prepositions of location	Poems/songs Information text Write a friendly letter Report information from an interview Write instructions collaboratively
34–47	3 Ready, steady, go!	Action verbs Parts of the body Numbers 1–20 Feelings (adjectives)	Imperatives *Can/can't* for ability Adverbs: *slowly, quickly* Conjunctions: *and, but, or* Determiners: *all, most, some* *I like /don't like* + verb + *-ing*	Poems/songs Information text Play: Native American tale Write information about birds Write an original song verse Write a riddle
48–61	4 The big sky	Weather Shadows Day and night: *Sun, moon, stars, planets* Time phrases: *Yesterday, in the morning, at night* Movement verbs	Past simple regular (*-ed*) and irregular forms Past simple of *be* Past simple question forms Time expressions: in the *morning/afternoon/evening; at night*	Poems/songs Information text Read and follow instructions Write informational sentences Report interview information (past tense)
62–75	5 Let's count and measure	Numbers 1–100 *How many? How far? How long?* *Metres, centimetres* Shapes Tell time to the hour	Past simple regular and irregular forms Countable and uncountable nouns with *some, a/an* *What (a)* + adj. + noun! *When* -clause	Poems and song Information text Traditional stories from India and Africa Write personal information Write a new verse
76–89	6 Bugs: Fact and fiction	Insects and spiders Parts of insects (wings, legs, antennae) Actions verbs	Prepositions: *above, under, near, on* Determiners: *all, some, most* Subject/verb agreement Regular and irregular past tense *How, What, How many, Do/Does?*	Poems/songs Information text Traditional story from Mexico Story elements: Plot (story map) Describe insects and what they do Write questions
90–103	7 Our green earth	Parks, leisure time Parts of a tree Fruits and vegetables Environmental issues *Would you like … I'd/We'd like…* *How about …?* *What does … mean?*	*-ing* forms as nouns (*no* + *-ing* form) *Must/mustn't* with rules/instructions *Can* for permission *Will* for future intentions/promises Determiners: *this, these, that, those*	Poems/songs Information text Write promises/intentions Write a poem Write your autobiography
104–117	8 Home, sweet home	Parts of a building Kinds of homes Climates (hot, cold, warm, cool, wet, dry) Rooms and furnishings Animal homes Construction materials *What is it made of?*	Present perfect *have* + object + infinitive *Have you ever…?* *Let's* and *How about* + *-ing* for suggestions *Would you like ___ or ___ ? I'd like…* *Too* to add information *Will* for future intention	Poems Narrative song Information text Information from diagrams Write descriptions of things Narrative writing (retell story)
118–131	9 Inside and outside cities	Buildings and other city words Holiday places and leisure activities Food and drink Opposites	*here/what would you like to …?* Comparative adjectives: *-er* and *more* + adjective; *better* Expressing agreement/disagreement: *So do I! I don't*	Poems/songs Information text Fable from Aesop (contemporary retelling) Write a poem (*haiku*) Write a picture caption (stating and explaining a preference)
132–143	Picture dictionary	Review of vocabulary and themes		

Listening/Speaking	School subjects	Phonics / Word study	Critical thinking / Values
Listen for information Follow instructions Ask and answer questions Collaborative problem solving Memory games Ask about an unknown word	Maths: Counting Using a contents page Using a dictionary	Letter names and sounds Vowels and consonants Sounds: *sh, ch, th* Short vowel sounds in initial and middle position Spelling dictation Compound words	*What can you find in a book?* Classifying Main ideas and details Values: Taking care of books and school supplies (responsibility, respect)
Listen for information Ask for, give and follow directions Roleplay + guessing game Interviews	Social studies: Communities Geography: Reading maps, using a map grid	Occupation words ending with *-er*: *singer, writer*, etc. Prefix *un-*	*Who lives in your neighbourhood?* Asking interview questions Interpreting maps Values: In a caring community, people help each other
Listen to and give instructions Discuss likes and dislikes Discuss and act out poems, song and play	Science: Different bird species; interpreting a chart Maths: Counting Physical education: Moving different parts of the body	Long vowel sounds and spellings: *ai, ay*; silent *e*	*How can we move in different ways?* Comparing and contrasting Classifying Values: Teamwork; an active life style keeps us healthy and happy
Listen for information Ask/answer questions Partner interviews Discuss and act out poems and song	Science: Shadows; weather; day and night; earth, moon, sun and planets	Long *i* spellings: *i, igh* Rhyming words Spelling dictation Compound words	*What is the sky like?* Making and using a sundial Comparing and contrasting Values: Appreciating and learning about the natural world
Listen for information Ask/answer questions Memory games Discuss and act out poems, songs and stories	Maths: Counting in 2s; measuring, completing chart, telling the time (to the hour); shapes	Homophones	*How do we use numbers?* Problem solving Sequencing Estimating Values: We can work together to help ourselves learn
Listen for information Ask/answer questions Discuss and act out poems, songs and stories Insect game	Science: Insects and spiders	Long *e* spellings (*-ee, -ea, me, s/he*) Rhyming words	*How are bugs special?* Classifying Comparing Study skills Graphic organisers Values: Appreciating and learning about the natural world
Listen for information Give/follow instructions Ask/answer questions Discuss and apply information Discuss and act out poems and song	Science and Social studies: Environmental issues; uses of trees Social studies: International signs Science: Plants; growing food	Long *o* spellings (*ou* and *ow*) Variant sounds of *ow*	*How can we care for the earth?* Problem solving Sequencing Study skills Values: We are responsible for taking care of the earth
Listen for information Ask/answer questions Share information Make decisions and choices Recite and discuss poems and song	Social studies: Homes around the world Geography: World places and climates Science: Homes built by animals; building materials	Long *u* spellings: Variant sounds of *oo* Rhyming words	*What kinds of homes do people and animals build?* Collaborative learning Values: Homes offer shelter and safety. Homes around the world are both similar and unique
Listen for information Recognise speaker's opinion Problem solving Discuss preferences Roleplay: Ask for food and drink Discuss and act out poem, song, and story	Geography: Mountains, beach, desert, etc. Social studies: Community places in a city	Identify opposites Count syllables Variant sounds of *c*	*What can we do in the town and countryside?* Comparing Supporting an opinion with reasons Values: Respecting different opinions and preferences

Map of the Learner's Book

Introduction

Welcome to *Cambridge Global English Stage 2*

Cambridge Global English is an eight-stage course for learners of English as a second language. The eight stages range from the beginning of primary to the penultimate year of junior secondary (roughly ages 6–13). The course has been designed to fulfil the requirements of the Cambridge English as a Second Language curriculum framework developed by Cambridge English Language Assessment. These internationally recognised standards provide a sequential framework for thorough coverage of basic English concepts and skills.

The materials reflect the following principles:

- *An international focus.* Specifically developed for young learners throughout the world, the themes, and situations and literature covered by *Cambridge Global English* strive to reflect this diversity and help learners find out about each other's lives through the medium of English. This fosters respect and interest in other cultures and leads to awareness of global citizenship.
- *An enquiry-based, language-rich approach to learning. Cambridge Global English* engages children as active, creative learners. As learners participate in a wide variety of curriculum-based activities, they simultaneously acquire content knowledge, develop critical thinking skills and practise English language and literacy. The materials incorporate a 'learning to learn' approach, helping children acquire skills and strategies that will help them approach new learning situations with confidence.
- *English for educational success.* To meet the challenges of the future, children need to develop facility with both conversational and academic English. From the earliest level, *Cambridge Global English* addresses both these competencies. *Cambridge Global English* presents authentic listening and reading texts, writing tasks, and culminating unit projects similar to those learners might encounter in English-medium and international schools. Emphasis is placed on developing the listening, speaking, reading and writing skills learners will need to be successful in using authentic English-language classroom materials. At Stage 2; the basic learning strategies introduced in Stage 1 are developed and practised. These continue the foundations for future language learning and development.
- *Rich vocabulary development.* Building a large and robust vocabulary is a cornerstone to success in both conversational and academic English. *Cambridge Global English* exposes learners to a wide range of vocabulary. Many opportunities for revising these words and using them in personalised, meaningful ways are woven into the activities and lesson plans.

- *Individualised learning.* We approach learning in an individual way by both acknowledging the individual nature of the knowledge and background of each child and encouraging their specific input. We also provide for differentiated learning in the classroom by offering a range of activities of varying difficulty and extra challenges. Unit by unit support for this is provided in the unit notes in this book.
- *Integrated assessment*. Throughout the course, teachers informally assess their learners' understanding of language and concepts. The Teacher's Resource provides suggestions for extending or re-teaching language skills based on learners' demonstrated proficiency. At the end of each unit, learners apply the skills and knowledge they have acquired as they work in groups to create and present a project of their choice. This provides teachers with an excellent performance assessment opportunity. An end-of-unit quiz in the Activity Book provides another evaluation measure: a quick progress check on learners' understanding of key ESL and early literacy skills.

Cambridge Global English can be used as a stand-alone ESL curriculum, or it can be used as part of an innovative suite of materials created by Cambridge University Press for young learners at international primary schools:

- *Cambridge Primary Science*
- *Cambridge Primary Mathematics*
- *Cambridge Primary English (L1)*
- *Cambridge Global English.*

We encourage you to learn more about these complementary courses through the Cambridge University Press website: education.cambridge.org

We hope that you and your learners will enjoy using these materials as much as we enjoyed developing them for you.

The *Cambridge Global English* team

How to use Cambridge Global English

A Components

Cambridge Global English offers the following components:

- The **Learner's Book** provides the core input of the course and consists of nine thematic units of study. Each unit contains six lessons developed around a unifying theme, and linked to a main question at the beginning of the unit. The materials cater for the needs of learners studying in a primary context, they feature skills-building tasks for listening, reading, writing and speaking, as well as language focuses. In addition, there is a strong vocabulary-building element to the course. Ways of introducing basic learning awareness skills are also explored through features such as:
  - Language tips
  - Words to remember
  - Language detective
  - Look what I can do!

  Materials are aimed at the learner with all the experiences that they bring to the classroom. Learners are encouraged to see the moral and social values that exist in many of the course texts, and find opportunities to reflect on these. We feel that the learner needs to be exposed to many different forms of text topics and styles in order to develop the skills of assessing, interpreting and responding appropriately to content. Therefore the course aims to provide a variety of factual and fictional texts, dialogues and poetry, on a range of different topics, at the appropriate level.

- The **Audio CDs** include all the listening material needed for the Learner's Book and Activity Book. The listening material supports the Learner's Book with listening, pronunciation and phonics activities, as well as songs and read-along stories. We recommend that learners also use the Audio CDs at home to practise the songs and stories, and to show their parents what they know.

- The **Activity Book** provides additional practice activities, deepening the understanding of language skills and content material introduced in the Learner's Book.

- The **Teacher's Resource** provides valuable guidance and support for using *Cambridge Global English* in your classroom. We understand that within each class there are learners of different abilities. It is very important to support differentiated work in the classroom and we do this through suggestions in the unit notes and additional differentiation 'challenge' activities in the Activity Book. The production skills required in the project work at the end of each unit can also be graded in terms of ability.
  At the end of the Teacher's Resource, photocopiable activities, cross-referenced in the unit notes, are provided to give additional work for each lesson.

A selection of lesson-by-lesson spelling words, which can be photocopied, cut out and given to the children to learn, are also included in the end section.

B Learner's Book structure

Cambridge Global English consists of nine thematic units of study, designed to cover approximately three units per term, in most educational systems. The Stage 2 Learner's Book is structured as follows:

- **Units:** Nine thematic units provide a year's worth of curriculum lessons.
- **Picture dictionary:** At the end of the book there is a thematically arranged Picture dictionary. This dictionary can be used for a number of activities, such as reviewing material at the end of terms, but its main aim is to introduce the concept of using a dictionary in order to look up the meaning of words. This should be done on a fairly regular basis, so that the learners become accustomed to the idea.

C Unit structure

Each unit is divided up into six lessons. The length of lessons will vary from school to school, so a strict time limit for each lesson has not been prescribed. Lessons are structured as follows:

- **Lesson 1 Think about it:** Lesson 1 introduces the main topic, in the form of a question, which should be a trigger for input from the learners in line with the enquiry-led approach of the course. A short poem and main picture lead into the topic of the unit, giving learners an opportunity to identify key vocabulary items. This leads to vocabulary practice tasks and culminates in a productive task.
- **Lesson 2 Find out more:** Lesson 2 is geared to deeper learning about a curriculum topic. It usually involves a short listening or reading passage followed by critical thinking skills and guided writing tasks.
- **Lesson 3 Words and sounds:** Lesson 3 focuses on the mechanics of reading and pronunciation, including phonics, alphabet skills, reading, listening and writing skills. It usually contains a song or simple phonics story and a range of activities.
- **Lesson 4 Use of English:** Lesson 4 focuses on developing language skills through contextualised activities. It involves combinations of speaking, writing and reading activities.
- **Lesson 5 Read and respond:** Lesson 5 focuses on literacy and reading stories, poems and factual texts. It allows the learner to explore a variety of text types and develop comprehension and writing skills through related activities.

- **Lesson 6 Choose a project:** Lesson 6 is the consolidation and production section of the unit. Learners produce a project related to the unit content. Lesson 6 begins with a restatement of the initial unit question and leads to a review of what has been learned in the course of the unit. Learner independence is enhanced by allowing choice. Learners choose one of three projects to complete. At the end of the lesson they carry out a short activity (*Look what I can do!*) where learners can be encouraged to identify and demonstrate skills they have accumulated during the course of the unit.

D Activity Book

Each lesson in the Learner's Book is supported by two Activity Book pages that reinforce learning through activities, clearly framed within the 'I can' objectives of the course. The Activity Book provides basic practice and reinforcement of vocabulary, use of English, writing and concepts. It also provides opportunities for personalisation and creative work, as well as activities that can offer a higher level of challenge to support differentiated classroom situations. The last lesson of each unit in the Activity Book is devoted to an end-of-unit quiz, offering more in-depth assessment of what the learners have achieved.

E Customising your lessons

Support for planning each lesson and teaching objectives are provided in the main unit notes of this book. When planning, please also bear in mind the following:

- These are ideas and guidelines only, you should adapt them to your situation and the needs of your learners. Do not be afraid of changing things and bringing in to the classroom additional elements of your own.
- Monitor your learners. If they need additional support for some aspect of the book or particular skills work, tailor the material to their needs.
- Learners of this age group need repetition and revision. Do not be afraid of going over material several times. We would encourage you to continue singing songs, reading stories and playing games throughout the year. Create routines and chants that learners can join in with.
- Be creative in developing craft activities and role-plays. Some suggestions are given but there is much more that can be done. Try combining English with arts and crafts classes.
- Try to encourage learning/teaching/showing between classes of different age groups.
- Draw on parental support where possible. There are 'home–school link' suggestions in every unit.

When using the book, the following guidelines might also be useful:

Before using the Learner's Book

- Engage in warm-up activities (songs, total physical response (TPR), vocabulary games, alphabet chants, etc.).
- Pre-teach and practise key language learners will encounter in the Learner's Book and Audio CDs.

While using the Learner's Book

- Keep learners actively engaged.
- Use the artwork in Lesson 1 as a conversation starter: ask learners to name everything they see in the picture; play *I Spy*, etc.
- Vary the group dynamics in the lesson: move from whole group response to individual response to pairwork, etc.
- Provide opportunities for learners to ask questions as well as answer them.
- Encourage learners to act out the language in the lessons.
- Encourage learners to use language structures and vocabulary to talk about their own ideas, opinions and experiences.
- In class discussions, write the learners' ideas on class charts. You can refer back to these charts in later lessons.
- Adjust your reading and writing expectations and instructions to suit the literacy level of your learners.

Using the Activity Book and further suggestions

- Use the Activity Book pages related to the Learner's Book pages.
- Depending on the ability of the learners, use the 'Additional support and practice' activities and/or 'Extend and challenge' activities suggested in the Teacher's Resource at the end of every lesson.
- Do a Wrap up activity or game at the end of every lesson.
- Give homework assignments at the end of every lesson, especially vocabulary reinforcement activities:
  - Learners draw and label a picture scene with vocabulary items
  - Learners write and illustrate several sentences using vocabulary items
  - Learners create flash cards
  - Learners play games such as *What's Missing?* or *Concentration* with a family member using a set of learner-made Word flashcards (*Concentration* requires a double set of flashcards – 6–10 pairs of words)
  - Learners make 'favourite word' posters where they draw a picture of their favourite word from each lesson/unit.

We would strongly recommend that you supplement this core material with the following:
- An extended reading programme to provide learners with practice of different types of books, leading ultimately to reading independence. It is recommended that you regularly set aside time for the learners to read books of their choice in class and that they are encouraged to read at home.
- 'Real' materials incorporated into the classroom as far as possible in order to create more interest in the lessons.
- Exposure to additional audiovisual material such as television programmes, songs and film excerpts so that the learners begin to feel confident in their ability to decode and understand a range of media in English.
- Supplementary handwriting and phonics materials to help build on those skills at this crucial time in the learner's linguistic development.

F Setting up the primary classroom

While there is not always a lot of flexibility in setting up the primary classroom, it would be useful to arrange the learning space in the following way:
- Set up tables in groups so learners can work together and have a bigger surface to do so when doing end-of-unit projects and craft activities.
- Set aside uncluttered spaces for learners to move around in, do circle activities, role-plays, etc.
- Designate a reading corner in the room in which you read to the learners and they also read independently. Make a space for a 'class library' with a variety of books that changes all the time.
- Reserve wall space to make displays of the learners' work, show words to remember, etc. Change these regularly to maintain learner interest.

G Assessment

We recommend that you take the time and opportunity to observe and monitor the progress and development of your learners. Many opportunities for informal assessment are provided through the projects, as well as in the self-assessment sections (*Look what I can do!*) in the Learner's Book. A restatement of the objectives is provided at the top of most pages in the Activity Book and in the 'Look what I can do!' statements and end-of-unit quizzes in the Activity Book.

At the beginning of the year, create individual portfolio folders to keep work that shows how the learners have been meeting the curriculum objectives. Use the portfolio to create a feeling of achievement and pride in learners about what they have achieved over the year. Keep this portfolio for parent–teacher meetings and send it home to show the parents/carers either at the end of each term or the end of the year. You might also want to include a letter to parents/carers outlining what the learners have achieved over the year.

If you would like further learner assessment opportunities, a table of how the Cambridge English Language Assessment exams for primary stages fit in with the *Cambridge Global English* levels is set out below:

Cambridge English Language Assessment exams for primary stages

Stage	Assessment	CEFR level
6		
5	Cambridge English: Key (KET) for Schools	A2
4		
3	Cambridge English: Flyers (YLE Flyers)	
2	Cambridge English: Movers (YLE movers)	A1
1	Cambridge English: Starters (YLE starters)	

H The home–school relationship

Support and encouragement at home is extremely important at this age. Encourage parents either face-to-face or via letter/email to become as involved as possible in their child's learning process by asking them what they have learned after every lesson, allowing children to 'teach' them what they have learned, taking an interest in what they bring home or want to perform for them and supporting any work the learners might try to do at home.

I Icons

The following icons have been used to clearly signpost areas of special interest or as shorthand for specific instructions:

Audio and track number reference. These appear in the Learner's Book, the Activity Book and the Teacher's Resource.

Speaking opportunity / activity recommended for pairwork or small group work. These appear in the Learner's Book, the Activity Book and Teacher's Resource.

Cross-curricular maths and science topics. These appear in the Learner's Book, the Activity Book and the Teacher's Resource.

Links directly to Activity Book activity and references it. These appear in the Learner's Book and the Teacher's Resource.

Activity to be written in the learner's notebook. These appear in the Learner's Book and the Activity Book.

Activity to be done out of the book, in a more active classroom setting. These appear in the Teacher's Resource.

Activity incorporating a song. These appear in the Learner's Book and in the Activity Book.

Framework correlations

Learning objectives from the Cambridge Primary English as a Second Language Curriculum Framework:
Stage 2 correlated with *Cambridge Global English*, Stage 2

Below you will find a table setting out specifically where to find coverage of the framework objectives for Stage 2.

Cambridge Primary English as a Second Language Framework: Stage 2	CGE Unit 1	CGE Unit 2	CGE Unit 3	CGE Unit 4	CGE Unit 5	CGE Unit 6	CGE Unit 7	CGE Unit 8	CGE Unit 9
Reading									
R1 Recognise, identify and sound, with support, a limited range of language at text level	✓	✓	✓	✓	✓	✓	✓	✓	✓
R2 Read and follow, with support, familiar instructions for classroom activities	✓	✓	✓	✓	✓	✓	✓	✓	✓
R3 Begin to read, with support, very short simple fiction and non-fiction texts with confidence and enjoyment	✓	✓	✓	✓	✓	✓	✓	✓	✓
R4 Understand the main points of very short, simple texts on some familiar general and curricular topics by using contextual clues	✓	✓	✓	✓	✓	✓	✓	✓	✓
R5 Understand, with support, some specific information and detail in very short, simple texts on a limited range of general and curricular topics	✓	✓	✓	✓	✓	✓	✓	✓	✓
R6 Understand the meaning of very short, simple texts on familiar general and curricular topics by rereading them	✓	✓	✓	✓	✓	✓	✓	✓	✓

Cambridge Primary English as a Second Language Framework: Stage 2	CGE Unit 1	CGE Unit 2	CGE Unit 3	CGE Unit 4	CGE Unit 5	CGE Unit 6	CGE Unit 7	CGE Unit 8	CGE Unit 9
R7 Understand the meaning of simple short sentences on familiar general and curricular topics	✓	✓	✓	✓	✓	✓	✓	✓	✓
R7 Use, with more infrequent support, a simple picture dictionary	Opportunities throughout to use picture dictionary in back of book								
Writing									
W1 Plan, write and check, with support, short sentences on familiar topics	✓	✓	✓	✓	✓	✓	✓	✓	✓
W2 Write, with support, short sentences which give basic personal information	✓	✓	✓	✓	✓		✓		✓
W3 Write short familiar instructions with support from their peers		✓					✓		
W4 Begin to use joined-up handwriting in a limited range of written work	Opportunities provided but not taught specifically								
W5 Link with support words or phrases using basic coordinating connectors	✓		✓	✓			✓	✓	
W6 Use upper and lower case letters accurately when writing names, places and short sentences during guided writing activities	✓	✓	✓	✓	✓	✓	✓	✓	✓
W7 Spell a growing number of familiar high-frequency words accurately during guided writing activities	✓	✓	✓	✓	✓	✓	✓	✓	✓

Cambridge Primary English as a Second Language Framework: Stage 2	CGE Unit 1	CGE Unit 2	CGE Unit 3	CGE Unit 4	CGE Unit 5	CGE Unit 6	CGE Unit 7	CGE Unit 8	CGE Unit 9
W8 Include a full stop and question mark during guided writing of short, familiar sentences	✓	✓	✓	✓	✓	✓	✓	✓	✓
Use of English									
UE1 Use singular nouns, plural nouns – including some common irregular plural forms – and uncountable nouns, genitive 's/s' to name and label things	✓	✓	✓	✓	✓	✓	✓	✓	✓
UE2 Use numbers 1-50 to count	1-15		1-20		✓	✓		✓	
UE3 Use adjectives, including possessive adjectives, on familiar topics to give personal information and describe things	✓	✓	✓	✓	✓	✓		✓	✓
UE4 Use determiners *a, the, some, any, this, these, that* to refer to familiar objects	✓	✓	✓	✓	✓	✓	✓	✓	
UE5 Use *who, what, where, how many* to ask questions on familiar topics; use impersonal *you* in the question: *How do you spell that?*	✓	✓	✓	✓	✓	✓	✓	✓	✓
UE6 Use demonstrative pronouns *this, these, that, those* and object pronoun *one* in short statements and responses	✓				✓		✓	✓	

Cambridge Primary English as a Second Language Framework: Stage 2	CGE Unit 1	CGE Unit 2	CGE Unit 3	CGE Unit 4	CGE Unit 5	CGE Unit 6	CGE Unit 7	CGE Unit 8	CGE Unit 9
UE7 Use personal subject and object pronouns, including possessive pronouns *mine, yours* to give basic personal information and describe things	✓	✓	✓	✓	✓	✓	✓	✓	✓
UE8 Use imperative forms [positive and negative] to give short instructions		✓	✓				✓		
UE9 Use common simple present forms, including short answer forms and contractions, to give personal information	✓	✓	✓	✓		✓			✓
Use common past simple forms [regular and irregular] to describe actions and narrate simple events including short answer forms and contractions				✓	✓	✓	✓	✓	
UE10 Use common present continuous forms, including short answers and contractions, to talk about what is happening now on personal and familiar topics		✓	✓	✓			✓		✓
Use *–ing* forms *swimming, spelling* as nouns to describe familiar and classroom activities			✓		✓		✓		✓
UE11 Use *there is/are* to make short statements and descriptions	✓	✓		✓	✓		✓		

Cambridge Primary English as a Second Language Framework: Stage 2	CGE Unit 1	CGE Unit 2	CGE Unit 3	CGE Unit 4	CGE Unit 5	CGE Unit 6	CGE Unit 7	CGE Unit 8	CGE Unit 9
Use *Have you [ever] been?* to talk about experiences								✓	✓
UE12 Use adverbs of time and place *now, today, over, there*, to indicate when and where				✓	✓			✓	
Use common *–ly* adverbs to describe actions			✓		✓				
Use the adverb *too* to add information					✓			✓	
UE13 Use *can* to make requests and ask permission and use appropriate responses *here you are, OK*					✓		✓	✓	✓
Use *must* to express obligation;					✓		✓		✓
Use *have + object + infinitive* to talk about obligations								✓	
Use *will* to talk about future intention							✓	✓	
Use *What/How about* + noun/-ing to make suggestions							✓	✓	✓
UE14 Use prepositions of location, position and direction: *at, behind, between, in, in front of, near, next to, on, to*		✓		✓	✓	✓	✓	✓	✓
Use prepositions of time: *on, in, at*, to talk about days and times;				✓	✓				✓
Use *with* to indicate accompaniment and instrument and *for* to indicate recipient	✓			✓	✓	✓	✓	✓	

Cambridge Primary English as a Second Language Framework: Stage 2	CGE Unit 1	CGE Unit 2	CGE Unit 3	CGE Unit 4	CGE Unit 5	CGE Unit 6	CGE Unit 7	CGE Unit 8	CGE Unit 9
UE15 Use *Would you like to …* to invite and use appropriate responses *yes please, no thanks*							✓	✓	✓
Use declarative *what [a/an]* + adjective + noun to show feelings					✓		✓		
UE16 Use conjunctions *and, or, but* to link words and phrases	✓	✓	✓	✓	✓	✓			✓
UE17 Use *when* clauses to describe simple present and past actions on personal and familiar topics	✓			✓			✓	✓	
Use *so do I* to give short answers									✓
Listening									
L1 Understand an increased range of short, basic, supported classroom instructions	✓	✓	✓	✓	✓	✓	✓	✓	✓
L2 Understand a growing range of short supported questions which ask for personal information	✓	✓	✓	✓	✓	✓	✓	✓	✓
L3 Understand an increasing range of short supported questions on general and curricular topics	✓	✓	✓	✓	✓	✓	✓	✓	✓
L4 Understand the main points of short supported talk on an increasing range of general and curricular topics	✓	✓	✓	✓	✓	✓	✓	✓	✓

Cambridge Primary English as a Second Language Framework: Stage 2	CGE Unit 1	CGE Unit 2	CGE Unit 3	CGE Unit 4	CGE Unit 5	CGE Unit 6	CGE Unit 7	CGE Unit 8	CGE Unit 9
L5 Understand some specific information and detail of short, supported talk on an increasing range of general and curricular topics	✓	✓	✓	✓	✓	✓	✓	✓	✓
L6 Use contextual clues to predict content and meaning in short supported talk on an increasing range of general and curricular topics	✓	✓	✓	✓	✓	✓	✓	✓	✓
L7 Understand short, supported narratives on an increasing range of general and curricular topics	✓	✓	✓	✓	✓	✓	✓	✓	✓
L8 Recognise words that are spelled out in a limited range of general and curricular topics	✓			✓		✓			
L9 Identify initial, middle and final phonemes and blends	✓	✓	✓	✓	✓	✓	✓	✓	
Speaking									
S1 Make basic statements which provide personal information on a limited range of general topics	✓	✓	✓	✓	✓	✓	✓	✓	✓
S2 Ask questions to find out about an increasing range of personal information	✓	✓	✓	✓	✓	✓	✓	✓	✓
S3 Describe basic present and past actions on a limited range of general and curricular topics	✓	✓	✓	✓	✓	✓	✓	✓	✓

Cambridge Primary English as a Second Language Framework: Stage 2	CGE Unit 1	CGE Unit 2	CGE Unit 3	CGE Unit 4	CGE Unit 5	CGE Unit 6	CGE Unit 7	CGE Unit 8	CGE Unit 9
S4 Use basic vocabulary for a limited range of general and curricular topics	✓	✓	✓	✓	✓	✓	✓	✓	✓
S5 Give short, basic descriptions of people and objects	✓		✓	✓	✓	✓	✓	✓	✓
S6 Contribute a growing range of suitable words, phrases, and sentences during short pair, group and whole class exchanges	✓	✓	✓	✓	✓	✓	✓	✓	✓
S7 Take turns when speaking with others in a growing range of short, basic exchanges	✓	✓	✓	✓	✓	✓	✓	✓	✓
S8 Relate very short, basic stories and events on a limited range of general and curricular topics	✓	✓	✓	✓	✓	✓	✓	✓	✓

Common European Framework of Reference (CEFR) guidelines

The Cambridge Primary English as a Second Language Curriculum Framework is mapped to the Council of Europe's Common European Framework of Reference for Languages (CEFR). For more information about the CEFR framework, please visit its website. The framework correlation to the *Cambridge Global English* stages (or levels) is set out in the table below. However, since the course material has been written for an ESL context (which has less rigid conceptions about language level) it can move more fluidly between CEFR levels.

Comparative CEFR levels for CGE stages

	Cambridge Global English stage					
	1	2	3	4	5	6
Reading CEFR level	Working towards A1	Low A1	High A1	Low A2	Mid A2	High A2
Writing CEFR level	Working towards A1	Low A1	High A1	Low A2	Mid A2	High A2
Use of English CEFR level	Low A1	High A1	Low A2	Mid A2	High A2	Low B1
Listening CEFR level	Low A1	High A1	Low A2	Mid A2	High A2	Low B1
Speaking CEFR level	Low A1	High A1	Low A2	Mid A2	High A2	Low B1

1 Look in a book

Big question What can you find in a book?

Unit overview

In this unit learners will:
- discuss what books are for and what types of books there are
- identify and describe different types of objects
- ask each other questions: *What's your name? Can you spell your name please?*
- introduce a new friend: *This is my friend. His/Her name is ...*

Learners will build communication and literacy skills as they read and listen to a poem and a song, recite a poem about books, sing a song about books, talk about different types of books and books they like, identify sounds at the beginning and in the middle of words, spell words and count up to 15.

At the end of the unit, they will apply and personalise what they have learned by working in small groups to complete a project of their choice: making a poster about things they like to read about, making word cards for things in the classroom or interviewing a friend.

Language focus
Singular and plural nouns: *There is/There are*
Possessive *'s*
Use of articles: *a/an*
Possessive pronouns: *mine, yours, one*
Compound nouns: *lunchbox, classroom, bedroom, bookshop, backpack, hairbrush*
Sight words: *open, read, when*
Review of: present tense and imperative, personal pronouns, possessive adjectives
Vocabulary topics: number and colour review, classroom objects, books

Critical thinking
- Analysing what makes a poem
- Predicting
- Memorising.

Self-assessment
- I can write about myself.
- I can talk about a book.
- I can name the vowels and read words with short vowel sounds.
- I can say who things belong to.
- I can understand the words of a song.

Teaching tips

Provide opportunities for extended reading by bringing in different books suitable for the level of learners. Encourage learners to handle them, look at the covers and illustrations, read extracts, and if possible, borrow the books for home reading. If it is not possible to take the books home, you may wish to allocate a few minutes at least once a week to reading a story in class.

Review learners' work on the quiz, noting areas where they demonstrate strength and areas where they need additional instruction and practice. Use this information to customise your teaching as you continue to **Unit 2**.

Lesson 1: Think about it

What can you find in a book?

Learner's Book pages: 6–7
Activity Book pages: 4–5

Lesson objectives

Listening: Listen to a poem and a conversation.

Speaking: Ask and answer questions, practise theme vocabulary, talk about yourself.

Reading: Recite and read a poem, read and identify key vocabulary.

Writing: Write about yourself.

Critical thinking: Discuss what makes a poem; fill information in a chart and interpret the results.

Language focus: Singular and plural nouns: *book, books*; possessive *'s*: *Nick's backpack*; *There is/There are*.

Vocabulary: Colour and number review; *bookcase, cupboard, tablet, e-book, book cover, pages*

Materials: A calendar, a set of weather symbols, a jar, craft sticks, chart paper, coloured card, staples and markers, photos (optional), enough copies of **Photocopiable activity 1** for the class.

Learner's Book

Warm up

- Ask each learner *What's your name?*
- Establish a warm-up routine for learners to do at the beginning of each class. Each day, learners identify the day of the week and describe the weather, e.g. *Today is Tuesday. It is cold and cloudy.*
- Give learners a copy of **Photocopiable activity 1** to make the weather icons.
- Then help learners to keep count of how many days of school there have been so far. To do this, they add a craft stick to a jar each school day. When ten sticks have accumulated, wrap an elastic band around the bundle of ten sticks. The next day there will be one bundle of ten plus one single stick.
- Write the learners' responses on a chart and then add one or more Learning Objectives. These will often match the 'I can' statements at the end of the unit. A daily chart might look like this:
Today is Tuesday.
It is cold and cloudy.
It is the 14th day of school.
Today we will read and talk about the parts of a book.

Introduce vocabulary

- Ask learners if they read and what they like reading. Ask them what they can find in a book. Elicit answers and write them on the board.
- Open the Learner's Book at page 6. Learners point to and name objects they see in the picture which they know the names of in English. Write the objects they name on a chart. Read the chart together.

Answers
Learners' own answers.

1 Read and listen

- Ask learners: *Which book has stayed inside your head?* Tell them which one has stayed inside your head. Elicit answers from learners.
- Point to the poem. Say: *Read and listen.*
- Play the audio a few times. Pause for learners to repeat each line.
- Practise reciting the poem together.
- **Critical thinking:** Ask learners to read the poem again and ask what makes a poem: *rhyming words, text divided into verses*. Ask them to find words that rhyme: *read, head*.

Audioscript: Track 2. See Learner's Book page 6.

Answers
Learners' own answers.

2 Which book?

- Point to the picture and focus on the children and the title of the book each child is reading.
- Ask learners to predict what the books may be about, e.g. *'The Snowy Day' is about a rabbit and a duck. They are playing in the snow.* Help learners with additional vocabulary they may need.
- In pairs, learners ask each other which one they would like to read. Encourage them to give reasons for their answer, e.g. *Which one do you want to read? I want to read The Snowy Day. I like stories with animals.*
- Tell learners they are going to listen to the children talking about the books. They listen and point to the correct book.
- Play the audio at least twice.

Audioscript: Track 3

Boy 1: I'm reading a story about two boys – the boys are friends. They play together, and they have a lot of adventures. It's a very exciting book.

Boy 2: My book tells you how to make things from paper. You can make a paper plane, a paper bird, and lots of other things. I want to make a paper plane.

Girl 1: I'm reading a story about two friends: a rabbit and a duck. It's a funny story. Look what they're making with snow!

Girl 2: I'm learning some interesting things about sharks. Look, here's a picture of one. This shark is very big and very scary.

Boy 3: There are lots of songs in this book. I can play them on my guitar. And I can sing the words too.
Old Macdonald had a farm e i e i o.

Answers
Boy 1 *Two Friends*
Boy 2 *Fun with Paper*
Girl 1 *The Snowy Day*
Girl 2 (girl bottom left with tablet)
Boy 3 *Play and Sing*

3 Topic vocabulary

- Play the audio once up to the pause.
- Play the first part of the audio again. Pause after each sentence for learners to repeat and point to the object.
- Write the words on the board. Read the words together.
- Tell learners to look at the big picture on page 6. Play the last part of the audio once.
- Play the last part of the audio again and tell learners to listen and follow the instructions.

Audioscript: Track 4

Bookcase. There are lots of books in the bookcase.

Book cover. The name of a book is on the book cover.

Tablet. You can read books and play games on a tablet.

E-book. This e-book is about sharks.

Cupboard. There are some pens and a book in the cupboard.

Pages. There are lots of pages in a book.

[*PAUSE*]

Point to a tablet with an e-book on it. What colour is the shark?

Find a book inside the cupboard. Point to it. What colour is the book?

Point to a book called *Play and Sing*. What colour is the book cover?

Point to the book with the most pages. It's a big fat book! What colour is it?

Answers
What colour is the shark? Grey
What colour is the book? Purple
What colour is the book cover? Green
What colour is it? Blue

4 Colours and numbers

- Review colour words. Play a game, e.g. *I spy*. Say: *I spy with my little eye something (blue)*. After a few rounds, ask a few learners to take the leading role.
- Review numbers and colours. Ask learners about objects in the classroom, e.g. *How many tables/yellow pencils are there?*
- Focus on the activity. In pairs, learners look at the big picture and ask and answer questions about the colour and number of objects.
- Circulate, checking for correct pronunciation and use of language, especially the use of *There is/There are*.
- Encourage learners to ask as many questions as possible since the picture offers a lot of possibilities.

Answers
Learners' own answers.

 For further practice, see Activities 1, 2 and 3 in the Activity Book.

5 Make a book about you!

- Tell learners they are going to make a book about themselves. You could have one ready to show learners so it is easier for them to grasp the idea.
- Provide plenty of practice by asking questions about their possessions, e.g. *This is Susan's book; Is this Cheng's notebook?* Encourage learners to describe each other's possessions to the class in this way.
- Guide learners through the instructions to make their book.
- Learners make the book cover. If appropriate, they may add a photograph to it.

Answers
Learners' own answers.

 For further practice, see Activity 4 in the Activity Book.

Wrap up

- Collect all the books and ask learners to help you prepare a book fair to display their work. You may wish to invite parents or other classes to see the fair. Each learner describes their book.
- **Home–school link:** Learners show the book to parents and explain what they did in class. They can also make a similar book about one of their parents, or someone in their family, and bring it to the class.
- **Portfolio opportunity:** Collect the books learners have made. Write the date and keep them in their portfolios.

Activity Book

1 Draw and colour

- Direct learners' attention to the picture and read the instructions. They draw the objects.
- After they have finished drawing, ask them to add up the number of books and answer the question.
- After they have answered the question, ask them to colour in the books according to the instructions.

Answer
9

2 Write about yourself

- Ask learners to speak about themselves and revise: *How old are you? I'm ... , How old is (Lisa)? She's ... .*
- Tell learners to answer the questions. Explain that they are going to use this information to make a book later on.

Answers
Learners' own answers.

3 What do you like?

- Ask learners questions about what they like and don't like. Ask learners to read the sentences and tick what is true for them.

- **Challenge:** Tell learners to think about what they like. Tell them to look in the **Picture dictionary** on page 133 for some ideas and then write a sentence.

> **Answers**
> Learners' own answers.

4 Draw and write

- Tell learners to draw a picture of something that belongs to them.
- Ask learners to write a label with their name and the name of the object.

I can write about myself.

- Direct learners' attention to the self-evaluation question at the top of page 4. Ask them to think and answer. Emphasise the importance of giving an honest answer.

> **Answers**
> Learners' own answers.

Differentiated instruction

Additional support and practice

- Create a favourite colour chart with the class. Ask: *What colour do you like best?*
- Learners write their name on a square of coloured paper then place the paper in the appropriate row. Discuss the completed chart: *How many children like purple best? What is X's favourite colour?*
- **Critical thinking:** Explain that you use a table or a chart to organise information. Ask how many columns and rows there are in this chart. What other types of information can they organise in this way?

Extend and challenge

- Give each learner eight index cards for a vocabulary concentration activity. They write and illustrate eight vocabulary words, e.g. colours, numbers, new vocabulary. In pairs, lay cards face down in four rows of four cards. Learners take turns turning over two cards, one at a time, saying the words aloud. If two matching cards are turned over, the player keeps the pair of cards. If the cards do not match, the player turns them face down again and it is the next player's turn.

Lesson 2: Find out more

Inside a book

Learner's Book pages: 8–9
Activity Book pages: 6–7

Lesson objectives

Speaking: Discuss the contents of a book.
Reading: Read about different types of books.
Writing: Guided writing.
Critical thinking: Understanding the difference between fiction and non-fiction, predicting, giving opinions.

Language focus: Possessive adjectives: *my, your*
Review of: *present simple tense, imperative*
Vocabulary: *author, title, inside, contents, chapter, fiction, non-fiction, character, information, scary, story*

Materials: A choice of different types of children's books, one copy of **Photocopiable activity 2** for each learner, chart paper, sheets of paper, card, staples and markers.

Learner's Book

Warm up

- Learners identify the day of the week and describe the weather and add a craft stick to the jar.
- Write the learners' responses on a chart and then add one or more Learning Objectives.
- Divide the class into small groups and ask them to recite one line of the poem in **Lesson 1** each. Do several rounds until all the groups have recited a line. Then ask the class to recite the whole poem together.

Introduce vocabulary

- Review with learners the names of their favourite books. Write the titles on the board. Explain the meaning of *title*.
- Ask learners if they know who the author is. Explain the meaning of *author*. Say: *The author is the person who …* Point at a book and mime 'write' to encourage learners to complete the sentence.
- You could mention popular authors of children's books the learners may know.

1 A book cover

- Tell learners to look at the book cover on page 8.
- Ask them who the author is and to identify the title.
- **Critical thinking:** Ask learners to predict what the book is about. Write the following phrases on the board and encourage learners to use them: *I agree / I don't agree / I think …*
- Ask learners to look at the cover of their own Learner's Book and answer the same questions.
- Ask them to look for more books in the classroom or in their Learner's Book and choose one. Ask them to answer the questions again.

> **Answers**
> **Author:** Jack Adler
> **Title:** *Busy Boats*
> **What is the book about?** Boats – the picture on the cover would suggest that it's about working boats, for example those used to catch fish.

For further practice, see Activity 1 in the Activity Book.

2 Inside a book

- Focus on the illustration of the **Contents page** and ask learners what information this page gives about a book. Elicit the words *page* and *chapter*.

22   Cambridge Global English Stage 2 Teacher's Resource

- Read the sentences together and ask learners to work in pairs to find the answers to the questions.
- After they have finished, ask them to choose one of the books available to them in the class and look for the contents page. Ask them to find out how many chapters there are and whether they have titles or numbers.

> **Answers**
> a small boat: Chapter 1 'Little boats' page 2
> b big boat: Chapter 2 'Big boats' page 5
> c new boat: Chapter 4 'New boats' page 10
> d an old boat: Chapter 3 'Old boats' page 8

3 Fiction or non-fiction?

- Use the books available in the class to introduce the concepts of *fiction* and *non-fiction*. Read the explanations with the class.
- Focus on *The Snowy Day*. Ask learners to identify the characters.
- Focus on the books on the page and ask learners to classify them as either *fiction* or *non-fiction*.
- Ask learners to look at the other books they have in the class. Tell them to classify them into fiction and non-fiction.
- **Critical thinking:** Provide plenty of opportunities for learners to examine and discuss the contents of books to decide if they are fiction or non-fiction. You could bring other books from the school library for learners to examine.

> **Answers**
> **Who are the characters?** A rabbit and a duck
> **Fiction books:** *The Elves and the Shoemaker, The Flying Panda, Four Friends Have an Adventure*
> **Non-fiction books:** *Make Fantastic Cakes, The Elephants of India, How Do Planes Fly?*

 For further practice, see Activity 2 in the Activity Book.

4 Choose a book

- Ask learners to read what the two children say. What sort of books do they like?
- Ask them to look back at the selection of books in **Activity 3** and choose a book the children would like to read. Encourage them to justify their choice.
- Ask them which of these books they would like to read and why.

> **Answers**
> **Rasha:** Perhaps *How Do Planes Fly?* – but others are possible if learners can justify their choice.
> **Miguel:** Perhaps *The Flying Panda* – but others are possible if learners can justify their choice.

 For further practice, see Activity 3 in the Activity Book.

5 A book about your school

- Tell learners they are going to write a book about their school

- Explain what the title and the main chapters might be. Ask them to suggest more chapters and what they may write in them.
- Possible chapters and ideas for writing are given in the table below. You could copy the table on the board.
- Elicit answers to the questions and review possessive adjectives. Focus on *your* (plural) and *our*.
- Encourage learners to describe the school in as much detail as possible, e.g. *There _____ in my (class/classroom). We go to school on _____. We do not go to school on _____.*
- Go through the questions and suggestions from learners and write the text for each chapter on the board with their help.
- Make the book with card, sheets of paper and staples.
- Ask learners to work in small groups to draw illustrations for the chapters. Then they cut them out and glue them in the book.
- Each group then copies in the text for the chapter they have illustrated.

Welcome to our school	
1 Our school	What is the name of your school? How many rooms are in your school?
2 Our class	How many children are in your class? How many boys? How many girls?
3 Our teacher	What is your teacher's name? What colour does your teacher like best? What does your teacher like to read about?
4 Our classroom	How many chairs, desks, and tables are in your classroom? How many windows and doors are in your classroom?
5 Our school week	Which days do you go to school? Which days do you **not** go to school?
6 Our busy day	What do you do in school? What subjects do you learn?

 For further practice, see Activities 4, 5 and 6 in the Activity Book.

Wrap up

- Once learners have finished doing their project, invite another class to come and see the book and ask learners to explain what they have done.
- **Home–school link:** Learners take it in turns to take the book home and show it to their family.

Activity Book

1 Titles and authors

- Tell learners to look at the book covers. They identify titles and authors.
- Tell them to draw a circle round each title and a line under the name of each author.

UNIT 1 Look in a book Lesson 2 23

> **Answers**
> Each book title should be circled; each author name should be underlined.

2 Sorting books

- Focus on the chart and the books in **Activity 1**. Ask learners to decide which books are fiction and which are non-fiction. They write the titles in the chart.
- Then they decide which books are scary and which are funny. They write the titles in the chart.
- As regards the concept of *scary*, even if snakes can be scary for many people, there might be learners who don't find them so. Accept an alternative answer.

> **Answers**
> **Fiction: c d** [*The Snowy Day, Look out!*]
> **Non-fiction: a b** [*Snakes, Silly Cats*]
> **Scary: a d** [*Snakes, Look Out!*]
> **Funny: c b** [*The Snowy Day, Silly Cats*]

3 Which book do you want to read?

- Learners write their choice of book.

> **Answers**
> Learners' own answers.

4 Which days do you go to school?

- Ask learners to read and circle the days they go to school. Then they cross out the days they don't go to school.

> **Answers**
> Learners' own answers.

5 What do you do at school!?

- Ask learners to look at the activities listed in the exercise. Ask them to circle the ones they do and cross out the ones they don't do.

> **Answers**
> Learners' own answers.

6 What subjects do you learn at school?

- Learners look at the list of school subjects. Tell them to circle the subjects they learn in school and to cross out the subjects they don't learn in school.

> **Answers**
> Learners' own answers.

I can talk about a book.

- Direct learners' attention to the self-evaluation question at the top of page 6. Ask them to think and answer. Emphasise the importance of giving an honest answer.

> **Answers**
> Learners' own answers.

> **Differentiated instruction**
> **Additional support and practice**
> - Give each learner a copy of **Photocopiable activity 2**. Learners work in groups to find answers to the six activities from your supply of children's books.
> - Provide additional support by having a spelling competition. Divide the class into two groups. They take it in turns to spell new words, e.g. the days of the week, topic vocabulary.
>
> **Extend and challenge**
> - If possible, give learners a copy of one of the books included in the lesson. Otherwise, make books in English suitable for the age and level available to them. Ask them to choose one and read it. When they have finished, they tell the class about the book they have read.

Lesson 3: Words and sounds

Review of short vowels

Learner's Book pages: 10–11
Activity Book pages: 8–9

> **Lesson objectives**
> **Listening:** Listen to a song and identify the letters of the alphabet, identify words with short vowel sounds, review **sh**, **ch**, **th**.
> **Speaking:** Sing a spelling song, spelling words, blend words with short vowel sounds, review **sh**, **ch**, **th**; counting.
> **Reading:** Recognise letters of the alphabet.
> **Writing:** Spelling dictation.
> **Critical thinking:** Memorise a song.
> **Language focus:** Spelling words, use of *a/an*, Counting from 1 to 15, questions: *How many __ are there?*
> **Vocabulary:** Letters of the alphabet, numbers 1–15
>
> **Materials:** Card, markers, enough copies of **Photocopiable activity 3** for the class.

Learner's Book

Warm up

- Learners identify the day of the week and describe the weather and add a craft stick to the jar.
- Write the learners' responses on a chart and then add one or more Learning Objectives.
- Play a spelling game with names. Ask a learner: *What's your name?* Learner answers, e.g. *Carlos*. Pretend to write and ask: *Can you spell it, please?* Learner spells the name.

1 Vowels and consonants 5

- Ask learners if they can remember the alphabet. Tell them to say it as a class.

- Tell them they are going to listen and sing an alphabet song. Point to the alphabet letters and play the audio.
- Play the audio, pausing after the song. Learners point to the letters as they listen and sing along.
- Read about vowels and consonants. Ask learners to look at the alphabet and identify and say the vowels.
- Play the last part of the audio for learners to check if they are correct.
- Play the ABC song again. Ask learners to clap when they hear each vowel.
- **Critical thinking:** Practise the song until learners have memorised it. Then ask pairs or groups to sing it.

Audioscript: Track 5

A B C D E F G

H I J K L M

N O P

Q R S T U

V W X Y Z

[*PAUSE*]

The English language has 5 vowels:

a, e, i, o, u … and sometimes y.

Answers

a, e, i, o, u and sometimes y

AB For further practice, see Activity 1 in the Activity Book.

2 Vowels at the beginning 6

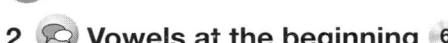

- Give learners card and markers and ask them to make six cards with a different vowel on each card.
- The letter *Y* can sometimes be considered a vowel, for example in *my*, but would be a consonant in words like *young, yellow.*
- They show each vowel in turn and say it.
- Tell them they are going to listen to an audio. They listen and look at the pictures.
- They identify the vowel at the beginning and hold up the correct card.
- Ask learners to spell the words as a class.

Audioscript: Track 6

a octopus

b egg

c insect

d apple

e umbrella

Answers

octopus – o, egg – e, insect – i, apple – a, umbrella – u

3 Vowels in the middle 7

- Tell learners they are going to listen to another set of words. They listen and look at the pictures.
- They identify the vowel in the middle and hold up the correct card.
- Then ask them to say a sentence to go with each picture. Elicit a variety of simple present tense sentences for each picture:
  This is a … I see a …
  The (hen/dog/fish) has (6 eggs/a ball/green fins).
  The (cat) is in a (box).
  The (cat/fish is orange/yellow and green).

Audioscript: Track 7

a hen

b cat

c dog

d fish

e duck

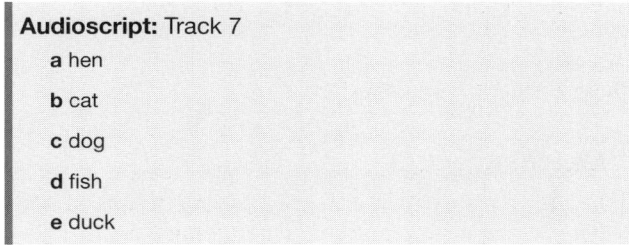

Answers

hen – e; cat – a; dog – o; fish – i; duck – u

4 How do you spell it?

- Focus on the pictures. Learner A chooses one picture. Learner B asks for the spelling. Learner A spells the word and Learner B writes it down in their notebook and finds the correct matching picture.
- Model the activity with one learner first.
- Circulate, checking for correct spelling and pronunciation.
- Ask learners to add more words of their choice and continue playing.

AB For further practice, see Activities 2, 3 and 4 in the Activity Book.

5 Numbers 1 to 15 8

- Ask learners if they remember the numbers. Ask them to count from 1 to 10.
- Tell them they are going to listen and to count along.
- They listen and count from 1 to 10.
- Then they listen and point to the numbers 11 to 15.
- Focus on the pictures and ask them to work with a partner and count the number of people they can see in each.

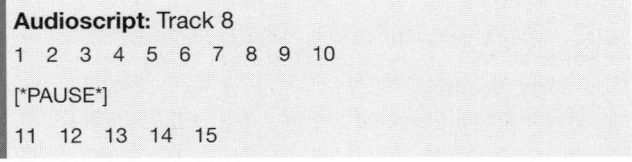

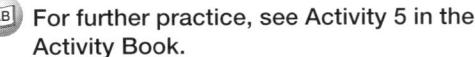

Audioscript: Track 8

1 2 3 4 5 6 7 8 9 10

[*PAUSE*]

11 12 13 14 15

Answers

A 10 people **B** 14 people

AB For further practice, see Activity 5 in the Activity Book.

Wrap up

- Pass out paper and pencils, markers, or crayons. Learners choose and write words and numbers.

They add the number and a picture for the words. They show them to the class and say and spell them.

Activity Book

1 Find the vowels

- After learners have practised the ABC song a few times, focus on the activity and ask them to circle the vowels and cross out the consonants.
- When they have finished, check as a class.

> **Answers**
> Vowels: a e i o u A E I O U

2 Matching words

- Focus on the exercise and ask learners to look at each picture and draw a line to the matching word.
- When they have finished, check as a class and ask learners to spell each word.

> **Answers**
> 1 ship 2 think 3 shop 4 chips

3 Read and draw

- Tell learners to read the instructions and complete the pictures.
- Ask them to say the sentences as fast as they can as a tongue twister, e.g. *a big black bug in a pink box, three red pens in the pan.*

4 What is it?

- Focus on the activity and ask learners to write what each thing is using the correct article *a/an.*
- Elicit from learners when they use *a* and when *an.*
- Ask learners to give more examples of the use of *a/an.* They draw a picture, show it to the class and say what it is, e.g. *It's an umbrella.*

> **Answers**
> 1 It's an octopus. 2 It's a fish. 3 It's an ant.

5 Crossword puzzle

- Ask learners if they have ever solved a crossword puzzle. Focus on the exercise and mime *across* and *down.*
- Tell learners to look at the clues then write the words.
- Some learners may need additional support with this activity. You may wish to group them together and supervise their work directly, helping as necessary.
- Check as a class. Ask for the correct word and the spelling.
- **Informal assessment opportunity:** Take advantage of this activity to assess learners' spelling.

> **Answers**
> Across:
> 2 clap 4 fifteen 6 pens 7 duck
> Down:
> 1 eleven 3 ships 5 neck

I can name the vowels and read words with short vowel sounds.

- Direct learners' attention to the self-evaluation question at the top of page 8. Ask them to think and answer. Emphasise the importance of giving an honest answer.

> **Answers**
> Learners' own answers.

Differentiated instruction

Additional support and practice

- Do **Photocopiable activity 3**. Review words beginning with each letter, e.g. *Find the picture of the table. What is the first letter in table? How do you spell table? Can you think of another word that begins with the* **t** *sound?*
- Ask learners to look for more words beginning with vowels in the **Picture dictionary** on pages 132–143. Can they spell them? How do they pronounce them?

Extend and challenge

- Ask learners to look back at **Activity 4** in the Learner's Book and put together words that sound similar then add one more word to each group. They say the words and spell them.

Lesson 4: Use of English

Talking about possessions

Learner's Book pages: 12–13
Activity Book pages: 10–11

Lesson objectives

Listening: Listen and identify, listen and answer.
Speaking: Say what you remember, describe a picture, speak about your possessions.
Reading: Read and follow instructions.
Critical thinking: Memorising.

Language focus: *have got* + noun to describe and ask about possessions: *She's got a pink hairbrush;* singular/plural nouns: *pencil, pencils;* subject pronouns: *he, she, you, I;* compound words, possessive pronouns
Vocabulary: colour names *(review),* backpack, hairbrush, skipping rope, camera, jumper, pencil, lunchbox, shoe, jacket, book, sock

Materials: Enough copies of **Photocopiable activity 4** for the class, pictures of camping equipment or real small camping equipment items.

Learner's Book

 Warm up

- Do the warm-up routine.
- Sing the ABC song. Ask learners to clap each time they say a vowel.

26 Cambridge Global English Stage 2 Teacher's Resource

- Divide the class into two groups. They take it in turns to sing and clap. Round 1: Group A sings and Group B stands up and claps the vowels, Round 2: Group B sings and Group A stands up and shouts the vowels.

1 Whose backpack? 9

- Ask learners if they like going camping. Ask them what they need to put in their backpack when they go camping. Display the objects or the pictures and elicit some vocabulary.
- Focus on the picture. Encourage learners to describe it in as much detail as possible.
- Tell learners that they are going to listen to the audio and find out which backpack belongs to which child.
- Play the audio at least twice. Learners identify the backpack owners.
- Play the audio again and ask the class to help you write the dialogue on the board by filling in the words.
- Practise the dialogue with the class.
- Divide the class into small groups and ask learners to act the dialogue out.
- Still in groups, learners collect their backpacks or school bags. They try to match them up with their owners by using the target language.
- Circulate, checking for correct language use and pronunciation.

Audioscript: Track 9

Woman: Jill, is this backpack yours?
Jill: Yes, it's mine.
Woman: OK, here you are ... Nick, is this red one yours?
Nick: No, mine is the blue one with the stars.
Woman: This one? OK ... Jack, which backpack is yours?
Jack: The black one is mine.
Woman: So which one is Lucy's?

Answers
Orange and yellow-striped backpack – It's Jill's.
Blue with white stars – It's Nick's.
Black – It's Jack's.
Red with a picture of a monkey – It's Lucy's.

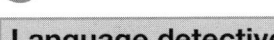 For further practice, see Activity 1 in the Activity Book.

Language detective

- Write the word *backpack* on the board and explain what a compound noun is. Draw a line between *back* and *pack* to make the concept clear to learners.
- Look at the other examples and ask learners to complete the explanations.
- Discuss more compound vocabulary words: *hairbrush (a brush for your hair)*, *toothbrush (a brush for your teeth)*, *a notebook (a book in which you write notes)*.

Answers
A classroom is a room with a **class** inside.
A bedroom is a room with a **bed** inside.
A bookshop is a shop that sells **books**.

2 What's in the backpack?

- Ask learners to look at the picture of Jill's backpack. Read the sentence and the question.
- Remind them of the use of personal pronouns. Draw a girl on the board and write *she* next to it. Draw a boy and elicit the correct pronoun from the class. Write it next to the picture.
- In pairs, learners take it in turns to describe the contents of each backpack using *He's got/She's got*.
- Circulate, checking for correct pronunciation and use of the target structure.

Answers
She's got …
a blue shoe
a red and yellow skipping rope
three yellow pencils
a blue jacket
a red lunchbox
a pink hairbrush

He's got …
a white jumper
a green lunchbox
a yellow book
a silver camera
four red pencils
two white socks

 For further practice, see Activity 2 in the Activity Book.

3 Can you remember?

- Divide the class into pairs. Learners choose one of the backpacks and decide if it is Jill's or Nick's. They look at the things inside, close their eyes and tell their partner what is in the backpack.
- They win a point for each thing they remember.

 For further practice, see Activity 3 in the Activity Book.

 Wrap up

- Learners draw the imaginary backpack of a fictional character they like and describe the contents.

Activity Book

1 Colour the pictures

- Focus on the activity. Tell learners to read the instructions and colour the backpacks.
- Check as a class.

Answers
Learners colour according to instructions.

2 Whose backpack?

- Tell learners to read the sentences and fill in the missing words using the words that are in the **Word box**.
- When they have finished, they write the names below the backpacks in the picture in **Activity 1**.

> **Answers**
> **Teacher:** Jill, is this backpack yours?
> **Jill:** Yes, it's **mine**.
> **Teacher:** Nick, is this red one **yours**?
> **Nick:** No, mine is the blue **one** with the stars.
> **Teacher:** Which one is Lucy's?
> **Nick:** The red one with the **monkey**.
>
> Nick's backpack, Lucy's backpack, Jill's backpack.

3 What's in the backpack?

- Ask learners to look at Lucy's and Nick's backpacks and write what's in them.
- Check as a class.
- **Challenge:** Learners write sentences about what they have in their own backpacks.

> **Answers**
> She's got a jumper, two shoes and a hairbrush.
> He's got a ruler, a camera and an apple.

I can say who things belong to.

Direct learners' attention to the self-evaluation question at the top of page 10. Ask them to think and answer. Emphasise the importance of giving an honest answer.

> **Answers**
> Learners' own answers.

Differentiated instruction

Additional support and practice

- Learners do a variation of **Activity 3** in the Learner's Book. Instead of a learner saying what they remember, the partner asks them questions. e.g. *Is there a yellow jacket? Are there two white socks? How many pencils are there?*
- Play a matching game in pairs or small groups. Ask learners to make word cards and picture cards. They put them face down on the table. They take it in turns to turn over two cards. If they have a match of picture and words, they say, e.g. *I've got a (toothbrush)*

Extend and challenge

- Give each learner a copy of **Photocopiable activity 4**. They cut out the nine word cards and place them face down.
- Learners play the game with a partner. Learner A chooses three cards and holds them in his/her hand. Say: *Don't let your partner see your cards!*
- Learner B gets six chances to guess which three pictures Learner A is holding.
  Learner B: *Have you got (a book)?*
  Learner A: *No, I haven't.*
  Learner B: *Have you got (a camera)?*
  Learner A: *Yes, I have.* (Learner A places the correctly guessed picture face up on the table.)
  Learner B continues to ask questions (a total of six questions). Write the number of pictures correctly guessed on a score board. Partners reverse roles for the next round of the game.

Lesson 5: Read and respond

Learner's Book pages: 14–17
Activity Book pages: 12–13

Lesson objectives

Listening: Listen to a song, listen and sing.
Speaking: Speak about books and reading.
Reading: Read along as you listen to the song, recognise the sight words *open, read* and *when*.
Writing: Write an original verse for a song.
Critical thinking: Predicting; learning ways to find the meaning of words.

Language focus: *When* clause
Vocabulary: *recipe, dinosaur, to whisper, sport, train, monkey, king, amazing, dictionary, computer, mobile, phone, volcano*

Materials: Writing supplies, pieces of paper.

Learner's Book

Warm up

- Do the warm-up routine.
- Remind learners of the poem in **Lesson 1**. What was it about? (stories). Ask the class to recite it.
- Ask learners what stories they have read lately. Encourage them to tell the class about them.

1 Before you read 10

- Tell learners to look at the picture and the title of the song and say why they think a book is like a window. Elicit as many suggestions as possible, e.g. *we can look at different worlds, we can 'meet' new people*.
- Tell learners that a book helps you discover new things you would not otherwise 'see'. It's like looking through a window and seeing something new and exciting. For example, you can read for fun or to learn new things.
- Ask learners if the book in the picture is a fiction or a non-fiction book. Ask them to find the characters.
- Ask the class if they would like to read the book. Encourage them to justify their answer.
- Tell the class they are going to listen to a song. While they listen, they read the text in their books.
- Play the song a few times and encourage learners to sing along as they grow more confident.
- Ask learners to look at the illustrations on page 15 and point to the pictures as they hear the words in the song.

Audioscript: Track 10. See Learner's Book pages 14–16.

> **Answers**
> It's a fiction book. The characters are a girl, a boy and a monster.

 For further practice, see Activities 1, 2 and 3 in the Activity Book.

28 Cambridge Global English Stage 2 Teacher's Resource

2 How do you say it in English?

- In pairs, learners draw something that they like reading about on pieces of paper.
- Ask them if they know how to say those things in English.
- Ask them how they can find out if they don't. Elicit answers from the class.
- Focus on the target question. Practise with the whole class.
- Tell learners to write the English word on the back of each picture.
- Then they teach their words to their partner.

3 Write your own verse!

- Remind learners of what they like reading about.
- Tell them to use the words that they looked up in **Activity 2** to finish the sentences in **Activity 4** in their Activity Book.
- They write words in the spaces to make a new verse. Then sing their new verse.
- **Informal assessment opportunity:** Take advantage of this activity to circulate and check how well learners are performing. Pay special attention to vocabulary use.
- **Portfolio opportunity:** You could collect the poems, write the date and the name of the learner and display the poems in the classroom. Later, you can file them in learners' portfolios.

Answers
(Example answer)
When I open up a book
Each page whispers, 'Look! Look! Look!'
Football and horses,
Superheroes and dragons,
Stories of scary adventures.

Words to remember

- Write the words *open, read* and *when* on the board.
- Learners look for these sight words in the song. How many times do they see the word?
- Ask them to take it in turns to practise spelling the sight words.

Wrap up

Ask learners to write their new verse on a sheet of paper. Collect all the verses and make a poster. All the class sings the new song together.
- **Home–school link:** learners show and teach their poems to their family.

Activity Book

1 Things we can read about

- Focus on the activity and ask learners to match the books with the pictures.

Answers
1 d 2 f 3 b 4 a 5 e 6 g 7 c

2 What do you like reading about?

- Ask learners to look at **Activity 1** and decide which things they like reading about. Tell them to draw a face in each circle above to show their answer.

Answers
Learners' own answers.

3 Where do you read books?

- Ask learners where they read books. They look at the options and tick the places where they like reading.
- Ask them if there are other places where they like reading that are not included in the list.
- When they have finished, ask learners to help you collect the results on the board and see which the place is the most popular to read in.
- Take advantage of this conversation to emphasise the importance of taking care of books and school supplies, showing responsibility and respect for the property of others and their own.

Answers
Learners' own answers.

4 Write your own verse

- Remind learners of what they like reading about.
- Learners use the words that they looked up in **Activity 2** in the Learner's Book to finish the sentences.
- They write words in the spaces to make a new verse. Then sing their new verse then draw pictures of things in the verse.

Answers
Learners' own answers.

I can understand the words of a song.

- Direct learners' attention to the self-evaluation question at the top of page 12. Ask them to think and answer. Emphasise the importance of giving an honest answer.

Answers
Learners' own answers.

Differentiated instruction

Additional support and practice

- Pairs of learners open their books to the corresponding section of the **Picture dictionary** (page 137). They point to and say the words they know.
- Spelling dictation: in pairs, learners take it in turns to choose two or three words they have learnt in this lesson and spell them. They write them down in their notebooks.

Extend and challenge

- 💬 In pairs, learners take it in turns to choose two or three words they have learnt in this lesson. They write a new poem containing these words.
- Ask learners if they know a song in English. If they do, they can learn a verse that they like and teach it to the class.
- Alternatively, bring two or three songs to the class. Give learners a copy of the lyrics and they choose the verses which they like the most.

Lesson 6: Choose a project

What can you find in a book?

Learner's Book pages: 18–19

Activity Book pages: 14–15

Lesson objectives

Listening: Listen and follow instructions, listening comprehension items in Activity Book quiz.

Speaking: Present your project to the class.

Reading: Read word cards, instructions, quiz items.

Writing: Write word cards, an interview, write answers in Activity Book quiz.

Language focus: Unit 1 Review

Materials

A Make a poster: Writing/drawing supplies, A4 sheets of paper.

B Word cards in your classroom: File cards, writing supplies, Learner's Book.

C Introduce your partner: Writing supplies, a sheet of paper.

Learner's Book

Warm up

- Do the warm-up routine.
- Play a guessing game: What's in the backpack? Put a backpack on your table and fill it with different classroom objects.
- Learners ask up to five questions to find out what object you have in your hand. Encourage them to ask a variety of questions, e.g. *Is it big/small/blue? How many are there? Have you got a …?*

Choose a project

- Learners will choose an end-of-unit project to work on. Look at the examples in the pictures and help learners to choose. Provide materials.
- Subdivide learners working on Project C so that there are pairs working on the interview.

A Make a poster

- Read the directions. Give out drawing and writing supplies.
- Learners write the things they like reading about. Tell them to look up the words they don't know in English.
- When they have finished, they present their poster to the class: they talk about the poster, why they included certain things, etc.
- Then, they teach the class the new words on their poster.

B Word cards in your classroom

- Read and explain the instructions.
- Learners write the word cards. Encourage learners to find out words for things they don't already know by looking them up in the **Picture dictionary** on page 137.
- When they have finished, they stick the word cards on or near the corresponding objects in the classroom.
- They teach the words to the class. Then they practise them by playing '*Please say please*'. The learner chooses a card and reads the words to the class. If he/she says *please*, the class must do the action or point at the object. If he/she doesn't say *please*, they must stay still.

C Introduce your partner

- Read the instructions. Learners ask their partner the questions and write down the answers.
- When they have finished, they introduce their partner to the class.
- **Informal assessment opportunity:** Circulate as learners work. Informally assess their receptive and productive language skills. Ask questions. You may want to take notes on their responses.

Look what I can do!

- Review the *I can …* statements. Learners demonstrate what they can do.
- Review the Big question. Ask learners what they have found in a book and what new things they have learnt about books. Elicit what they liked most about this unit and encourage them to explain why. This may also be a good opportunity for learners to reflect on what aspects of the unit they have found most difficult and why.

Activity Book

Unit 1 Quiz: Look what I can do!

Listen 90 [CD2 Track 39]

- Learners listen and tick the correct picture. Do the first item as a class. Play the audio several times.

Listen and write

- Learners listen, write the word and then tick the correct picture.

Read and write

- Learners read the question and write their answer.
- **Portfolio opportunity:** If possible, leave the learners' projects on display for a short while, then consider filing the projects, photos or scans of the work in learners' portfolios. Write the date on the work.

- If you have been filing learners' work all through this unit, you may find it useful to put all the work of this unit together. You could ask learners to make a cover for their Unit 1 work decorating it with an image that represents what they have learnt.

Audioscript: Track 90

1 **Woman:** Tell me about your book, Danny.
  Boy: It's a fiction book about a baby shark and a baby turtle.
  Woman: Is it a scary book?
  Boy: Oh no, it's not scary. It's funny. The shark and the turtle are friends.

2 **Man:** Is this your lunchbox, Shu Ling?
  Girl: Yes, that's mine. It's got stars on it.

3 **Man:** Is there a bookcase in your classroom?
  Girl: Yes, there is.
  Man: How many books are in the bookcase?
  Girl: Hmmm. Let me count: 1, 2, 3, 4, 5, 6, 7, 8, 9, 10, 11, 12. There are 12 books in the bookcase.

4 **Girl:** Hello, Tom. What are you doing?
  Boy: I'm reading.
  Girl: But you haven't got a book.
  Boy: No, I've got a tablet. I'm reading an e-book on my tablet.
  Girl: Oh, I see! That's cool!

5 Lucy has got 2 pencils, a book and an apple. She hasn't got a ball.

6 P-E-N. Listen again: P-E-N.

7 D-U-C-K. Listen again: D-U-C-K.

Answers
1 b
2 c
3 b
4 b
5 c
6 a
7 b
8 a
9 Acceptable answers: learner's first name, learner's full name, full sentence: *My name is…*
10 Acceptable answers: *funny, scary, funny books, scary books, I like funny books. I like scary books.*

2 Good neighbours

Big question Who lives in your neighbourhood?

Unit overview

In this unit learners will:
- talk about family and neighbours
- identify and describe different types of shops
- talk and write about jobs
- ask for and give directions
- read and talk about a poem.

Learners will build communication and literacy skills as they read and listen to a poem and a song, recite a poem about their neighbourhood, sing a song about taking care of the planet, talk about different types of jobs and jobs they like, identify places on a map and ask for and give directions, say where things are and write a letter to a friend.

At the end of the unit, they will apply and personalise what they have learned by working in small groups to complete a project of their choice: making a book about what they can be when they grow up; doing a survey about what they want to be when they grow up; and drawing a school map and giving directions.

Language focus
Present continuous
Irregular plurals
Question forms
Ordinal numbers
Suffix *-er*
Present simple third-person endings
Prepositions of location
Prefix *un-*
Sight words: *friends, some, there, city*
Review of: imperatives
Vocabulary topics: jobs, family, neighbourhood, geography words
Critical thinking
- Compare and contrast the neighbourhood in the picture with learners' own neighbourhood
- Map-reading skills, awareness of the world around us
- Spatial orientation
- Awareness of and respect for people around us
- Memorising.

Self-assessment
- I can name people and things in my neighbourhood.
- I can talk about where I live.
- I can talk and write about different jobs.
- I can ask for and give directions.
- I can read and talk about a poem.

Teaching tips

Encourage learners to peer review their work. This will help them develop awareness of mistakes and also cooperation among peers.

Review learners' work on the quiz, noting areas where they demonstrate strength and areas where they need additional instruction and practice. Use this information to customise your teaching as you continue to **Unit 3**.

Lesson 1: Think about it

Who lives in your neighbourhood?

Learner's Book pages: 20–21
Activity Book pages: 16–17

Lesson objectives

Listening: Listen to a description, listen and answer questions.

Speaking: Ask and answer questions, practise theme vocabulary, talk about your family.

Reading: Read and recite a poem, read and identify key vocabulary.

Writing: Write about your family.

Critical thinking: Compare and contrast the neighbourhood in the picture with learners' own neighbourhood.

Language focus: Present continuous; irregular plurals: *woman – women;* question forms

Vocabulary: *neighbours, neighbourhood, police officer, nurse, street cleaner, young, old, people, apartment building, balcony, street*

Materials: Chart paper, coloured card, staples and markers, family photos (optional).

Learner's Book

Warm up

- Do the warm-up routine.
- Focus on the picture and ask learners to describe it in as much detail as possible. Help with some questions, e.g. *Who can you see in the picture? Are there any children/adults? What are the people doing? What kind of buildings can you see?*
- Explain the meaning of *neighbourhood*. Ask learners who lives in their neighbourhood. Do they know their neighbours?

1 Read and listen 11

- Ask learners to look at the picture again and find neighbours helping neighbours.
- Tell learners you are going to play an audio. Ask them to listen and follow in their books.
- Play the poem '*My neighbourhood*' at least twice.
- Play the poem again, stopping after each verse for learners to repeat.
- Ask learners to read the poem as a class. Practise reciting the poem together.

Audioscript: Track 11. See Learner's Book page 20.

2 Ben's neighbourhood 12

- Ask learners to look at the picture carefully while they listen to Ben talking.
- Play the audio once. Ask what is Ben describing (his neighbourhood).
- Play the audio again at least twice. Ask learners to identify Ben.
- Tell learners to listen again and point to the people and things Ben describes.
- **Critical thinking:** Ask learners to compare and contrast the neighbourhood in the picture with theirs. How similar or different are they? What makes them different? What are people like in their neighbourhood?

Audioscript: Track 12

Hi! Welcome to my neighbourhood! My name is Ben. I live in apartment building number 12 with my family. Lots of other families live in the building, too. Can you see me in the picture? I'm opening the door for my neighbour, Mrs Tran. She's carrying some big bags.

Can you see a little boy on the bicycle? His name is Tommy. My cousin Josie is helping Tommy ride his bicycle.

My grandpa is helping our neighbour plant some flowers. And look up, on the balcony: that's my aunt!

In our neighbourhood, there are old people and young people. Can you see a nurse helping an old woman? Her name is Mrs Ortega. In the road, a police officer is stopping the traffic. A young woman is crossing the road with a small baby.

Sometimes the street gets dirty. A street cleaner is cleaning the pavement. His name is Mr Sands, and his job is very important.

Answers
Ben is the child holding open the door of apartment building 12 for the woman carrying bags of shopping.

3 Topic vocabulary 13

- Play the audio once, up to the pause.
- Play the audio again. Pause after each sentence for learners to repeat them.
- Write the words on the board. Read the words together.
- Encourage learners to guess the meaning of *traffic*. Ask them to look at the pictures to help them understand.
- Ask them to compare the word to an existing word in their language. How similar or different is it?
- Tell learners to look at the big picture. Play the last part of the audio once.
- Play the audio again and tell learners to listen and answer the questions.

Audioscript: Track 13

Young people. Children are young people.

Police officer. The police officer is stopping the traffic.

Nurse. The nurse is helping an old woman.

Street cleaner. The street cleaner is cleaning the pavement.

Old people. My grandma and grandpa are old people.

[*PAUSE*]

What is the police officer doing?

Who is the nurse helping?

How many women can you see?

What is the street cleaner doing?

> **Answers**
> **What is the police officer doing?** She's stopping the traffic. She's helping a woman with a baby to cross the road.
> **Who is the nurse helping?** She's helping an old woman, Mrs Ortega.
> **How many women can you see?** Seven women if they include Josie (young woman/teenager).

4 Ask questions

- Elicit from learners some common plural forms of nouns, e.g. *boy/boys, girl/girls, friend/friends*.
- Explain that there are some nouns that have different plural forms. Use the illustration to elicit or explain *woman/women*.
- Focus on the activity. In pairs, learners look at the big picture and ask and answer questions about it using the questions in the activity as a model.
- Circulate, checking for correct pronunciation and use of language.
- Encourage learners to ask as many questions as possible since the picture offers a lot of possibilities.

> **Answers**
> Learners' own answers.

[AB] For further practice, see Activity 1 in the Activity Book.

5 My family

- Tell learners to look at the family tree and at the photo. Ask them who the people in the photo are.
- Talk about the photo in relation to Ben, e.g. *This is Ben's grandma/uncle/cousin.*
- If appropriate, ask learners to show photos of their family. Ask questions about the families, e.g. *Have you got an aunt/uncle/cousin? How many … ?*
- If appropriate, ask learners to draw a picture of their family. When they have finished, ask them to show the picture to the class and talk about their family if they are happy to do so.

> **Answers**
> Learners' own answers.

[AB] For further practice, see Activity 2 in the Activity Book.

Wrap up

- Discuss with learners what makes a good neighbour and a good friend. Emphasise the importance of helping each other and taking care of each other.
- Elicit examples of good friend and good neighbour behaviour.
- **Informal assessment opportunity:** Take advantage of this discussion to informally assess correct grammar and vocabulary use.
- **Home–school opportunity:** Learners show the family tree in the Learner's Book to their parents/family and explain what they did in class. If appropriate, they can make a similar family tree about their own family with the help of their parents.

Activity Book

1 Yes or no?

- Ask learners to look at the picture (or the same big picture in the Learner's Book). Ask them to read each sentence and write *yes* if the sentence is true and *no* if the sentence is not true.
- Check as a class and ask learners to correct the sentences that are not true.

> **Answers**
> Ben lives in apartment building number twelve. **yes**
> There is a man on the balcony. **no**
> A nurse is helping an old woman. **yes**
> A police officer is stopping the traffic. **yes**
> Three children are crossing the street. **no**
> Ben's aunt is cleaning the pavement. **no**

2 Josie's family tree

- Ask learners to look at Josie's family tree. They write the missing words from the **Word box**.
- **Challenge:** If appropriate, ask learners to answer the questions about their own families.

> **Answers**
> grandma + grandpa;
> uncle + aunt;
> dad + mum;
> cousins

I can name people and things in my neighbourhood.

- Direct learners' attention to the self-evaluation question at the top of page 16. Ask them to think and answer. Emphasise the importance of giving an honest answer.

> **Answers**
> Learners' own answers.

> ### Differentiated instruction
> **Additional support and practice**
>
> - Give each learner eight index cards for a vocabulary concentration activity. They write and illustrate eight vocabulary words, e.g. family members, topic vocabulary. In pairs, lay cards face down in four rows of four cards. Learners take turns turning over two cards, one at a time, saying the words aloud. If two matching cards are turned over, the player keeps the pair of cards. If the cards do not match, the player turns them face down again and it is the next player's turn.
>
> **Extend and challenge**
>
> - In pairs, learners write one or two more verses for the '*My neighbourhood*' poem including some of the topic vocabulary. Then they read the poem with the new lines.

Lesson 2: Find out more

Where do you live?

Learner's Book pages: 22–23
Activity Book pages: 18–19

Lesson objectives

Listening: Listen for specific information.
Speaking: Answer questions and talk about your home town.
Reading: Read a letter.
Writing: Guided writing: write a letter.
Critical thinking skills: Map-reading skills, awareness of the world around us.
Language focus: Ordinal numbers; Present simple tense review
Vocabulary: *geography, city, country, continent, address, lift*

Materials: Globe or map of the world.

Learner's Book

 Warm up

- Divide the class into small groups and ask them to recite one line of the poem in **Lesson 1** each. Do several rounds until all the groups have recited a line. Then ask the class to recite the whole poem together.
- Ask learners where they live. Elicit the name of the town or city and the name of the neighbourhood.
- Display a map of the world or a globe and ask learners if they can find their country and their city on the map/globe.

1 A letter from Fiona

- Tell learners to look at the illustration. Introduce Fiona and ask them to predict what Fiona's letter will be about. Elicit some suggestions.
- Tell them to listen and read the letter. Play the audio at least twice.
- Ask learners if their predictions were correct.
- In pairs, learners answer the first question.
- Ask learners if they can find a city in square D-1 of the map. (London).
- Look at Fiona's address together. Elicit what is included in each line (building/street or road/city or town/country).
- **Critical thinking:** Take advantage of this activity to develop learners' map-reading skills.

Audioscript: Track 14. See Learner's Book page 22.

Answers
Can you find the city? London
What's your address? Learner's own answers.

 For further practice, see Activity 1 in the Activity Book.

2 Continents

- Show learners the map/globe again. Use the map to elicit *city, country, continent*. Ask: *Is (name of a city) a city or a country?* Point at a country on the map. Say: *Look, this is (name of a continent/country). Is it a country or a continent?*
- Look at the illustration. Read the introduction together. Ask learners to look for the UK on the map/globe. Elicit which continent it is in (Europe).
- Ask learners to answer the questions, helping learners with their country/continent if necessary.

Answers
How many continents are there? Seven – North America, South America, Europe, Africa, Asia, Australia with Oceania, Antarctica.
Note: Some nations don't consider Antarctica to be a continent; others consider North and South America which one do you live in? Learners' own answer. to be a single continent. Oceania is often given with Australia to include the Pacific Islands.
Which one do you live in? Learners' own answer.

3 In the lift: Going up!

- Focus on the illustration and ask learners what they see. Elicit the word *lift*. Ask them what they use a lift for.
- Do learners live in an apartment building or in a house? Is there a lift in their building? How many floors are there in the building?
- Read the sentences and ask learners to decide which buttons Fiona has to press.
- Write some more numbers on the board and ask them what floor they are going to, e.g. 11, the eleventh floor

Answers
fourth floor 4, second floor 2, first floor 1, third floor 3

For further practice, see Activity 2 in the Activity Book.

4 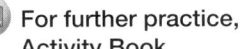 A letter to Fiona

- Tell learners they are going to write a letter to Fiona.
- Read the instructions together.
- Learners can write their letters on paper or use **Activity 3** in the Activity Book.

For further practice, see Activity 3 in the Activity Book.

Wrap up

- Once learners have finished writing and drawing, ask them to read their letters to the class. If they have

written the letters on separate sheets of paper, you may wish to make a class display.
- **Portfolio opportunity:** Collect the letters, write the date on them and file them in the learners' portfolios.

Activity Book

1 Where do you live?
- Tell learners to look at the letter in the Learner's Book again. Identify the parts of the letter. Ask: *Why does Fiona use 'everybody' instead of a name? How does she say goodbye? What information does she include in the letter?*
- Ask learners to write their own address. Model first writing your address, real or imaginary.
- Ask if it is necessary to write *Earth*. Elicit why not.
- Circulate, checking that learners fill in the information correctly.

2 How about you?
- Focus on the questions. Remind learners of their previous answers and ask them to write them.

> **Answers**
> Learners' own answers.

3 A letter to Fiona
- Focus on the questions in the activity. Tell learners to use them as a guide to plan their letter.
- Allow plenty of time for them to write and draw the picture.
- Circulate offering help.

I can talk about where I live.
- Direct learners' attention to the self-evaluation question at the top of page 18. Ask them to think and answer. Emphasise the importance of giving an honest answer.

> **Answers**
> Learners' own answers.

> **Differentiated instruction**
>
> **Additional support and practice**
> - Ask learners to locate their country on the map. Is it far away from or near Fiona's house in the United Kingdom? Also develop their awareness of the world around them. What countries can they find near theirs? What continent is their country in?
>
> **Extend and challenge**
> - Tell learners to search the Internet and find information about the solar system. In small groups or pairs, they choose a planet, look for some information about it and make a model. When all the planets and the sun are ready, help learners mount a mobile solar system. Then, each pair or group presents their planet.

Lesson 3: Words and sounds

Jobs that end in *-er*
Learner's Book pages: 24–25
Activity Book pages: 20–21

> **Lesson objectives**
>
> **Listening:** Listen and identify the sound of the ending *-er*, listen for information.
>
> **Speaking:** Talk about jobs people do, act out a dialogue, interview the teacher.
>
> **Reading:** Recognise letters of the alphabet.
>
> **Writing:** Guided writing, taking notes.
>
> **Language focus:** Present simple third person singular; review of questions
>
> **Vocabulary:** *singer, teacher, dancer, window cleaner, writer, painter, clothes designer, baker, taxi driver, street cleaner, firefighter, fire station, uniform, fire alarm, fire engine, ladder, rescue*
>
> **Materials:** Enough copies of **Photocopiable activity 5** for the class.

Learner's Book

Warm up
- Do the warm-up routine.
- Play a spelling game to review vocabulary from Lessons 1 and 2. Divide the class into two teams. Learners take it in turns to dictate a word to a learner from the other group. If the spelling is correct, the group gets a point.
- Ask learners what their parents' job is. How many job words do they know? Brainstorm job words and write them on the board.

1 What is your job? 15
- Focus on the pictures. Can learners name the jobs?
- Tell them they are going to listen to some sentences. Say: *Listen and repeat.*
- Play the audio at least twice. Ask learners how *-er* is pronounced. Repeat the sound in isolation several times. This sound can be difficult to produce for speakers of some languages.
- Focus on the question. Elicit answers from learners.
- If they don't like any of these options, invite them to say what they would like to be when they are older. Supply any additional vocabulary as necessary.

> **Audioscript:** Track 15
> I'm a singer. I sing.
> I'm a teacher. I teach.
> I'm a dancer. I dance.

> **Answers**
> Learners' own answers.

2 What do you do?

- Ask learners to look at the sentences and complete them.
- Tell them to write the sentences in their notebooks.
- Focus on the picture. In pairs learners ask and answer where the people are, e.g. *Where is the painter? He's on the second floor.*

Answers
1 I am a window cleaner. I **clean** windows.
2 I am a writer. I **write** books.
3 I am a painter. I **paint**.
4 I am a clothes designer. I **design** clothes.
5 I am a baker. I **bake** bread.
6 I am a taxi driver. I **drive** a taxi.
7 I am a street cleaner. I **clean** the street.

[AB] For further practice, see Activity 1 in the Activity Book.

3 Who am I?

- In small groups, learners take it in turn to act out a worker at work. The group asks questions to guess the job.
- Circulate, checking for correct pronunciation and use of the language.

Answers
Learners' own answers.

[AB] For further practice, see Activity 2 in the Activity Book.

4 The firefighter 16

- Focus on the picture and ask: *What is his job? What do firefighters do?*
- Ask learners to listen and point to the things Mr Lucas talks about.
- Ask learners to look at the questions and play the audio again for learners to answer the questions.
- Elicit the answers from learners.

Audioscript: Track 16

Mr Lucas is a firefighter and he works at a fire station. He wears a firefighter's uniform: a jacket, trousers, gloves, boots and a helmet. When the fire alarm rings, he quickly puts on this uniform. He jumps on the fire engine and rushes to the fire. The light on the fire engine flashes and you can hear a loud siren.

Mr Lucas and the other firefighters fight the fire. Mr Lucas uses water to put out the fire. Sometimes he uses a ladder to rescue people from buildings.

Sometimes Mr Lucas goes to schools and talks to the children. He teaches them about fire safety.

Firefighters help to keep our neighbourhood safe. Thank you, firefighters!

Answers
1 **Where does Mr Lucas work?** He works at a fire station.
2 **What clothes does a firefighter wear?** A firefighter wears a firefighter's uniform: a jacket, trousers, gloves, boots and a helmet.
3 **What does Mr Lucas do when the fire alarm rings?** He quickly puts on this uniform. He jumps on the fire engine and rushes to the fire.
4 **What do firefighters use to put out a fire?** They use water to put out a fire.
5 **Why does Mr Lucas go to schools?** He goes to schools to teach the children about fire safety.

[AB] For further practice, see Activity 3 in the Activity Book.

5 Interview your teacher

- Tell learners to imagine they are working in a TV programme called '*Jobs*'. They are going to interview their teacher.
- Tell them to use the questions in the activity and write down the answers. Then, they use these to write their TV report.

Answers
Learners' own answers.

Wrap up

- When they have finished writing their TV report, learners read it to the class.
- **Home–school opportunity:** Learners use the questions in **Activity 5** to interview a parent or relative. They write down their answers and tell the class about it.
- **Portfolio opportunity:** Collect the interviews learners have brought from home, write the name and date and file them in their portfolios.

Activity Book

1 Jobs

- Ask learners to look at the **Language tip** box. Can they add more jobs that follow the rule?
- Ask them to write the name of the job to complete the sentences. Then draw a line to the correct picture.

Answers
1 painter, 2 singer, 3 dancer, 4 taxi driver

2 Who am I?

- Tell learners to look at the picture on page 24 of the Learner's Book. They write the name of the relevant person.

UNIT 2 Good neighbours Lesson 3 37

> **Answers**
> 1 clothes designer, 2 writer, 3 baker

3 A busy morning

- Focus on the activity. Tell learners that they are going to write about what Mr Lucas, the firefighter, does in the morning.
- Look at the **Language tip** and the examples together. Encourage learners to say the sounds and the verbs, e.g. *-sh, I brush, he brushes*.
- They look at the sentences and write the missing words.

> **Answers**
> 1 Mr Lucas **eats** his breakfast.
> 2 He **washes** his hands.
> 3 He **brushes** his teeth.
> 4 He **watches** TV.
> 5 Oh no! It's late! Mr Lucas **rushes** out of his house.
> 6 He **catches** a bus and he goes to the fire station.

I can talk and write about different jobs.

- Direct learners' attention to the self-evaluation question at the top of page 20. Ask them to think and answer. Emphasise the importance of giving an honest answer.

> **Answers**
> Learners' own answers.

> **Differentiated instruction**
>
> **Additional support and practice**
> - Learners read and practise the punctuation and structures on **Photocopiable activity 5**.
>
> **Extend and challenge**
> - Ask learners to use the questions in Learner's Book **Activity 5** to interview somebody from another profession. If appropriate, they may ask their family doctor, neighbourhood police officer, baker, etc. Then they illustrate their interview and present it to the class.

Lesson 4: Use of English
Saying where things are

Learner's Book pages: 26–27
Activity Book pages: 22–23

> **Lesson objectives**
>
> **Listening:** Listen and follow directions.
> **Speaking:** Ask for and give directions, give instructions.
> **Reading:** Read and follow instructions.
> **Writing:** Write instructions.
> **Critical thinking:** Spatial orientation.

> **Language focus:** Imperatives; prepositions of location: *next to, between, opposite, behind, inside, under, on, left/right, straight ahead, over there.*
>
> **Vocabulary:** *pet shop, bookshop, toyshop, sweet shop, café, shoe shop, clothes shop, sports shop, bicycle shop, phone shop, computer shop, treasure hunt, treasure, clue, bridge, log.*
>
> **Materials:** Map or street plan of the city, slips of paper, writing supplies, a 'treasure' (a small box or bag of sweets or chocolates or something similarly attractive but inexpensive), enough copies of **Photocopiable activity 6** for the class.

Learner's Book

Warm up

- Do the warm-up routine.
- Play a mime game. A learner mimes a job and the class guesses what the job is. You may turn this game into a competition by dividing the class into two groups.
- Show the map of the city and ask learners to locate the school, their home, a relative's home.
- Ask them what other places they can locate on the map. Elicit names of places in town and write them on the board.
- Ask if there is a shopping centre and what shops they can find there.

1 At the shopping centre

- Revise *left* and *right*. Practise simple instructions using parts of the body, e.g. *Put your left hand on your right knee.*
- Focus on the map of the shopping centre. Read the instructions and ask learners to follow on their maps.
- As they go, learners identify the shops. Tell them to use the pictures to identify each one. Say: *Look, a rabbit and a fish. What shop is it?*
- Elicit the answer and write the name of the shop on the board.

> **Answers**
> **Which shops are on your right?** Shoe shop, clothes shop, sports shop
> **Which shops are on your left?** Pet shop, book shop, toy shop, sweet shop, café
> **Now which shops are on your left?** Phone shop, computer shop
> **Which shop is on your right?** Bicycle shop

2 Find the mystery shop

- Ask learners to look at the **Language tip**. Provide plenty of examples of the prepositions. Ask learners to draw pictures on the board to illustrate the meaning.
- Focus on the clues. Tell learners to read them and find the mystery shops on the map.

- When they have found the three places, ask them to write one more clue and read it aloud. The class tries to find the shop.
- **Critical thinking:** All these activities provide plenty of opportunities to help develop spatial awareness and map reading skills.

> **Answers**
> 1 the toy shop
> 2 the clothes shop
> 3 the bicycle shop

[AB] For further practice, see Activities 1 and 2 in the Activity Book.

3 Asking for directions 17

- Tell learners they are going to listen to a dialogue. They listen and follow the directions.
- Play the dialogue at least twice.
- Learners practise the conversation with their partner. They choose a shop from the map in **Activity 1** and give directions.

> **Audioscript : Track 17**
> **Woman 1:** Excuse me, where is the computer shop?
> **Woman 2:** Go straight ahead, then turn right at the corner. It's opposite the bicycle shop.
> **Woman 1:** Thank you very much.

[AB] For further practice, see Activity 3 in the Activity Book.

4 Behind, between, inside, on, under 18

- Turn learners' attention to the pictures. Use the pictures to revise the prepositions.
- Say: *Listen and follow the instructions.*
- Learners can look at the pictures to check they are making the correct movements.
- Play the audio a few times while learners mime the actions and positions.

> **Audioscript: Track 18**
> **behind** – Look behind you. Then put your arm behind your back.
> **between** – Put your hand between your knees.
> **inside** – Wiggle your finger. Then put your finger inside your book.
> **on** – Put your right hand on your book. Put your left hand on your right hand.
> **under** – Wave your left hand. Wave your right hand. Put your left hand under your right hand.

5 Find the treasure 19

- Tell the class that they are going to listen to two children going on a treasure hunt.
- Ask if they have ever been on a treasure hunt. What is it? Elicit some explanations. Make sure they all understand what the game consists of.

- Focus on the map and tell them to follow the clues as they listen.
- Play the audio a few times.

> **Audioscript:** Track 19
> **Boy:** This is Clue number 1. Look under the table.
> **Girl:** I've got it! Clue number 2 is under the table.
> **Boy:** Great! Read Clue 2.
> **Girl:** Look on the bridge. Where is the bridge?
> **Boy:** I can see a bridge over there. Let's go!
> **Girl:** I've got it. Here's Clue number 3, on the bridge.
> **Boy:** OK! Read Clue 3.
> **Girl:** Look between two trees.
> **Boy:** I can see two trees over there. Let's go!
> **Girl:** Here it is! Clue 4 is between the trees.
> **Boy:** Fantastic! Read Clue 4.
> **Girl:** Look inside the log. Hmmm … Look inside the log.
> **Boy:** Can you see a log?
> **Girl:** Yes, over there!
> **Boy:** Clue 5 is inside the log.
> **Girl:** Good! Read it.
> **Boy:** Look behind the big rock. Look behind the big rock.
> **Girl:** There's a big rock over there. Let's go!
> **Boy:** Look at this! It's a treasure box.
> **Girl:** It's a box of balloons! Hooray, I love balloons!
> **Boy:** Me, too!

> **Answers**
> They look under the table, on the bridge, between the two trees, inside the log and behind the big rock.
> The treasure is behind the big rock.

6 Make up a clue

- Play the audio again to remind learners of the clues.
- Ask them to work in pairs and take it in turns to say a clue and find a place on the map.

> **Answers**
> Learners' own answers.

7 Classroom treasure hunt

- Divide the class into small groups. Each group writes four clues for the rest of the class.
- They hide clues 2 to 4 and give clue 1 to another group.
- Remind learners that clue 2 should be placed in the location suggested by clue 1, clue 3 in the location suggested by clue 2 and clue 4 in the place suggested by clue 3. Clue 4 leads to the treasure.
- Some kind of 'treasure' needs to be provided in the final location.

Wrap up

- In small groups, learners draw the map of an imaginary place with clues to find treasure.
- They show the map to the class and the class guesses where the treasure is.

Activity Book

1 Where are the shops?

- Tell learners to look at the map and read the questions and answers. They identify the missing shops and draw a line from each picture to the map of the shopping centre.

> **Answers**
> **left:** pet shop, book shop, toy shop, sweet shop
> **right:** shoe shop, clothes shop, bicycle shop, phone shop

2 Find the mystery place

- Tell learners to look at the street plan and follow the instructions to find the places.

> **Answers**
> It's next to the library. fire station
> It's opposite the park. school
> It's between the sports shop and the computer shop. café
> It's opposite the café. bicycle shop
> It's next to the school. bus stop

3 What are they saying?

- Tell learners to read the dialogue. Remind them of the dialogue they listened to and then practised in **Activity 3** in their Learner's Books.
- Tell them to write the missing words from the **Word box**.
- Check as a class.

> **Answers**
> – Excuse **me**. Where **is** the **fire station**?
> – **Go** straight ahead. Then **turn** left at the corner.
> It's **next** to the library.
> – Thank **you**!

I can ask for and give directions.

- Direct learners' attention to the self-evaluation question at the top of page 22. Ask them to think and answer. Emphasise the importance of giving an honest answer.

> **Answers**
> Learners' own answers.

Differentiated instruction

Additional support and practice

- Do **Photocopiable activity 6**.

How to Play

Each partner has a copy of the Treasure Map.

Partner 1: Draw a sweet in one square. Draw a balloon in one square. Do not show your partner your map!

Partner 2: You want to find the treasures! Ask your partner 'Is there a treasure in A2?' If your partner says 'No,' draw an X in that square and ask your partner another question. If your partner says 'Yes,' ask 'Is it a sweet or a balloon?' Draw the picture in the square.

When you have found both treasures, show your map to your partner. Are the two maps the same? Play the game again! Switch roles.

Extend and challenge

- Learners work in pairs. They use a street map of the city and prepare clues. They take it in turns to read the clues and discover the shops.

Lesson 5: Read and respond

Learner's Book pages: 28–31
Activity Book pages: 24–25

Lesson objectives

Listening: Listen to a poem and a song.
Speaking: Recite a poem, sing a song, talk about a poem, make up a conversation.
Reading: Read along as you listen to the poem and the song, recognise the sight words *friends, some, their, city.*
Writing: Write an original verse for a song.
Critical thinking: Awareness of the difference between formal and informal language; awareness of and respect for people around us.

Language focus: Prefix *un-*; formal and informal language

Vocabulary: *kid, friendly, unfriendly, unhappy, world, sun, rain, moon, stars, wind, clouds*

Materials: Map of the world, writing supplies, pieces of paper.

Learner's Book

Warm up

- Do the warm-up routine.
- Play a game of '*Simon Says*' to revise prepositions.
- Ask learners how many countries they think there are in the world. Do they know what countries are near theirs? Can they name some cities in their country?

1 Before you read 20

- Tell learners to look at the picture and the title of the poem and predict what the poem is about. Elicit as many suggestions as possible.
- Elicit from them what 'kids' means. Do they know another word for *kids*? (*children*)

- **Critical thinking:** Discuss with learners when they would use *kids* and when they would use *children*. Ask them if they use the same language with a friend, their parents, their teachers, etc. Discuss the idea of 'informal' language and when they would use it. Elicit other words that have an informal equivalent, e.g. *dad – father*, *mum – mother*.
- Tell the class they are going to listen to the poem. While they listen, they read in their books.
- Play the poem a few times and encourage learners to say the verses as they listen.

Audioscript: Track 20. See Learner's Book page 28.

2 Talk about the poem

- Focus on the questions and discuss them with the class.
- With the last questions, learners may not think either word applies, or perhaps both. Encourage them to explain their answers, e.g. *She's happy thinking of all the children in the world she could play with – but then she may never meet her best friend.*

Answers
1 **Where does the girl in this poem live?** She lives in an apartment building.
2 **Are there many apartment buildings on her street?** Yes. She says there are '*a lot of apartment buildings on my street*'.
3 and 4 Learners' own answers.

Language detective

- Focus on the question and on the example. Remind learners of the adjectives beginning with *un-* in **Activity 2**. Elicit the meaning of *un-*
- Provide more examples, e.g. *kind – unkind, real – unreal, safe – unsafe*

Answers
What is the meaning of *un-* at the beginning of a word? It means *not* (i.e. the opposite of the word).
Can you think of another word for sad, which begins with *un-*? unhappy

3 Friends around the world

- Focus on the picture and ask learners to describe it.
- Tell them to look at the children and say where they think they might come from. (There are no 'right answers' here.) Tell the class to pretend they are meeting a friend from another country. They choose one of the photos and make a name card for the child.
- They complete the information on the card. They also add some information about what the child likes.
- Remind learners of the use of *he/his, she/her*.
- With a partner, learners take it in turns to pretend they are meeting the new friend.
- They complete the dialogue in the Activity book and then act out the dialogue with their partner.
- Take advantage of this activity to create awareness of different ethnic groups, how people from different parts of the world may look different, e.g. somebody from Iceland and somebody from Senegal, and also and most importantly, respect for different ethnic groups. Note: The World map on page 132 of the Learner's Book will provide learners with English names and spellings of countries used in this stage.

For further practice, see Activity 1 in the Activity Book.

Words to remember

- Write the word *friends, some, there* and *city* on the board.
- Learners look for these sight words in the song. How many times do they see each word?
- Ask them to take it in turns to practise spelling them.
- Remind them of the sight words in **Unit 1**. Ask learners to look for them in this unit.

4 The world is our neighbourhood 21

- Focus on the introductory sentences and the concept of '*neighbours on Planet Earth*'. Ask learners what they think this means.
- Tell them they are going to listen to the song. They follow in their books.
- Point out that the pictures relate to the last verse, which is not printed. Ask learners to point at the correct picture as they listen.
- Play the song a few times and encourage learners to start singing along as they grow more confident.
- Look at the meaning of this song and the values it represents. The words in this song say, '*We've got the whole world in our hands.*' What do learners think about this? What is the message of the song? (It means it is our job to take good care of the world and all the people who live with us in our 'world neighbourhood').

Audioscript: Track 21
For verses 1 and 2, see Learner's Book page 31.
(final verse)
We've got the rivers and the mountains in our hands,
We've got the seas and the oceans in our hands,
We've got the towns and the cities in our hands,
We've got the whole world in our hands.
We've got the whole world in our hands …

For further practice, see Activities 2 and 3 in the Activity Book.

Wrap up

- Sing the song once as a class.
- Then divide the class into three groups. Each group sings a verse. They sing the chorus all together.
- **Home–school opportunity:** Learners teach the family the song they have learnt.

Activity Book

1 Hello, friend!
- Learners choose one of the children and complete the dialogue.
- **Challenge:** Tell learners to write sentences about their new friend.

> **Answers**
> Learners' own answers.

2 🎵 We've got the whole world in our hands
- Ask learners to draw a line from each sentence to the matching picture.
- Then they sing the song again.

> **Answers**
> Line 1 c   Line 2 a   Line 3 b   Line 4 d

3 Read and draw
- Tell learners to look at the landscape and draw the elements listed. When they have finished, ask them to describe their picture to the class.

I can read and talk about a poem.
- Direct learners' attention to the self-evaluation question at the top of page 24. Ask them to think and answer. Emphasise the importance of giving an honest answer.

> **Answers**
> Learners' own answers.

> **Differentiated instruction**
>
> **Additional support and practice**
> - 💬 In pairs, learners take it in turns to choose two or three words they have learnt in this lesson and spell them. They write them down in their notebooks. Then check with the **Picture dictionary**.
>
> **Extend and challenge**
> - Ask learners to work in groups and add one more verse to the song, e.g. with animals, plants.

Lesson 6: Choose a project

Who lives in your neighbourhood?
Learner's Book pages: 32–33
Activity Book pages: 26–27

> **Lesson objectives**
>
> **Listening:** Listen and follow instructions, listening comprehension items in the Activity Book quiz.
> **Speaking:** Present your project to the class.
> **Reading:** Read instructions.
> **Writing:** Write sentences, make a chart, write questions and answers, draw and label a map, write answers in the **Activity Book** quiz.

Language focus: Unit 2 Review

> **Materials**
> **A Make a book:** writing/drawing supplies, A4 sheets of paper.
> **B Do a survey:** sheets of paper, writing supplies.
> **C Draw a school map:** writing supplies, a sheet of paper.

Learner's Book

↪ Warm up
- Do the warm-up routine.
- Play a guessing game with the places in the shopping centre. Learners take it in turns to give clues and the rest of the class finds the shop.
- Learners take it in turns to mime jobs. The class guesses what job it is.

Choose a project
- Learners choose an end-of-unit project to work on. Look at the examples in the pictures and help learners to choose. Provide materials. Remember that all the projects are group projects.

A Make a book
- Read the directions in the Learner's Book. Give out drawing and writing supplies.
- Learners think of interesting jobs and make a page for each.
- Tell them to look at the **Picture dictionary** for vocabulary and ideas.
- Learners write sentences and draw a picture.
- When they have finished, they show their book to the class and explain what it is about.

B Do a survey
- Read and explain the instructions. Ask learners to look at the chart and answer the question.

> **Answers**
> The most popular job is a doctor.

- Learners make the chart and go round the class asking the questions and recording the answers.
- Once learner's own chart is completed, encourage them to present the information to the class, explaining what it means (e.g. *Four people want to be … The most popular job is …*).
- Encourage the class to add follow up questions, (e.g. *How many children want to be a pilot?*), to check understanding.

C Draw a school map
- Read the instructions. Elicit the meaning of *hall*, *office* and *toilets* as these words are new vocabulary.
- Learners draw the map of their school and label it.
- When they have finished, they demonstrate how they would tell a visitor to get to different places in the school.

42   Cambridge Global English Stage 2 Teacher's Resource

- You may wish to invite other learners to play the visitor and role-play the dialogues.
- **Informal assessment opportunity:** Circulate as learners work. Informally assess their receptive and productive language skills. Ask questions. You may want to take notes on their responses.
- **Portfolio opportunity:** If possible, leave the student projects on display for a short while, then consider filing the projects, photos or scans of the work, in students' portfolios. Write the date on the work. Ask learners to review the work filed in their portfolios. Ask them to make a cover and decorate it with an illustration that shows how they feel about what they have learnt in this unit. Encourage them to write a sentence to go with the illustration, e.g. a verse of a song or a line of a poem they remember.

Look what I can do!

- Review the *I can …* statements. Learners demonstrate what they can do.
- Remind learners of the Big question: Who lives in your neighbourhood? What did they say about this? Do they remember anything special about their neighbourhood that they want to share with the class?

Activity Book

Unit 2 quiz: Look what I can do!

Listen 91 [CD2 Track 40]
- Do the first item as a class. Play the audio several times.

Listen and write
- For items 6, 7 and 8 learners read the questions, listen and write the job.

Write about you
- For items 9 and 10, learners read the question and write their answer.

Audioscript: Track 91

1. Ben likes helping. His neighbour Mrs Tran is carrying lots of bags. Ben is opening the door for Mrs Tran.
2. **Woman:** Hello, Nora.
   Girl: Hello Mrs Marcos. Are you going to your apartment?
   Woman: Yes, I am. Can you press the button for me please?
   Girl: Yes, I can! I like pressing the buttons on the lift. Which floor do you live on?
   Woman: I live on the fourth floor.
   Girl: The fourth floor. Going up!
3. **Girl:** Hello. My name is Lena.
   I live in an apartment with my family.
   I live with my mum and my dad, my baby brother, and my grandma.
   I love my family!
4. **Man:** Where do you live, Ramón?
   Boy: I live in an apartment building. It's next to the book shop.
5. **Boy:** My name is Tony. My dad's a baker.
   Girl: What does he bake?
   Boy: He bakes lots of bread.
   Girl: Mmm. I love bread.
6. **Woman:** Hi. My name is Mrs Garcia. I teach children.
7. **Woman:** Hello. How are you? My name is Mrs Wong. I paint pictures.
8. **Woman:** Hello, children. My name is Mrs Demir. I write stories.

Answers
1. c
2. b
3. c
4. a
5. a
6. teacher
7. painter
8. writer
9. Learners' own answers.
10. Learners' own answers.

UNIT 2 Good neighbours Lesson 6 43

3 Ready, steady, go!

Big question How can we move in different ways?

Unit overview

In this unit learners will:
- use action words to give instructions
- count up to 20
- talk about birds and what they can and can't do
- read and write words with long vowel sounds
- say what they like and don't like doing
- read, talk about and act out a play script.

Learners will build communication and literacy skills as they read and listen to a poem and a song, act out a story, learn action words and use them to give instructions, talk about birds and what they can or can't do, identify words with long vowel sounds, count up to 20 and speak about what they like and don't like doing.

At the end of the unit, they will apply and personalise what they have learned by working in small groups to complete a project of their choice: leading an action game, writing animal riddles or making a counting book.

Language focus
Action verbs
Adverbs *slowly, quickly*
Can/can't for ability
Conjunctions: *and, but, or*
Determiners: *all, most, some*
I like/I don't like
Sight words: *know, when, good*
Review of: present simple tense, present continuous tense and imperative, personal pronouns *it, they, -ing* forms
Vocabulary topics: body, numbers 1–20, birds, feelings

Critical thinking
- Understanding the structure of a text
- the purpose of headings
- using context and illustration to understand the meaning of words
- making deductions to work out spelling rules
- predicting
- making inferences
- memorising.

Self-assessment
- I can use action words to give instructions.
- I can talk about birds and what they can and can't do.
- I can read and write words with long vowel sounds.
- I can say what I like and don't like doing.
- I can read, talk about and act out a play script.

Teaching tips

As far as possible, encourage learners to explain and give reasons for their answers. This will help them begin to analyse and reflect even if it is on very simple things.

Review learners' work on the quiz, noting areas where they demonstrate strength and areas where they need additional instruction and practice. Use this information to customise your teaching as you continue to **Unit 4**.

Lesson 1: Think about it

How can we move in different ways?

Learner's Book pages: 34–35
Activity Book pages: 28–29

Lesson objectives

Listening: Listen to a poem, listen and follow instructions, listen and count.

Speaking: Ask and answer questions, practise theme vocabulary.

Reading: Recite and read a poem, read and identify key vocabulary.

Writing: Complete sentences.

Critical thinking: Memorise and recite.

Language focus: Singular and plural nouns; imperative; adverbs: *slowly, quickly*

Vocabulary: numbers 1–20, *wave, stand, hop, flap, wiggle, nod, fall, shake, clap, tap, roll, body, nose, foot, head, hand, tummy, fingers, toes, leg, arm*

Materials: Enough copies of **Photocopiable activities 7 and 8** for the class.

Learner's Book

Warm up

- Do the warm-up routine.
- Play a few rounds of '*Simon says*' to revise action verbs the class has learnt so far.
- Discuss with learners ways in which we can move.
- Focus on the picture and ask learners to move in the same way.

1 Read and listen 22

- Tell learners they are going to listen to a poem. They listen and join in.
- Play the audio a few times. Pause for learners to repeat each line.
- Play the poem again and ask learners to do the actions.
- Play the poem one last time and learners say the poem along and point at the children who are doing the action in the picture.
- Point at the children in the picture in random order and elicit the correct action word from the class.
- **Critical thinking:** encourage learners to memorise the poem. When they feel confident enough, invite them to recite it either individually or in pairs.

Audioscript: Track 22. See Learner's Book page 34.

2 'Get up and move' day 23

- Point to the picture and tell learners they are going to listen to Julia.
- They listen and say what the children are doing.
- Play the audio at least twice.
- Ask learners if they can wave their hands, hop on one foot and nod their heads.
- Invite them to try to do it.

Audioscript: Track 23

Julia: It's 'Get up and move' day at our school. Moving is good for us: it keeps our bodies healthy and strong. We are moving in lots of different ways!

Those two children are having a duck race. Look! They are flapping their arms and walking like ducks.

That boy over there is jumping very high. He's trying to reach the balloon. I think he's done it!

These children are playing a game. Let's listen to them.

Child 1: Wave your hands!

Children 2 and 3: We're waving our hands!

Child 4: Wave your hands and hop on one foot!

Children 2 and 3: We're waving our hands and hopping on one foot!

Child 5: Wave your hands and hop on one foot and nod your head!

Children 2 and 3: We're waving our hands and hopping on one foot and nodding our heads!

Child 6: Ooo… I'm falling o-v-e-r …!

Julia: Well done, everyone! OK, it's your turn now. Can you wave your hands, hop on one foot and nod your head? Try it!

Answers
Learners' own answers from the children's activities in the audioscript above.

3 Topic vocabulary 24

- Focus on the pictures. Tell learners that they are going to listen to the audio and follow the instructions. Play the audio once and mime the movements.
- Review the meaning of *both*. Say and mime, e.g.: *Show me both hands.*
- Play the audio again and ask learners to follow the instructions.
- Play it again. Pause after each sentence for learners to say the sentence and do the action.
- You may wish to play the audio again, pause after each instruction and ask a different learner each time to say it. The class follows the instructions.
- Review the parts of the body. Focus on the picture and give some instructions, e.g. *Point to your nose, wiggle your fingers.*
- In pairs, learners take it in turns to give instructions to the class using parts of the body.

Audioscript: Track 24

Wave. Wave one hand. Now wave both your hands!

Stand. Stand up! Now stand on one leg!

Hop. Hop on one foot! Hop three times!

Fall. Fall over!

Flap. Flap your arms. Flap like a bird!

Wiggle. Wiggle your fingers. Wiggle your toes. Can you wiggle your nose?

Nod. Nod your head, up and down.

4 Say it and do it

- Go through the actions in the activity. Say, e.g. *Clap your hands, shake your head, roll your eyes.*
- In pairs, learners take it in turns to give an instruction to their partner and follow it.

Answers
Learners' own answers.

[AB] For further practice, see Activities 1, 2 and 3 in the Activity Book.

5 Counting to 20

- Revise the numbers learnt so far.
- Pre-teach *slowly/quickly*. Say e.g. *Let's run slowly.* Then mime as in slow motion. Then, do the same with *quickly–Let's run quickly.* Then mime as if running very fast.
- Play the audio at least twice so that learners familiarise themselves with the instructions.
- Play the audio again and invite the class to follow the instructions as they count.

Audioscript: Track 25

Let's count to 20 slowly. 1, 2, 3, 4, 5, 6, 7, 8, 9, 10, 11, 12, 13, 14, 15, 16, 17, 18, 19, 20.

Now let's count to 20 quickly. 1, 2, 3, 4, 5, 6, 7, 8, 9, 10, 11, 12, 13, 14, 15, 16, 17, 18, 19, 20.

Tap your tummy … and stand on one leg … and count to 15 quickly. 1, 2, 3, 4, 5, 6, 7, 8, 9, 10, 11, 12, 13, 14, 15. Did you do it?

Wiggle your fingers … and shake your head … and count to 10 slowly and *quietly*. 1, 2, 3, 4, 5, 6, 7, 8, 9, 10. Well done!

Wrap up

- Divide the class into two groups. Each group will say one line of the poem in turn while the other group carries out the instructions. Groups take turns to be the first to start saying the poem. When they become more confident, you may ask groups to say the whole poem while the other groups mime the actions.
- **Home–school opportunity:** Learners teach parents and siblings the actions and play an instructions game with them following the model of **Activity 5**.

Activity Book

1 My body

- Ask learners to look at the pictures and write the words on the lines.

Answers
1 head 2 nose 3 arm 4 hand 5 leg 6 toes 7 tummy
8 fingers 9 foot

2 Try this!

- Ask learners to read the instructions and follow them. Then they answer if they could or couldn't do as instructed.
- Take advantage of this opportunity to emphasise the importance of giving an honest answer.

Answers
Learners' own answers.

3 Read and write

- Tell learners to look at each picture. They complete the sentences with the missing words from the **Word box**.
- **Challenge:** Ask learners to complete the sentences saying what they can do with their hands.

Answers
1 **Touch** your nose.
2 **Wave** your hand.
3 **Wiggle** your finger.
4 **Hop** on one foot.
5 **Stand** on your toes.
6 **Flap** your arms.

I can use action words to give instructions.

- Direct learners' attention to the self-evaluation question at the top of page 28. Ask them to think and answer. Emphasise the importance of giving an honest answer.

Answers
Learners' own answers.

Differentiated instruction

Additional support and practice
Do Photocopiable activities 7 and 8.

How to open and close the 'chatterbox':

1 Pinch each thumb and pointer finger together; to open, pull left and right. Close by bringing all four finger tips together.

2 Put your thumbs together and your pointer fingers together; to open move your thumbs away from your pointer fingers. Close by bringing all four finger tips together.

How to play the game:

1 Say to your partner: *Choose a colour*.
2 Spell the colour aloud: *P-I-N-K*. Open and close the chatterbox as you say each letter. (See directions above.) Leave the cootie catcher open as you say the last letter.
3 Say to your partner: *Choose a number*.
4 Count to that number: *1, 2, 3 …* . Open and close the chatterbox as you say each number. Leave the chatterbox open as you say the last number.
5 Say to your partner: *Choose a number*. Open that flap. Read the directions for that number. Your partner will do what the directions say. You can do it too!

Extend and challenge

- Give each learner eight index cards for a vocabulary concentration activity. They write and illustrate eight vocabulary words, e.g. numbers and topic vocabulary. In pairs, lay cards face down in four rows of four cards. Then take turns turning over two cards, one at a time, saying the words aloud. If two matching cards are turned over, the player keeps the pair of cards. If the cards do not match, the player turns them face down again and it is the next player's turn.

Lesson 2: Find out more

What can birds do?

Learner's Book pages: 36–37
Activity Book pages: 30–31

Lesson objectives

Listening: Listen for information.
Speaking: Talk about birds.
Reading: Read about different types of birds.
Writing: Guided writing: write about a penguin.
Critical thinking: understanding the structure of a text; the purpose of headings; using context and illustration to understand the meaning of words.

Language focus: *Can /Can't* for ability; pronouns: *it, they;* conjunctions: *and, but, or;* determiners: *all, most, some*
Vocabulary: *amazing, lay eggs, feathers, humming bird, fingernail, ostrich, nest, penguin, swan, kiwi, goose, falcon, parrot, crane.* Review: colours, *big, small*

Materials: File cards, writing supplies.

Warm up

- Learners do the warm-up routine.
- With the class, recite the poem '*Reach for the sky*' on page 34 of the Learner's Book making all the necessary movements.

- Ask the class if they like birds. Look at the pictures and ask them if they know the names of the birds. Elicit names from the class and write them on the board.
- What can birds do? Elicit a few answers and write them on the board.

Answers
Learners' own answers.

1 Before you read 26

- Tell learners to look at the picture again and ask them what they know about birds in general. Elicit answers from the class.
- Direct their attention to the headings and ask them where they would find the answer to *Can all birds fly?* What helped them find the information? (the headings). Introduce the word *heading*.
- Ask learners to look at the headings. Ask them to focus on the colour, size and type of letters. Elicit from learners what the purpose is of headings in a text (to organise the text into sections, show where key information is).
- Tell learners that they are going to listen to the audio and follow in their books. Play the audio a few times.
- Elicit from learners the meaning of the new words. Encourage them to guess the meaning of the words using the illustrations and the context to help them.

Audioscript: Track 26. See Learner's Book page 36.

Answers
You will find the answer under the heading 'Flying'.

2 Talk about it

- Talk with learners about the information in **Activity 1**. Discuss what new information they have learnt about birds.
- Ask which of the birds live in their area or country.

Answers
Learners' own answers.

3 True or false?

- Ask learners to read the sentences and decide if they are true or false.
- Tell them to refer back to the text in **Activity 1** if they are not sure.
- When they have finished, check as a class. Then, ask learners to correct the false sentences to make them true.

Answers
1 true 2 true 3 false 4 true 5 false

4 All, most, some

- Refer back to the text and ask learners to make sentences using these determiners.

- For example, say: *Can all birds fly? (no) Which birds can't fly?* (The penguin and the ostrich.) *So, most birds can fly.*
- Proceed in a similar way to make the meaning of all the determiners clear to learners.
- Ask learners to make as many sentences as possible.

> **Answers**
> (Examples, based on text)
> All birds … have feathers; lay eggs.
> Most birds … build nests; can fly.
> Some birds … don't build nests; lay their eggs on the ground; can't fly; can swim.

[AB] For further practice, see Activity 1 in the Activity Book.

5 What can birds do?
- Focus on the **Language tip** box and explain the use of *and, but, or*.
- Ask learners to look at the table and say what the birds can and can't do using *and, but, or*.
- Then, ask them to write a sentence about each bird in their notebooks.

> **Answers**
> **hummingbird** A hummingbird can fly, but it can't swim or walk.
> **goose** A goose can fly, swim and walk.
> **falcon** A falcon can fly and walk, but it can't swim.

[AB] For further practice, see Activities 2 and 3 in the Activity Book.

Wrap up
- Learner A chooses a bird. Learner B asks questions, e.g. *Can it fly? Is it a …?* Learner A replies with short answer forms.
- Allow a limited number of questions to keep the activity interesting.
- **Informal assessment opportunity:** Circulate checking for correct pronunciation and use of language. You could take notes of the most common mistakes learners make for setting up some remedial work later.

Activity Book

1 What can birds do?
- Tell learners to look at the **Language tip** box and remind them of the use of determiners.
- Focus on the activity and ask them to match the sentence halves.
- When they have finished, ask individual learners to read the complete sentences.

> **Answers**
> 1 All birds have feathers.
> 2 All birds lay eggs.
> 3 Most birds can fly.
> 4 Most birds build nests.
> 5 Some birds can swim.
> 6 Some birds can't fly.

2 Which bird?
- Tell learners to look at the chart. They read the sentences and find the birds.
- **Challenge:** Learners use the chart to write about what a penguin can and can't do.

> **Answers**
> **This bird can walk, fly and climb trees, but it can't swim.** parrot
> **This bird can walk and fly, but it can't swim or climb trees.** crane
> **What can it do?** It can swim and walk.
> **What can't it do?** It can't fly or climb trees.

3 Draw a penguin
- Read through the instructions with the learners.
- Draw an example on the board as they read out the instructions and tell you what to do.
- Learners follow the instructions and draw their own penguin.

I can talk about birds and what they can and can't do.
- Direct learners' attention to the self-evaluation question at the top of page 30. Ask them to think and answer. Emphasise the importance of giving an honest answer.

> **Answers**
> Learners' own answers.

> **Differentiated instruction**
>
> **Additional support and practice**
> - Ask learners to choose one of the birds that appear in this lesson and search the Internet for information about it. Help them prepare a short information file about their bird. You may give them a set of guiding questions to help them, e.g. *Which bird? Where does it live? What does it eat? How many eggs does it lay? What can it do?* Learners can print or draw a picture to illustrate the file.
>
> **Extend and challenge**
> - Ask learners to work in pairs or small groups and search the internet for information about the birds that live in their country or region. They prepare a poster presentation about them.

Lesson 3: Words and sounds
Long vowel sounds
Learner's Book pages: 38–39
Activity Book pages: 32–33

> **Lesson objectives**
>
> **Listening:** Listen to a play; identify long vowels with silent *e*; long dipthongs *ai* and *ay*.
>
> **Speaking:** Read and say a play; act out words; sing a song.

Reading: Read a play.
Writing: Complete sentences.
Critical thinking: memorise a song.
Language focus: Adjectives to express feeling
Vocabulary: *scared, tired, unhappy, cross, puzzled, excited, surprised, hungry*
Materials: Pieces of paper, file cards, writing supplies.

Learner's Book

Warm up
- Learners do the warm-up routine.
- Ask learners to sing the ABC song (see Learner's Book page 10).

1 Which vowel sound? 27
- Ask learners to look at the pictures. Can they say the words?
- Tell learners to write the vowels **a**, **i** and **o** on three pieces of paper.
- Tell them you are going to play an audio recording.
- Learners listen for the sound in the middle of these words and hold up the vowel sound they hear.

Audioscript: Track 27

kite
rope
nine
cake
rice
line
name
page
home
phone

Answers
a kite - i
b cake - a
c page - a
d rice - i
e home - o
f line - i
g nine - i
h name - a
i rope - o
j phone - o

2 Silent e 28
- Ask learners to look at the words and say them in pairs.
- Ask them if they notice how the silent **e** changes the sound of the vowel.
- Play the audio recording at least twice for learners to check if they were right.

- Then ask learners to look at the pictures in **Activity 1** and write the words.

Audioscript: Track 28
Tim   time
Sam   same

Answers
It changes the vowel sound from short to long.

3 Revision of *ai* and *ay* 29
- Ask learners to read the play with their partner and identify words that have a long **a** sound.
- Tell them to circle these words.
- Play the audio recording. Learners listen to check their answers.
- Elicit from them what letters make this sound (**ai** and **ay**).

Audioscript: Track 29. See Learner's Book page 38.

Answers
Mr **Gray:** Let's **wait** for the **train**. **Stay away** from the wet **paint!**
Daisy Gray: There's a **snail** on the **railway**. I **hate snails**. I **hate rainy days**.
Mr **Gray:** Here comes the **train**. Move away, **Snail!**
What letters make this sound? **ay, ai, a-e**

[AB] For further practice, see Activity 1 in the Activity Book.

4 How are you feeling?
- Before doing this activity, go through and discuss the pictures with the class as several of the words are new. Encourage learners to guess the meanings using the pictures.
- Check that learners have understood the correct meaning of each word. Some of these facial expressions may vary between cultures.
- Learners work in pairs. They take it in turns to choose a word and mime it. The partner guesses what it is.

[AB] For further practice, see Activities 2 and 3 in the Activity Book.

5 Sing about it 30
- Focus on the song. Tell learners that they are going to listen to it and do the actions.
- Play the audio a few times and ask learners to join in and mime along.
- Tell learners to write more verses for the song. Work with learners to compile a list of actions they would like to use to express each feeling. Write the list on the board.
- Learners work in pairs and write their verses.
- When they have finished, they sing the new verses and the class mimes along.

UNIT 3 Ready, steady, go! Lesson 3   49

Audioscript: Track 30. See Learner's Book page 39.

[AB] For further practice, see Activity 4 in the Activity Book.

⮕ Wrap up

- Divide the class into two groups. Group A mimes an action in the song. Group B guesses the feeling it represents.
- **Home–school opportunity:** Learners can teach the song to their family and sing and mime together.

Activity Book

1 Word puzzle

- Focus on the puzzle. Tell learners to find and circle the words in the puzzle.
- Explain that some of the words go from left to right and some from top to bottom.
- Highlight the examples and let them work independently.
- When they have finished, you may ask them to check their answers with a partner. Then, check as a class.

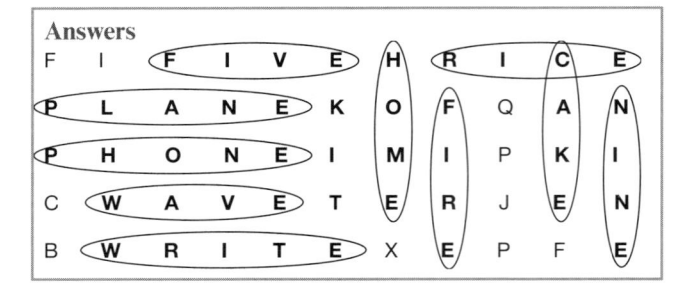

Answers									
F	I	F	I	V	E	H	R	I	C	E
P	L	A	N	E	K	O	F	Q	A	N
P	H	O	N	E	I	M	I	P	K	I
C	W	A	V	E	T	E	R	J	E	N
B	W	R	I	T	E	X	E	P	F	E

2 How are you feeling?

- Ask learners to draw a face in each circle.
- Then, they tick ✓ one of the faces to show how they are feeling today.

Answers
Learners' own answers.

3 How are these people feeling?

- Tell learners to look at the scrambled words. They put the letters in the correct order to make the word.
- Check as a class by asking individual learners to say and spell the words.

Answers
hungry   cross   puzzled

4 🎵 If you're unhappy and you know it ...

- Ask learners to draw a line from the beginning of the sentence to the best ending to make some more verses for the song.
- When they have finished they sing and mime along.

Answers
1 If you're scared and you know it, ... you can scream (quietly!).
2 If you're excited and you know it, ... shout 'Hooray!'
3 If you're hungry and you know it, ... say, 'Let's eat!'
4 If you're unhappy and you know it, ... you can cry. (Boo, hoo.)
5 If you're cross and you know it, ... say, 'Go away!'

I can read and write words with long vowel sounds.

- Direct learners' attention to the self-evaluation question at the top of page 32. Ask them to think and answer. Emphasise the importance of giving an honest answer.

Answers
Learners' own answers.

Differentiated instruction

Additional support and practice

- 💬 In pairs, learners write word cards for the feelings and the actions. They put the cards face down. They then take it in turns to turn a card and mime the action or feeling.

Extend and challenge

- Ask learners to look at the play in **Activity 3** in the Learner's Book and write the words that have a long **a** sound on a piece of paper. With a partner, they make a tongue twister.

Lesson 4: Use of English

Revision of –ing forms
Learner's Book pages: 40–41
Activity Book pages: 34–35

Lesson objectives

Listening: Listen and guess.
Speaking: Ask and answer questions.
Reading: Read and act out.
Writing: Write what you like and what you don't like.
Critical thinking: Making deductions to work out spelling rules.

Language focus:

Present continuous; spelling rules when adding *-ing*; *I like/I don't like* + verb *-ing*; conjunctions: *and, or*
Vocabulary: *waving, making, writing, ripping, cutting, swimming, watching TV, skipping, eating, shopping, playing, riding, clapping, hitting a ball, driving a car, running*

Materials: Sheets of paper.

Learner's Book

⇨ Warm up

- Do the warm-up routine.
- Sing 'If you're happy and you know it' as a class. Invite learners to mime along as they sing.
- Ask learners what they can do with a piece of paper. Elicit some answers.

1 What can you do with a piece of paper?

- Ask learners to look at the pictures and read. Tell them to mime the actions. Point at each picture in random order and ask: What's he/she doing?
- In pairs, ask learners to act out the sentences.
- Circulate, checking for correct language use and pronunciation.

Answers
Learners' own answers.

2 Listen and guess

- Ask learners to work in pairs and sit back to back with their partner. Give each one a piece of paper, e.g. old newspapers.
- Learner A does something with a piece of paper. Learner B has to listen carefully and guess what their partner is doing.
- Circulate, checking for correct pronunciation and use of language.

Answers
Learners' own answers.

[AB] For further practice, see Activities 1 and 2 in the Activity Book.

3 What do you like doing?

- Tell learners to look at the list of activities and decide which they like doing and which they don't like doing.
- Model a few examples and elicit answers from the class.
- Then, learners work independently in their notebooks.
- You may wish to extend the activity, e.g. *Where do you do these things? Swimming.* Learners answer: *I swim in the sea; watching TV – I watch TV at home.*
- Note that *shop* is a verb in itself although we more often say *go shopping*.

Answers
Learners' own answers.

Language detective

- Focus on the first set of verbs. Ask learners to look at them and find the answer to the question.
- Ask some learners to write the verbs + *ing* on the board.
- Ask the class to spell them.
- Proceed in the same way with the second set of verbs.
- **Critical thinking:** Focus on the words. Ask learners what they notice about the spelling. Can they make a rule? Ask them to look for more words to put in each group.

Answers
Look carefully. When we add -*ing*, which letter disappears?
Letter **e**
What happens when we add -*ing*?
The final consonant is doubled: *ripping, cutting*

[AB] For further practice, see Activity 3 in the Activity Book.

4 Interview your partner

- In pairs, learners ask and answer questions about what they like. Ask them to make notes.
- Circulate, checking for correct pronunciation and use of language.
- When learners have finished, they report back to the class.
- **Portfolio opportunity:** Note-taking is a useful ability learners need to develop. You may wish to collect the notes they have made, write the name and date on top and file them in their portfolios.

⇨ Wrap up

- Learners take it in turns to mime an activity they like doing, e.g. dance.
- The class has to guess what it is, e.g. *You like dancing!*

Activity Book

1 What are they doing?

- Ask learners to find the numbers next to the people and ask them to say what the people are doing.
- They write a sentence for each number.
- Remind them to use *He is, She is* or *They are* and words from the **Word box**.
- Remind learners of the information in the **Language detective box** and ask them to think about the spelling when they add -*ing*.

Answers
1 He is hitting a ball.
2 They are clapping.
3 They are waving.
4 She is running.
5 He is driving a car.

2 Having fun

- Ask learners to add -*ing* and write the words. Tell them to think about the spelling.

Answers
1 playing 2 swimming 3 riding 4 eating 5 dancing
6 shopping

3 Which do you like doing?

- Talk with learners about whether they like each activity in **Activity 2**.
- Focus on the **Activity 2** examples and elicit some more from learners before they write two examples independently.

> **Answers**
> Learners' own answers.

I can say what I like and don't like doing.

- Direct learners' attention to the self-evaluation question at the top of page 34. Ask them to think and answer. Emphasise the importance of giving an honest answer.

> **Answers**
> Learners' own answers.

Differentiated instruction

Additional support and practice

- Learners play a spelling game to revise different verbs + *ing*, e.g. *playing, running, hopping*

Extend and challenge

- Learners make a class survey of favourite activities. They make a chart with five activities of their choice. Encourage them to include action verbs they have learnt in this and other units.
- They circulate and ask at least five other learners and record the answers in their chart.
- They share the results with the class and collect them on a class chart. Then they see which activity is the most popular.

Lesson 5: Read and respond

Learner's Book pages: 42–45
Activity Book pages: 36–37

Lesson objectives

Listening: Listen to a story.
Speaking: Discuss a story, act out a play.
Reading: Read a story, read and answer questions.
Writing: Label a picture, fill in a chart, complete sentences.
Critical thinking: Predicting; making inferences; memorising their part in a play; using a chart to classify information.

Vocabulary: *narrator, character, fast, strong, brave, boasting, whisper, clever, ridiculous, race, pond, cheer, cave, winner, win, lose, rabbit, frog, deer, fox, crow*
Review adjectives to describe feelings (**Lesson 3**).

Materials: Map of the world.

Learner's Book

Warm up

- Do the warm-up routine.
- Remind learners of the adjectives for feelings they learnt in **Lesson 3**. Play a guessing game in teams.
- Team A draws a face showing a feeling and Team B says the correct word.

1 Before you read 31

- **Critical thinking:** Tell learners to look at the pictures and the title of the story and predict what the story will be about. Elicit as many suggestions as possible.
- Tell learners that this is a story from the Seneca Indians in the United States. If learners have not heard of the Seneca Indians, supply some information about them (see information box below) and ask learners to locate the US and Canada as well as other relevant places on a map.
- Read the introductory sentences and encourage learners to look at the pictures and find who the characters are.
- Tell the class they are going to listen to the story. While they listen, they read the text in their books.
- Play the story twice if necessary.

Audioscript: Track 31. See Learner's Book pages 42–45.

> **Answers**
> Bear, the turtles, Rabbit, Frog, Deer, Fox and Crow.

> **Background information on the Seneca nation**
> The Seneca Indians originally lived in the area that is now New York State. They were part of the Iroquois League, a union of six Native American nations. Today many Seneca people still live in New York State. Communities of Seneca people have also settled near Ottawa, Canada and in Oklahoma (as a result of forced migration).
> For child-appropriate information about the Seneca people, please see *http://www.bigorrin.org/seneca_kids.htm*. The official Seneca Nation website also provides useful information http://sni.org/culture/

2 Talk about it

- Focus on the questions. Tell learners to work in groups and discuss them.
- Tell them to make notes of their answers and be ready to justify them.
- Circulate offering help.
- When learners have finished, discuss the questions as a class.
- **Critical thinking:** These questions provide a good opportunity for learners to analyse, make inferences and come to conclusions as some of the answers cannot be readily found in the text. Learners are also required to give opinions and justify them, especially in the last question.

Suggested answers
1 Because he is always boasting/he thinks he is bigger, faster, stronger and braver than everyone else.
2 Rabbit, Frog, Deer, Fox and Crow.
3 Ready, steady, go!
4 unhappy, cross, tired
5 happy, excited
6 three (turtles 2, 3 and 4)
7 Learners' own answers.

[AB] For further practice, see Activities 1, 2 and 3 in the Activity Book.

3 Act out the play
- In groups, learners assign roles and rehearse the play.
- They act it out for the class.
- Check for correct pronunciation and intonation. Make notes about learners' weaknesses to set up some remedial work later.

Wrap up
- Ask learners if they know another story like *The Bear and the Turtle*, e.g. *The Hare and the Tortoise*. How similar or different are they? Learners tell their story to the class.
- **Home–school opportunity:** Learners can tell the story to their family and teach them the names of the animals.

Answers
Learners' own answers.

Activity Book

1 Where is Crow?
- Tell learners to look at the picture and write the correct words on the labels.
- Ask learners to answer the questions.

Answers
Crow is on the rock.
Bear is in the cave.
There are four holes.

2 Did you know …?
- Learners look at the pictures and write the names of two animals which are good swimmers.
- Ask learners the names of other animals which are good swimmers.

Answers
bear deer

3 Running, jumping and swimming
- Ask learners the names of animals which can run, jump and swim. Elicit some answers.
- Tell them to read and fill in the chart. They draw a tick ✓ if they think the animal **can** do the action and they draw a cross X if they think the animal **can't** do it.
- **Critical thinking:** Discuss with learners what they can use a chart for and what other information they can classify using it.

- **Challenge:** Ask learners to choose two other animals and find out and write about what they can or can't do.

Answers
Most likely responses are marked on the chart below but variations are also fine (since answers may vary across species).

	run	jump	swim
bear	✓	X	✓
turtle	X	X	✓
frog	✓	✓	✓
deer	✓	✓	✓
rabbit	✓	✓	X

I can read, talk about and act out a play script
- Direct learners' attention to the self-evaluation question at the top of page 36. Ask them to think and answer. Emphasise the importance of giving an honest answer.

Answers
Learners' own answers.

Differentiated instruction
Additional support and practice
- Play a mime game. Learners choose an animal and mime what it can do. The class guesses what animal it is and say, e.g. *A deer! A deer can jump!*

Extend and challenge
- Ask learners to search the Internet and find information about the Seneca Nation. They then prepare a poster about them.

Lesson 6: Choose a project
How can we move in different ways?
Learner's Book pages: 46–47
Activity Book pages: 38–39

Lesson objectives
Listening: Listen and follow instructions, listening comprehension items in the Activity Book quiz.
Speaking: Present your project to the class, teach a game to the class.
Reading: Read word cards, instructions, quiz items.
Writing: Write word cards and animal riddles, make a counting book, write answers in the Activity Book quiz.

Language focus: Unit 3 Review

Materials
A Lead an action game: writing/drawing supplies, file cards.
B Write an animal riddle: file cards, writing supplies.
C Make a counting book: writing supplies, sheets of paper, staples.

Learner's Book

▷ Warm up
- Do the warm-up routine.
- Ask learners to say the poem in **Lesson 1** as a class.
- Play a counting and miming game as in **Lesson 1 Activity 5**.

Choose a project
- Learners will choose an end-of-unit project to work on. Look at the examples in the pictures and help learners to choose. Provide materials.

A Lead an action game
- Read the directions in the Learner's Book. Give out drawing and writing supplies.
- Learners write the body words on cards.
- When they have finished, they take it in turns with another group to lead the game.

B Write an animal riddle
- Read and explain the instructions.
- Learners write the riddle on a card.
- They make an answer flap with the answer written underneath, as in the illustration.
- They say the riddle and the class guesses the animal.

C Make a counting book
- Read the instructions. Learners draw their book pages as instructed.
- They write the corresponding captions for each picture.
- They make a cover for the book and write the names of the authors.
- They present their book to the class.
- Circulate as learners work. Informally assess their receptive and productive language skills. Ask questions. Take notes on their responses.

> **Answers**
> How many legs do two frogs have? Eight

Look what I can do!
- Review the *I can …* statements. Learners demonstrate what they can do.
- Revisit the Big question: How can we move in different ways? Ask them to make different movements and say what they are doing.
- Elicit from learners what interesting facts they have learnt in this unit.
- **Portfolio opportunity:** While learners are engaged in oral work, circulate, listening to them and making notes on their progress and difficulties. Then write the information on a file card with the name and the date and file it in their portfolios. If possible, leave the student projects on display for a short while, then consider filing the projects, photos or scans of the work, in students' portfolios. Write the date on the work.

Activity Book

Unit 3 quiz: Look what I can do!

Listen 92 [CD2 Track 41]
- Do the first item as a class. Play the audio several times.

Listen and write
- Ask learners to look at the pictures of Lucy and John then listen and write.

Write and do
- Learners read the instructions then write and draw.

Write about you
- Learners read the question and write their answer.

> **Audioscript:** Track 92
> 1 Stand on one foot and flap your arms.
> 2 I am thinking of a bird. Here are some clues. This bird can run very fast, but it can't fly.
> 3 Now I am thinking of a different bird. Here are some clues. This bird can fly and walk, but it can't swim.
> 4 **Interviewer:** Hi, Lisa. What do you like doing?
> **Girl:** I like running and skipping.
> **Interviewer:** Do you like swimming and playing football?
> **Girl:** No, I don't like swimming or playing football.
> 5 **Narrator:** It is after the race. Frog is talking to Fox.
> **Frog:** Hello Fox. Where is Bear?
> **Fox:** He's in his cave.
> **Frog:** How is he feeling?
> **Fox:** He's feeling … puzzled.
> **Frog:** Is he feeling cross?
> **Fox:** No, he's not feeling cross. He's feeling puzzled and a bit unhappy.
> 6 **Lucy's dad:** Look, Lucy. Your friends are on their balcony.
> **Lucy:** Oh yes. I can see them.
> **Dad:** Wave to your friends.
> **Lucy:** OK. Hi Jill! Hi Alex!
> 7 **Boy:** John, please hop on one foot.
> **John:** OK! Hop, hop, hop!
> **Boy:** Very good! Thank you.

> **Answers**
> 1 c
> 2 b
> 3 c
> 4 c
> 5 a
> 6 Lucy is waving./She is waving./waving
> 7 John is hopping./He is hopping./hopping
> 8 Learner writes own name on the cake.
> 9 Learner draws a kite next to the cake.
> 10 Learners' own answers: *I like …*

4 The big sky

Big question What is the sky like?

Unit overview

In this unit learners will:
- speak about what makes day and night
- speak about what they did in the past
- read and write words with long vowel sounds
- learn about scientific developments in the past
- read and talk about an information text.

Learners will build communication and literacy skills as they read and listen to poems, read information texts, talk about the sky, clouds, day and night, identify words with long vowel sounds and speak about what they did yesterday.

At the end of the unit, they will apply and personalise what they have learned by working in small groups to complete a project of their choice: making a game, making a cloud-shaped book or making a poem.

Language focus
Simple past of *be*: regular and irregular forms, question forms

Question words

Compound nouns

Time expressions

Sight words: *many, people, about*

Review of: days of the week

Vocabulary topics: weather words, day and night words

Critical thinking
- memorising poems
- awareness of the world around us.

Self-assessment
- I can use *is* and *was*.
- I can talk about the sky.
- I can read and write words with the long **i** sound.
- I can say what I did yesterday.
- I can read and talk about an information text.

Teaching tip

Review learners' work on the quiz, noting areas where they demonstrate strength and areas where they need additional instruction and practice. Use this information to customise your teaching as you continue to **Unit 5**.

Lesson 1: Think about it

What is the sky like?
Learner's Book pages: 48–49
Activity Book pages: 40–41

> **Lesson objectives**
>
> **Listening:** Listen to a poem, listen and follow instructions.
>
> **Speaking:** Ask and answer questions, practise theme vocabulary.
>
> **Reading:** Recite and read a poem, read and identify key vocabulary.
>
> **Writing:** Complete sentences.
>
> **Critical thinking:** Memorise and recite a poem.
>
> **Language focus:** Past simple of the verb *to be*, third person
>
> **Vocabulary:** *sky, sun, cloud, shadow, long, short, clay, straw, plate*
>
> Review weather words: *sunny, cloudy, hot, cold, rainy, windy*
>
> **Materials:** Clay and straws for the sundial, file cards, writing supplies, a calendar, enough copies of **Photocopiable activity 9** for the class.

Learner's Book

Warm up
- Do the warm-up routine.
- Ask learners to choose a poem or a song from **Units 1** to **3**.
- Tell them to get together with other learners who have made the same choice and recite their poem or sing the song.
- Ask learners to look out of the window or, if the situation permits, take them to the school yard. Ask them what the sky is like. Elicit as many answers as possible.

> **Answers**
> Learners' own answers.

1 Read and listen 32
- Ask learners to look at the floor around them and find out if they have a shadow.
- Elicit the meaning of *shadow*.
- Ask them to jump. Does their shadow jump too? What else can their shadow do?
- Tell learners they are going to listen to a poem. They listen and read.
- Play the audio a few times. Pause for learners to repeat each line.
- Play the poem again and ask learners to do the actions.
- Play the poem one last time. Ask learners to say the poem and point at the girl who is doing the actions in the picture.
- Point at the pictures in random order and elicit the correct action word from the class.
- **Critical thinking:** Ask learners to memorise the poem and recite it to the class. Encourage them to use the gestures to help them memorise.

> **Audioscript:** Track 32. See Learner's Book page 48.

2 Looking at shadows 33
- Point to the picture and ask learners to describe what they see.
- Introduce *in the morning/afternoon, at midday,* e.g. *We're at home/at school in the morning.*
- Tell learners they are going to listen to Sally and her mother.
- They listen and point to the right pictures.
- Play the audio at least twice.
- Ask a few comprehension questions, e.g. *Is the shadow long or short?*

> **Audioscript:** Track 33
> **Sally:** Hi, Mum!
> **Mum:** Hi, Sally!
> **Sally:** I'm looking at my shadow. Look, my shadow is long!
> **Mum:** Oh yes, what a long shadow! It's a sunny afternoon, so we can see our shadows really well.
> **Sally:** I looked at my shadow in the morning too. In the morning my shadow was long.
> **Mum:** Yes, that's right.
> **Sally:** At midday it was cloudy, but sunny too. So I looked at my shadow again. At midday my shadow was short!
> **Mum:** Yes, at midday the sun was very high. So your shadow was very short.
> **Sally:** Now my shadow is long again!

> **Answers**
> Learners point to the relevant pictures.
> in the afternoon
> in the morning
> at midday
> in the afternoon

3 Topic vocabulary 34
- Focus on the pictures. Ask learners to listen to the audio recording, point to the correct picture and say the words.
- Play the audio up to the pause.
- Play it again. Pause after each sentence for learners to repeat.
- Play the rest of the audio recording. Ask learners to look through the window of their class, listen to the questions and think about the answers.
- Play the recording again. Stop after each question to give learners time to answer.

56 Cambridge Global English Stage 2 Teacher's Resource

Audioscript: Track 34

Speaker: Sky. The sky was blue.

Sun. The sun was high at midday.

Cloud. There were some clouds at midday.

Shadow. Sally looked at her shadow.

Long. In the morning, Sally's shadow was long.

Short. At midday, Sally's shadow was short.

[*PAUSE*]

Look through the window of your classroom.

What colour is the sky today?

Can you see the sun today?

Are there any clouds? What colour are they?

Are there any shadows?

Answers
Learners' own answers.

[AB] For further practice, see Activity 1 in the Activity Book.

4 Talk about the pictures

- Tell learners to look at each picture on page 48. Review weather vocabulary learners know, e.g. *rainy, windy, hot, cold*. Ask learners to spell the words and draw an icon for each on the board.
- Discuss the questions and elicit as many answers as possible.
- Talk to learners about the weather where they are, choosing time frames depending on the time of the lesson. It could be *now* and *this morning*, or *now* and *yesterday*. Use a calendar to make the meaning of *yesterday* clear.
- Focus on *is* (now) and *was* (specified time in the past).
- Ask learners to write their answers in their notebooks.

Answers
Sally is talking to her mum in the afternoon. Is her shadow long or short? Her shadow is long.
Is the weather sunny or cloudy? The weather is sunny.
Sally looked at her shadow in the morning. Was her shadow long or short? Her shadow was long.
In the morning, was the weather sunny or cloudy? The weather was sunny.
And at midday? Sally's shadow was short. The weather was cloudy.

[AB] For further practice, see Activity 2 in the Activity Book.

5 Make a sundial

- Give learners the materials to make the sundial.
- Read the instructions together and make the sundial.
- Go to the school yard with learners and see how it works.
- **Informal assessment opportunity:** Discuss with learners how the sundial works, encouraging them to voice their observations. Take notes of learners' strengths and weaknesses for future remedial work.

[AB] For further practice, see Activity 3 in the Activity Book.

Wrap up

- Collect all the sundials and ask learners to help you prepare a show to display their work. You may wish to invite parents or other classes to see the show. Each learner describes how they made the sundial.
- **Home–school link:** Learners show parents and siblings their sundial and show them how it works.

Activity Book

1 Label and colour

- Ask learners to look at the pictures and write the words on the labels.
- Then, they colour the pictures as instructed.

Answers
sun = yellow, shadows = black, sky = blue, cloud = grey

2 Today and yesterday

- Ask learners to look at the words in the **Word box** and answer the questions.
- Ask them to draw the picture.

Answers
Learners' own answers.

Challenge

- Ask learners what their favourite weather is. Elicit answers and invite learners to give reasons then write the answers in the Activity Book.

Answers
Learners' own answers.

3 How to make a sundial

- Ask learners to read the instructions and put them in the right order.
- They write the numbers 1, 2, 3 and 4 in the sun shapes.

Answers
Leave your sundial in a sunny place. 4
Push a straw into the clay. 3
Roll some clay into a ball. 1
Put the clay on a plate. 2

I can use *is* and *was*.

- Direct learners' attention to the self-evaluation question at the top of page 40. Ask them to think and answer. Emphasise the importance of giving an honest answer.

Answers
Learners' own answers.

UNIT 4 The big sky Lesson 1 57

> **Differentiated instruction**
>
> **Additional support and practice**
>
> - In small groups, learners write illustrated word cards of the new vocabulary they learnt in this lesson. Ask learners to post them on a noticeboard for future reference and revision.
>
> **Extend and challenge**
>
> - Do **Photocopiable activity 9**. Provide prompts to help learners explore how shadows change: Ask: *What happens to the shadow when you move your hand closer to / further from a light source? What happens to the shadow when you turn your hand? Can you use both hands to make a shadow of a duck/goose or rabbit ears?*

Lesson 2: Find out more

The sky by day and night

Learner's Book pages: 50–51
Activity Book pages: 42–43

> **Lesson objectives**
>
> **Listening:** Listen for information.
> **Speaking:** Talk about the sky, discuss why we have day and night.
> **Reading:** Read for information.
> **Writing:** Guided writing.
> **Critical thinking:** Using elements in a text to predict content.

> **Language focus:** Review of *can*
> **Vocabulary**: *sun, star, planet, drop, moon, sunlight, shine, turn round, light, dark*

> **Materials**: File cards, writing supplies, a globe, a torch, a ball.

Learner's Book

Warm up

- Learners do the warm-up routine.
- With the class, recite the poem *'Reach for the sky'* (page 34) making all the necessary movements.
- Ask learners to look at the photos on page 50 and describe what they see. Help with some questions, e.g. *What colour is the sky? Is it day or night?*

1 Before you read 35

- Tell learners to read the questions and discuss the answers with a partner. Elicit answers from the class. How much do they know? Write some answers on the board.
- Direct learners' attention to the headings in the text and ask them where they would find the answer to *What are clouds made of?* What helped them find the information? (the headings).

- **Critical thinking:** Remind learners of the importance of using headings and illustrations to help them look for information. What other things can help? (layout on the page, type of letters)
- Tell learners to listen to the audio and follow the text in their books. Play the audio a few times.
- Encourage learners to guess the meaning of any new words using the illustrations and the context to help them.
- Ask learners if they have found the answers to the questions. Elicit answers from the class.
- Tell learners to write the answers in their notebooks.

Audioscript: Track 35. See Learner's Book pages 50–51.

> **Answers**
> **Can we see the sun in the day or at night?** in the day
> **What are clouds made of?** water
> **Can we see the stars in the day?** The sun is a star, and we can see the sun in the day. But we can't see the other stars.

Try it out 36

- Ask learners to work in groups. Give each group a plastic ball and a torch and do the experiment. You may wish to model the activity yourself with a torch and a globe.
- Play the audio recording as you model the activity.
- Discuss with learners how light is reflected on different countries.

Audioscript: Track 36. See Learner's Book page 51.

For further practice, see Activities 1 and 2 in the Activity Book.

2 Write about it

- Talk about the information in **Activity 1**. Discuss what new information they have learnt about day and night.
- Ask them to write the sentences in their notebooks.
- When they have finished, they share the sentences with the class.
- **Portfolio opportunity:** You may ask learners to do this activity on a separate sheet of paper and make a picture to accompany it. Then, write the name and date and file it in the learners' portfolios.

For further practice, see Activity 3 in the Activity Book.

Wrap up

- **Spelling game**: Learners play in teams and review the vocabulary they have learnt in **Lessons 1** and **2**. Team A gives Team B a definition for a word. If team B guesses the word correctly they get a point. Then they provide a definition for Team A.
- **Home–school link:** Learners teach the new words to their family.

Activity Book

1 Yes or no?
- Tell learners to read the questions about the sky. They write **yes** or **no** for each question.

Answers
1 no
2 no
3 yes
4 yes
5 yes
6 no
7 no
8 yes

2 I live on planet Earth
- Ask learners to write the name of their country in the space then circle the correct answers.

Answers
1 Learners' own answers.
2 Planet Earth
3 light (usual answer, depending where learner lives)
4 dark (usual answer, depending where learner lives)
5 turns
6 day
7 night

3 Finish the picture
- Learners complete the picture by following the instructions.

Answers
Learners' own answers.

I can talk about the sky.
- Direct learners' attention to the self-evaluation question at the top of page 42. Ask them to think and answer. Emphasise the importance of giving an honest answer.

Answers
Learners' own answers.

Differentiated instruction

Additional support and practice
- Ask learners to search the Internet and find out what stars or groups of stars they can see in the sky, e.g. the Southern Cross. Can they see them from their home town?

Extend and challenge
- Ask learners to work in pairs or small groups and search the Internet for information about the sun, the moon and the clouds, e.g. types of clouds. They prepare a poster presentation about them.

Lesson 3: Words and sounds

Long *i* spellings
Learner's Book pages: 52–53
Activity Book pages: 44–45

Lesson objectives
Listening: Listen to a poem, identify long /i/ sounds and spelling, do a spelling dictation.
Speaking: Ask and answer questions about yesterday.
Reading: Read a poem.
Writing: Complete sentences.
Critical thinking skills: See patterns in words.

Language focus: Compound nouns; time expressions: *in the morning/afternoon/evening, at night*
Vocabulary: *sunlight, moonlight, daytime, night-time, nightclothes, daylight*

Materials: Pieces of paper, file cards, writing supplies.

Learner's Book

Warm up
- Learners do the warm-up routine.
- Ask learners to sing the ABC song (page 10).

1 Words with a long *i* sound 37
- Ask learners to look at the pictures and the words and find the words with each different ending: *-ite*, *-ine* and *-ight*.
- Tell learners to listen to the audio recording and find words that rhyme with *bite*.
- Focus on the pictures of the three things that rhyme with *bite*. Ask learners to say the words and spell them.

Audioscript: Track 37. See Learner's Book page 52.

Answers
-ite   bite, kite
-ine   line, shine
-ight   night, right
Which words rhyme with *bite*? night, right and kite
How do you spell these three words? a write **b** light **c** nine

2 Spelling dictation 38
- Ask learners to listen to the spelling and write the word. Play the audio at least twice.
- Then, ask them to point to the corresponding picture and say the word.
- Ask a few learners to write the words on the board.

UNIT 4 The big sky Lesson 3

> **Audioscript:** Track 38
> 1 n – i – g – h – t
> 2 w – r – i – t – e
> 3 k – i – t – e
> 4 l – i – g – h – t
> 5 s – h – i – n – e

> **Answers**
> 1 night 2 write 3 kite 4 light 5 shine

[AB] For further practice, see Activity 1 in the Activity Book.

3 Poem 🔊39

- Ask learners to look at the picture and describe it. Ask: *What's the sailor doing? Why is he looking at the sky?*
- Tell learners to read the poem while you play the audio recording.
- Play the recording once. Ask learners to identify words that have a long **i** sound. Tell them to point to the words.
- Play the audio recording again. Learners listen to check.
- Play the audio recording again and ask learners to answer the questions.
- Check as a class.
- Ask learners what they think the poem means. What other ways do they know of predicting the weather?

> **Audioscript:** Track 39. See Learner's Book page 52.

> **Answers**
> **Which words rhyme?** night, delight; morning, warning
> **Which words have a long *i* sound?** sky, night, delight
> **Which letter makes a long *i* sound in sky?** Letter y

[AB] For further practice, see Activity 2 in the Activity Book.

4 Compound words

- Focus on the picture. Ask learners to describe what they see. Ask: *What time of day is it? What's the boy wearing?*
- Ask them to read the sentence. Ask them to point to the very long words. What do they notice about them? (they are made up of two short words)
- Read the explanation of what a compound word is.
- **Critical thinking skills:** Focus on the list of compound words and ask learners to find the little words in each. Then, as a class, clap the syllables.
- Read the clues and ask learners to match them to the correct word. Check as a class.

> **Answers**
> 1 sunlight = sun + light
> 2 moonlight = moon + light
> 3 daytime = day + time
> 4 night-time = night + time
> 5 nightclothes = night + clothes
> 6 daylight = day + light
>
> **How many syllables are there in each word?** All the words have two syllables.
>
> a sunlight
> b night-time
> c daytime
> d nightclothes

[AB] For further practice, see Activity 3 in the Activity Book.

5 💬 Time expressions

- Focus on the question. Elicit simple phrases for where learners might have been: *at home, at school, at work, in bed*.
- Show a calendar to make the meaning of *yesterday* clear.
- Read the questions and give some examples about yourself, e.g. *I was at school in the morning. my sister/brother was at the club in the afternoon.*
- Write a few sentences with *I, He, She* on the board and elicit a simple rule from the class, e.g. *We use* **was** *with i, he and she.* Circle **was**.
- In pairs, learners talk about where they were. Circulate, checking for correct grammar and language.

> **Answers**
> Learners' own answers.

[AB] For further practice, see Activity 4 in the Activity Book.

↪ Wrap up

- Divide the class into pairs. Learner A mimes an action that can be associated with a place, e.g. play football = club. Learner B says *She was at the club*.

> **Answers**
> Learners' own answers.

Activity Book

1 Find the long *i* words

- Ask learners to look at the wordsearch and find and circle six words that make a long **i** sound.

> **Answers**
> top row: bite, light
> middle row: shine, night
> bottom row: write, kite

2 How many sounds?

- Ask learners to read the tongue twister and circle the long **i** sounds.

> **Answers**
> Five white tigers are driving in a line at night.
> **How many can you find?** 6

3 Make some compound words

- Ask learners to take one word from each half of the sun and put them together to make a longer word.

> **Answers**
> moon + light = moonlight
> day + time = daytime
> night + clothes = nightclothes
> day + light = daylight
> (Other answers are possible)

4 Read and draw

- Tell learners to draw something that they do *in the morning* and something that they do *in the afternoon*.
- **Home–school link:** Learners ask their parents what they do at different times of the day. They write the sentences and draw a picture. They may need words they still don't know, so tell them to write these words in their mother tongue. They can ask you when they go back to class. Then they draw a picture.

> **Answers**
> Learners' own answers.

Challenge

- Elicit some ideas about what people do in the evening. Learners write sentences about what they do.

> **Answers**
> Learners' own answers.

I can read and write words with the long *i* sound.

- Direct learners' attention to the self-evaluation question at the top of page 44. Ask them to think and answer. Emphasise the importance of giving an honest answer.

> **Answers**
> Learners' own answers.

Differentiated instruction

Additional support and practice

- In pairs, learners write word cards for the compound words. They cut each card in half with one half of the compound word on each card. They put them face down and take it in turns to turn the cards and find the matching pairs to form compound words.

Extend and challenge

- Ask learners to look at **Activities 1**, **2** and **3** in the Learner's Book and write the words that have a long **i** sound on a piece of paper. With a partner, they make a tongue twister.

Lesson 4: Use of English

Using the past simple

Learner's Book pages: 54–55
Activity Book pages: 46–47

Lesson objectives

Listening: Listen to a poem and do the actions.
Speaking: Ask and answer questions.
Reading: Read and act out a poem.
Writing: Write answers to an interview.

Language focus: Past simple regular forms: *-ed* forms; past simple question forms; question words
Vocabulary: *travel, spaceship, outer space, submarine, watch, talk, climb, wave, walk, bottom, use, help, brush*
Revision of weekdays

Learner's Book

Warm up

- Do the warm-up routine.
- Play a game of shadows. Ask learners to make shadows with their hands and the class guesses what the shadows are.

1 We travelled by spaceship 40

- Ask learners if they would like to travel in a spaceship. Ask: *Where would you go? How would you move in a spaceship? What would you eat?*
- Focus on the pictures and ask learners to describe them in as much detail as possible.
- Tell learners they are going to listen to a poem about two astronauts. Play the audio while learners follow in their books.
- Play the audio again. Learners mime the actions as they listen. Model the actions for learners to follow, e.g. wave goodbye, jump, climbing
- Play the audio again stopping after each exchange for learners to repeat.

Audioscript: Track 40. See Learner's Book page 54.

Language detective

- Ask learners to find a compound word in the poem.

Answer
spaceship

2 Verbs ending in *-ed*

- Ask learners to read the poem again and find all the words that describe what the children did. Remind them that they are reading about what happened in the past. Tell them that the words end in *-ed*.
- Elicit the answers from the class and write the verbs on the board.

> **Answers**
> travelled, waved, watched, jumped, walked, climbed

UNIT 4 The big sky Lesson 4   61

3 We travelled by submarine 41

- Tell learners that they are going to listen to a new poem but first, they read it and try to complete it by filling the gaps with the correct verb.
- Tell learners to copy the verbs onto slips of paper and move them around the sentences to decide which verbs fits best then write their final choice.
- Ask learners to check answers with a partner, then write them in **Activity 2** in their Activity book.
- Play the audio recording and learners check their answers.

Audioscript: Track 41. See Learner's Book page 55.

Answers
1 We **travelled** by submarine to the bottom of the sea.
2 We **waved** at the ship.
3 We **climbed** out of the submarine.
4 We **walked** on the bottom of the sea.
5 We **watched** the fishes.
6 We **talked/waved** to an octopus. Then we travelled back home.

[AB] For further practice, see Activities 1 and 2 in the Activity Book.

4 What did you do yesterday?

- In pairs, learners take it in turns to ask each other about what they did yesterday.
- Focus on the verbs and the question words between brackets. Model some questions and answers with learners.
- Learners work in pairs. Circulate, helping as necessary.
- Depending on the ability of the class, you can ask more questions, e.g. *What did you do in the morning/afternoon/evening? Did you …?*

Answers
Learners' own answers.

[AB] For further practice, see Activity 3 in the Activity Book.

Wrap up

- Learners circulate asking each other what they did on a particular day, e.g. yesterday. You may wish to set a limit to the number of learners they can ask questions to.
- When they have finished, they report their answers back to the class and see which activity was the most popular.
- Circulate, checking for correct use of language and pronunciation. Make notes for remedial work if necessary.

Answers
Learners' own answers.

Activity Book

1 We travelled by spaceship

- Ask learners to match a picture to a sentence then circle the words ending in *–ed*.

Answers
1 c   2 a   3 b

2 We travelled by submarine

- When learners have decided where to place the verbs in the poem, they write the answers.

Answers
1 We **travelled** by submarine to the bottom of the sea.
2 We **waved** at the ship.
3 We **climbed** out of the submarine.
4 We **walked** on the bottom of the sea.
5 We **watched** the fishes.
6 We **talked** to an octopus. Then we travelled back home.

3 What did you do yesterday?

- Ask learners to read the questions and write *yes* or *no* then answer the question using verbs from the word box. When they have finished, they draw a picture for each answer.

Answers
(Example answers)
Did you help? Who did you help?
Yes. I helped my dad.
Did you play? What did you play?
Yes. I played football with my brother.
Did you walk? Where did you walk to?
Yes. I walked to school.
Did you talk? Who did you talk to?
Yes. I talked to all my friends and my teacher at school.

I can say what I did yesterday.

- Direct learners' attention to the self-evaluation question at the top of page 46. Ask them to think and answer. Emphasise the importance of giving an honest answer.

Answers
Learners' own answers.

Differentiated instruction
Additional support and practice

- Make two lists. List A contains the words in the past tense which learners found in **Lesson 4**. Next to each one, build List B, the infinitive forms of the verbs.

Extend and challenge

- Learners search the Internet and find out what astronauts do when they are in outer space. They write a short paragraph.
- **Portfolio opportunity:** You may file this piece of written work in learners' portfolios.

Lesson 5: Read and respond

Learner's Book pages: 56–59
Activity Book pages: 48–49

Lesson objectives

Listening: Listen to an information text.
Speaking: Describe a picture.
Reading: Read a text and answer questions, recognise sight words: *many, people, about*.
Writing: Complete sentences.
Critical thinking: Predicting; using context to understand new words; making inferences.
Language focus: Past simple verbs, regular and irregular forms
Vocabulary: *astronomer, telescope, camera, astronomy, measure, planet, shine, year, month, calendar;* nationalities: *Egyptian, Mayan, Greek*

Materials: Map of the world.

Warm up

- Do the warm-up routine.
- In groups, ask learners to recite the poems they learnt in **Lesson 4**.

1 Before you read 42

- Tell learners to look at the map and find the countries. If their own country is not one of those mentioned, ask if the countries are far from theirs. Ask what they know about these countries. Elicit as much information as possible from learners.
- **Critical thinking:** Ask learners to look at the photographs and describe what they see. Can they predict what the text is about? What helped them?
- Read each extract and elicit the meaning of new words using the context and the pictures.
- Write the names of the countries on the board. Ask learners to find the word for the people in each country.

Audioscript: Track 42. See Learner's Book pages 56–58.

> **Answers**
> Learners' own answers.

Words to remember

- Write the words *many, people, about* on the board.
- Learners look for these sight words in the text. How many times do they see each word?
- Ask them to take it in turns to practise spelling them.

> **Answers**
> Learners' own answers.

2 True or false?

- Focus on the sentences. Ask learners to read them and decide if they are true or false. Tell them to go back to the text to check if they are not sure.

- When they have finished, check as a class. Ask learners to correct the false sentences to make true ones.

> **Answers**
> 1 false
> 2 true
> 3 false
> 4 false
> 5 true
> 6 true

For further practice, see Activities 1, 2 and 3 in the Activity Book.

3 Match the verbs

- Ask learners to look at the lists and match the verbs in the present with their past forms.
- Check as a class. Ask learners to find the verbs in the information text.

> **Answers**
> | Past | Present |
> |---|---|
> | learned | learn |
> | lived | live |
> | wrote | write |
> | made | make |
> | thought | think |
> | gave | give |
> | knew | know |

4 Spot the difference

- Ask learners to work in pairs. They look at the pictures and take it in turns to say one thing which is different.
- They write down the number of differences they can find.

> **Answers**
> (Example answers)
> **Picture 1** The girl has got long hair. The girl is wearing short socks. There are yellow stars on her red top. The girl is flying a kite. The weather is sunny. The girl's shadow is long. There is a bird in the tree.
> **Picture 2** The girl has got short hair. The girl is wearing long socks. There are no stars on her red top. The girl isn't flying a kite. The weather is cloudy. The girl's shadow is short. There is a bird behind the tree.

Wrap up

- Divide the class into pairs or small groups. Group or Pair A spells a verb in the past to Group or Pair B. They have to guess and say what verb it is. Then they switch roles. The pair or group that gets the most correct answers wins.
- **Home–school link:** Learners share with their family the information they have learnt about ancient civilisations.

Activity Book

1 Ancient astronomy

- Ask learners to read the sentences and write the missing words.
- Tell them to look at Learner's Book pages 56–58 to find the information. They use words from the **Word box**.

> **Answers**
> An astronomer is a person who looks at planets and **stars**.
> The people of ancient Egypt learned to tell the **time**.
> Hypatia wrote books about **maths** and astronomy.
> Mayan people made special **buildings** to watch the stars.
> The people of ancient Rome made a **calendar**.

2 Yes or no?

- Tell learners to read and circle **yes** or **no** next to each sentence.

> **Answers**
> 1 yes
> 2 no
> 3 no
> 4 yes

3 Mystery picture

- Ask learners to join the dots starting from number 1 to find out what the mystery picture is.

> **Answers**
> a telescope

I can read and talk about an information text.

- Direct learners' attention to the self-evaluation question at the top of page 48. Ask them to think and answer. Emphasise the importance of giving an honest answer.

> **Answers**
> Learners' own answers.

Differentiated instruction

Additional support and practice

- Ask learners to search the Internet and look for information about famous astronomers and answer three questions: *Who were they? Where did they live? What did they do?*
- Learners prepare a factsheet about their subjects.

Extend and challenge

- Ask learners to work in groups. They choose a country from those mentioned in the text. They search the Internet and find information about their chosen country. They write a short factsheet about them and present it to the class.

Lesson 6: Choose a project

What is the sky like?

Learner's Book pages: 60–61
Activity Book pages: 50–51

Lesson objectives

Listening: Listen and follow instructions, listening comprehension items in the Activity Book quiz.
Speaking: Present your project to the class, teach a game to the class.
Reading: Read word cards, instructions, quiz items.
Writing: Write word cards, make a book or write a poem, write answers in the Activity Book quiz.

Language focus: Unit 4 Review

Materials
A Make a game: writing/drawing supplies, file cards.
B Make a cloud-shaped book: card, writing supplies, sheets of paper, staples.
C Make a poem: writing supplies, sheets of paper.

Learner's Book

Warm up

- Do the warm-up routine.
- Play a few rounds of '*Simon says*' to review the verbs learnt in this unit.

Choose a project

- Learners choose an end-of-unit project to work on. Look at the examples in the pictures and help them choose. Provide materials. All the projects are done in groups.

A Make a game

- Read the directions in the Learner's Book. Give out drawing and writing supplies.
- Learners make the word cards and write the verbs, e.g. *walked, played, helped, made.* Then they make the time cards
- Play the game with the class. Take a verb card and a time card and ask learners to make up a sentence with those words in.

B Make a cloud-shaped book

- Read and explain the instructions. Look at the picture with learners so they know what their book will look like when finished.
- Learners cut out the picture of a cloud, trace it on paper or card and make them into a book.
- They make the cover and add the pages also shaped into a cloud.
- They write sentences about clouds.
- You may wish to extend the activity by asking learners to look for pictures of different types of clouds and add them to the book. If they did the **Extend and Challenge** activity in **Lesson 2**, they may re-use part of the information in this project.

C Make a poem

- Read the instructions. Learners choose a place to travel to. They could search the Internet to help them decide.
- They write the poem using the words listed and illustrate their poem.
- They read their poem to the class.
- Circulate as learners work. Informally assess their receptive and productive language skills. Ask questions. You may want to take notes on their responses.

Look what I can do!

- Review the *I can …* statements. Learners demonstrate what they can do.
- Discuss with learners what they have learnt in this unit. Ask: *What is the sky like?* Ask if they know something they didn't know before starting the unit.
- **Portfolio opportunity:** If possible, leave the student projects on display for a short while, then consider filing the projects, photos or scans of the work, in learners' portfolios. Write the date on the work.

Activity Book

Unit 4 quiz: Look what I can do!

Listen 93 [CD2 Track 42]

- Do the first item as a class. Play the audio several times.

Listen and write

- Learners listen and write the word then tick the correct picture.

Read and write

- Learners read and tick the correct picture.

Write about you

- Learners read the questions and write their answers.

Audioscript: Track 93

1 **Speaker 1:** It was sunny yesterday.
   Speaker 2: Today it is cloudy.
2 **Boy:** Mei, your shadow is very long.
   Girl: Yes, because it's morning. Shadows are long in the morning.
3 **Speaker 1:** It's very dark.
   Speaker 2: Yes, it's night-time, so we can't see the sun.
4 **Adult:** What did you do yesterday, Tom?
   Tom: I watched TV.
5 **Speaker 1:** What did you do yesterday, Lucy?
   Lucy: I travelled in a submarine!
6 l-i-g-h-t.
   Listen again: l-i-g-h-t.
7 k-i-t-e.
   Listen again: k-i-t-e.

Answers
1 c
2 a
3 a
4 c
5 c
6 a (light)
7 a (kite)
8 b (boy reading books about the sky)
9 Learners' own answers.
10 Learners' own answers.

5 Let's count and measure

Big question How do we use numbers?

Unit overview

In this unit learners will:
- count and read numbers to 100
- tell the time
- measure and say how long something is
- recognise words that sound the same, like *one/won* and *two/too*
- say and write what they did this morning
- read, discuss and act out a story.

Learners will build communication and literacy skills as they read and listen to poems and a song, read information texts and stories, talk about numbers, distances and size, identify words that sound the same, identify count and non-count nouns and speak about what they did this morning.

At the end of the unit, they will apply and personalise what they have learned by working in small groups to complete a project of their choice: making a picture with 100 objects, having a contest or making a measuring book.

Language focus
Past simple: regular and irregular forms, question forms
How many/How far …
What time is it? It's … + time to the hour
Countable and non-countable nouns
Exclamative *What a …!*
Sight words: *was, said, first, new*
Review of: shape words
Vocabulary topics: numbers up to 100, measure words

Critical thinking
- memorise poems
- awareness of the world around us
- making calculations
- awareness of distance and size
- making inferences.

Self-assessment
- I can count and read numbers to 100.
- I can measure and say how long something is
- I can recognise words that sound the same, like *one/won* and *two/too*.
- I can say and write what I did this morning.
- I can read, discuss and act out a story.

Teaching tip
Review learners' work throughout the unit, noting areas where they demonstrate strength and areas where they need additional instruction and practice. Make notes of each learner's performance and prepare personalised remedial work.

Lesson 1: Think about it

How do we use numbers?

Learner's Book pages: 62–63
Activity Book pages: 52–53

Lesson objectives

Listening: Listen to a song, listen for specific information, listen and follow instructions.
Speaking: Count, measure and tell the time.
Reading: Recite and sing a song, read and identify key vocabulary.
Writing: Complete sentences, complete a grid.
Critical thinking: Measure time, measure distances, make calculations.

Language focus: *How many …? How far … ? What time is it?* + time to the hour
Vocabulary: numbers to 100
Review of shapes: *circle, square, rectangle, triangle, star*

Materials: Pieces of paper, metre sticks or tape measures, a toy clock, enough copies of **Photocopiable Activity 10** for the class.

Learner's Book

Warm up

- Do the warm-up routine.
- Review the numbers 1 to 10. Say a number and ask learners to show it with their fingers. Then, you show a number with your fingers and they say it.
- Write the numbers 10, 20, 30, etc. on the board and ask learners to say them.
- Play a spelling game in groups. One group spells a number, e.g. *forty*, and the other group says the word and writes the number on the board.

1 Read and listen 43

- Ask learners to look at the picture and describe what they see. Can they see anything they know the names of? (shapes)
- Review words for shapes. Ask learners to point at the shapes and name them.
- Tell learners they are going to listen to a song. They listen and look for the children in the picture who are singing the song.
- Play the audio a few times. Learners identify the children.
- Play the audio again. Learners sing and join in the actions. Line up 10 learners and count in 10s by getting them to display all 10 fingers, one learner at a time.

Audioscript: Track 43. See Learner's Book page 62.

Answers
Learners' own answers.

2 A maths lesson 44

- Tell learners they are going to listen to the children in Class 2 having a maths lesson.
- They look at the picture, listen and point to the children they hear speaking.
- Play the audio at least twice.
- Play the audio again and ask learners to put up their hands each time they hear a number.
- Can they say the numbers they hear? Elicit the numbers and write them on the board.

Audioscript: Track 44

Girl 1: There are a lot of shapes on this chart.
Girl 2: Yes, there are! There are 10 big circles and 10 little circles.
Girl 1: There are 10 big squares and 10 little squares. There are 10 big triangles and 10 little triangles.
Girl 2: There are 10 big rectangles and 10 little rectangles. There are 10 big stars and 10 little stars.
[*PAUSE*]
Boy 1: OK, Carlos? Ready, steady, jump!
Boy 2: How far did I jump?
Boy 1: Just a moment … I'll measure. You jumped 52 centimetres.
Boy 2: How many?
Boy 1: 52 centimetres.
[*PAUSE*]
Girl: Look at this clock. What time is it?
Boy: Umm … Is it 11 o'clock?
Girl: No it isn't … try again.
Boy: It's 10 o'clock!
Girl: Yes, it is!

Answers
Part 1: two girls at the table, bottom left of picture.
Part 2: two boys with measure, centre of picture.
Part 3: boy and girl with clock, bottom right of picture.

3 Topic vocabulary 45

- Focus on the pictures. Tell learners that they are going to listen to the audio recording, point to the correct number and say it.
- Play the audio up to the pause.
- Play it again. Pause after each sentence for learners to repeat.
- Play the rest of the audio recording. Ask learners to listen and point to the numbers.
- Play the recording again. Stop after each number to give learners time to repeat.
- Play the audio once again and ask learners to count without help.

UNIT 5 Let's count and measure Lesson 1 67

> **Audioscript: Track 45**
> Ten, twenty, thirty, forty, fifty, sixty, seventy, eighty, ninety, a hundred.
> [*PAUSE*]
> Twenty, twenty one, twenty two, twenty three, twenty four, twenty five, twenty six, twenty seven, twenty eight, twenty nine, thirty.

[AB] For further practice, see Activities 1 and 2 in the Activity Book.

4 How far can you jump?

- Tell learners that they are going to listen again to the boys in **Activity 2**. They have to find out how far Carlos can jump.
- Play the audio recording at least twice. Elicit the answer from the class.
- In groups, learners try the activity and measure how far each of them can jump.
- Give each group a metre stick or tape measure. They write the numbers on pieces of paper. Learners ask and answer: *How far did x jump? S/he jumped … centimetres.*
- Then, they order the measures from smallest to biggest.
- **Critical thinking:** This activity will require learners to compare distances: *Who jumped the farthest?*

> **Audioscript: Track 46**
> **Boy 1:** OK, Carlos? Ready, steady, jump!
> **Boy 2:** How far did I jump?
> **Boy 1:** Just a moment … I'll measure. You jumped 52 centimetres.
> **Boy 2:** How many?
> **Boy 1:** 52 centimetres.

> **Answers**
> 52 centimetres

5 What time is it?

- Pre-teach the time using a toy clock or drawing a clock face on the board.
- Write *o'clock* on the board for learners to remember the phrase.
- Turn to the activity in the Learner's Book. In pairs, learners ask and answer questions about the time.
- **Critical thinking:** Learners become aware of the passing of time and also learn to measure time.

> **Answers**
> Clocks shown read 2 o'clock; 11 o'clock; 6 o'clock; 9 o'clock; 4 o'clock

[AB] For further practice, see Activity 3 in the Activity Book.

Wrap up

- Divide the class into two groups. Group A draws a clock on the board showing a time, e.g. 2 o'clock. They ask: *What's the time?* Group B answers. If the answer is correct they get a point. If it isn't, the point goes to Group A. Then, Group B asks.
- **Home–school opportunity:** Learners teach parents and siblings how to tell the time in English.

Activity Book

1 What time is it?

- Ask learners to look at the clocks and the sentences. They draw a line from each sentence to the two matching clocks.

> **Answers**
> 1 a, e
> 2 b, f
> 3 c, d

2 Count and write

- Explain the activity and ask learners to count the cubes. They write the number and the words.
- **Critical thinking:** Learners make calculations and solve problems: *How many … are there?* They have to count and add up.

> **Answers**
> 1 26 twenty-six
> 2 52 fifty-two
> 3 41 forty-one

3 Read and draw

- Read the instructions and ask learners to draw and colour the shapes.
- When they have finished, ask them to count how many there are and write the answers.
- Then, they draw the star.

> **Answers**
> How many stars are there altogether? 30
> How many shapes are there altogether? 100

I can count and read numbers to 100.

- Direct learners' attention to the self-evaluation question at the top of page 52. Ask them to think and answer. Emphasise the importance of giving an honest answer.

Answers
Learners' own answers.

Differentiated instruction
Additional support and practice
- 💬 Learners play '*What's the time Mr Wolf?*' One player is chosen to be Mr Wolf. Mr Wolf stands at the opposite end of the playing field from the other players, facing away from them. All players except for Mr Wolf chant in unison *What's the time, Mr Wolf?*, and Mr Wolf will answer in one of the two ways:
    1. Mr Wolf calls a clock time (e.g., *3 o'clock*). The other players will then take that many steps, counting out loud as they go (*One, two, three*). Then they ask the question again.
    2. Mr Wolf calls *Dinner Time!* Then Mr Wolf turns and chases the other players back to their starting point. If Mr Wolf successfully tags a player, that player becomes the new Mr Wolf for the next round.
- 💬 Play the game '*Smile*'. Give each learner a copy of **Photocopiable activity 10**. Tell learners to write a number from 50 to 99 in each square of the game board. Ask them to look at the example and make a similar one.
- Read a number. If that number is on the learner's game board, they put a marker on it.
- The winner is the first player to get five markers in a row. The markers can go across, down or diagonally.

Extend and challenge
- Ask learners to measure different things in their room, e.g. the distance between desks, between the board and a picture on the wall.
- They draw a simple plan and write in the distances.

Lesson 2: Find out more
How did people measure long ago?
Learner's Book pages: 64–65
Activity Book pages: 54–55

Lesson objectives
Speaking: Talk about different forms of measuring.
Reading: Read for information, read about ways of measuring in the past and in the present.
Writing: Guided writing.
Critical thinking: Apply information, global awareness.

Language focus: *How long …? It's x cm long; How many …?; was*
Vocabulary: *footsteps, metric system, centimetres, metres, school hall, leaf, fence, high, wide, long.*

Materials: File cards, writing supplies, a globe or map of the world, metre sticks, rulers of different kinds, tape measures, **Photocopiable activity 11**.

Learner's Book
Warm up
- Learners do the warm-up routine.
- Ask learners to look at the headings and the texts and to find names of countries and cities (Egypt, Rome). Ask them to locate the places on the map or globe.
- Elicit from learners information they have learnt about these countries in previous units, e.g. **Unit 4**.

1 Before you read
- Ask learners what we use to measure things. Elicit answers and show different things we use, e.g. rulers, tape measures.
- Ask learners if they think people measured things in the same way in the past. Elicit answers.
- Tell learners to read the texts and find out. Ask, e.g. *What did they use in ancient Egypt? Did they use rulers in ancient Rome?*
- Elicit from learners the meaning of the new words. Encourage them to guess the meaning of the words using the illustrations and the context to help them.
- Read each section together with the class and do the **Try it out!** activities together.
- Give learners different measuring equipment and encourage them to experiment and find the answers to the questions together and write the answers in their notebooks.
- **Critical thinking:** Learners will have to apply the information they have read to answer the questions. They will also need to reflect to solve problems like finding out why the number of footsteps is different between them and their teacher.

Answers
Learners' own answers.

For further practice, see Activity 1 in the Activity Book.

2 Centimetres or metres?
- As a class, read the questions and elicit the answers from learners.
- Ask them to show a metre and centimetres on the measuring things they have.

Answers
your school hall metres
a leaf centimetres
a fence metres

3 How long is it?

UNIT 5 Let's count and measure Lesson 2 69

- In pairs, learners use their rulers or the rulers in **Photocopiable activity 11** to measure the pictures. They ask and answer the question: *How long is it? It's … cm long.*
- They write down the results in their notebooks. Remind them to use the abbreviation *cm* for centimetres
- **Photocopiable activity 11** provides rulers for three learners. You may want to print it on stiff paper. Learners will use rulers to do measuring activities in **Lesson 2** and beyond.

Answers
paperclip 3 cm
paint brush 14 cm
fish 4 cm
shell 7 cm

[AB] For further practice, see Activities 2 and 3 in the Activity Book.

Wrap up
- Learners play a guessing game in small groups. They take it in turns to describe an object saying its measures, e.g. *It's 15 cm long, 10 cm high and 8 cm wide.* The other group members have to guess what it is, e.g. *Your pencilcase.*

Activity Book

1 Measuring with your body
- Tell learners to look at the activity and use their fingers, hands and arms to measure–like the ancient Egyptians did.

Answers
Learners' own answers.

2 Measuring with a ruler
- Focus on the activity. Elicit the meaning of *wide* and *high*.
- Tell learners to use a centimetre ruler to measure the stamps and then write the answers.

Answers
[Answers tbc]

3 Estimate … then measure
- Focus on the introduction to the activity and talk about what *estimate* means.
- Learners look at the picture of the phone and estimate the measures.
- Then, they measure a real phone or a toy phone and compare their estimates and the actual measures.

Answers
Learners' own answers.

I can measure and say how long something is.
- Direct learners' attention to the self-evaluation question at the top of page 54. Ask them to think and answer. Emphasise the importance of giving an honest answer.

Answers
Learners' own answers.

Differentiated instruction
Additional support and practice
- If learners are unfamiliar with the countries mentioned in the lesson, ask them to use the Internet to find out more information about Egypt, Mexico and Thailand. They prepare a short presentation.

Extend and challenge
- If appropriate, ask learners to work in pairs or small groups and search the Internet for information about the measurements of famous buildings in the places mentioned in the lesson, e.g. the Pyramids of Egypt, the Sphynx, the Mayan Pyramids, the Temple of Dawn in Thailand.
- They prepare a small poster with a picture of the monument they have chosen and a brief description.

Lesson 3: Words and sounds
Homophones
Learner's Book pages: 66–67
Activity Book pages: 56–57

Lesson objectives
Listening: Listen to a poem, identify homophones and spelling.
Speaking: Read and say a poem, counting in twos.
Reading: Read a poem, solve maths problems.
Writing: Complete sentences.
Critical thinking skills: Memorise a poem, solve problems.

Language focus: Exclamative *What a…* + adjective + noun!
Vocabulary: *prize, race, racehorse, win, eggs, every day, cottage, gate, cherries, fast, clever, heavy*

Materials: Pieces of paper, file cards, writing supplies.

Learner's Book

Warm up
- Learners do the warm-up routine.
- Remind learners of the poem and the words they learnt in **Unit 4**, **Lesson 3**.
- Ask them to recite the poem.
- Then, make a tongue twister with words from the lesson.

1 Words that sound the same 🔊 47

- Tell learners that there are words in English that sound the same even if the spelling is different.
- Write some examples on the board, e.g. *see – sea, right – write*. Ask learners to read the words aloud. Do they sound the same?
- Look at other homophones learners will have met e.g. *write/right, here/hear, wear/where, I/eye, know/no, buy/by, their/there*. Write them on the board and ask learners to read them aloud.
- Ask learners if there is a similar feature in their own language. If there is, elicit examples.
- Focus on the activity and ask learners to read the pairs of words aloud. Ask: *Are they the same or different?*
- Tell learners they are going to listen to a poem. They listen, read and find the words that sound the same. Play the audio at least twice.
- Play it again and pause after each verse for learners to repeat. Then ask them to read the poem independently.
- Ask learners to fill the missing words to complete the tongue twister.
- When they have finished, ask them to calculate the answer to the **Language detective** question.

Audioscript: Track 47. See Learner's Book page 66.

Answers
Find the words that sound the same. one and won; two and too
How many eggs did Ed eat in a week? 56 (8 eggs per day, 7 days per week)

[AB] For further practice, see Activity 1 in the Activity Book.

2 Counting in twos 🔊 48

- Ask learners to listen to the audio recording. They listen to the numbers and join in the counting.
- Play the audio at least twice. Learners count and point to the numbers they hear.
- Tell learners to read the poem while you play the audio recording.
- Play the audio recording. Learners listen and join in.

Audioscript: Track 48. See Learner's Book page 66.

Answers
Learners' own answers.

3 🔊 🎵 What an amazing animal! 🔊 49

- Read the explanation about the use of *What a …!*
- Play the audio up to the Pause. Ask learners to repeat after each. Check for correct pronunciation and intonation. Elicit the meaning of the new adjectives.
- Play the rest of the recording. Ask learners to follow in their books. In each exchange, stop before the exclamation and encourage learners to supply the correct one.

Audioscript: Track 49

What a fast animal!

What a big animal!

What a clever animal!

What a heavy animal!

[*PAUSE*]

Speaker 1: 1 The blue whale is the biggest animal on Earth. It is about 30 metres long. That's as long as two buses parked end to end.

Speaker 2: What a big animal!

Speaker 1: 2 A parrot can learn to talk. It can count, name colours and do maths.

Speaker 2: What a clever animal!

Speaker 1: 3 An African elephant weighs the same as 100 men.

Speaker 2: What a heavy animal!

Speaker 1: 4 A very good runner can run 12 metres in a second. A cheetah can run 30 metres in a second.

Speaker 2: What a fast animal!

Answers
1 d What a big animal! (blue whale)
2 a What a clever animal! (parrot)
3 b What a heavy animal! (elephant)
4 c What a fast animal! (cheetah)

[AB] For further practice, see Activities 2, 3 and 4 in the Activity Book.

Wrap up

- Ask learners to choose a tongue twister from this lesson or from **Unit 4 Lesson 3**. They try to say them as fast as possible. You may wish to do this as a competition and provide some small prizes for the winners, e.g. some sweets.

Activity Book

1 Words that sound the same

- Tell learners to read the words and draw a circle around the number words. Then they draw a line between each pair of words that sound the same.

Answers
one	won
two	too
four	for
eight	ate

2 Tongue twisters

- Ask learners to write the correct words on the lines and then finish the drawing.
- Ask them to say each tongue twister three times quickly.

> **Answers**
> These **four** frogs are **for** Fran's friend.
> (Learners draw a fourth frog in the box.)
> Tim has **two** turtles, **too**.
> (Learners draw two turtles in the glass tank.)

3 A maths poem

- Ask learners to read Finn's poem about his family. They work out the problem.
- **Critical thinking:** Learners will have to understand the clues to work out and write how old each person is. Ask them to reason the clues aloud.

> **Answers**
> Mary: 5 Bea: 3 Billy: 9 Grandpa: 60

Challenge

- Learners work out the answers to the questions by making the necessary calculations.

> **Answers**
> 1 7
> 2 53

4 Draw Finn's family

- Learners draw people in the poem from youngest to oldest, labelling each with their name and age.

> **Answers**
> Bea: 3 Mary: 5 Finn: 7 Billy: 9 Grandpa: 60

I can recognise words that sound the same, like *one/won* and *two/too*.

- Direct learners' attention to the self-evaluation question at the top of page 56. Ask them to think and answer. Emphasise the importance of giving an honest answer.

> **Answers**
> Learners' own answers.

Differentiated instruction

Additional support and practice

- Learners look for information about nature records, e.g. the most intelligent dog, the smallest bird, the longest river. They choose one or two and make or print a picture. They show it to the class and explain what it is following the example of **Activity 3** in the Learner's Book. The class makes a suitable exclamation.
- Supply adjectives as necessary.

Extend and challenge

- Ask learners to work in small groups. They use the words from **Lesson 3** in **Units 3**, **4** and **5** and try to make a poem.
- **Portfolio opportunity:** File the poem in learners' portfolios.

Lesson 4: Use of English

Countable and non-countable nouns

Learner's Book pages: 68–69
Activity Book pages: 58–59

Lesson objectives

Listening: Listen to a story.
Speaking: Speak about breakfast, ask and answer questions, play a memory game.
Reading: Read and act out a story.

Language focus: Countable and non-countable nouns with *some, a/an;* past simple regular and irregular forms: *-ed* forms

Vocabulary: *breakfast, grapes, bread, juice, milk, tricky, chalk, rub out*

Materials: Map of the world.

Learner's Book

⇨ Warm up

- Do the warm-up routine.
- Play a counting game to review numbers to 99.

1 Morena's breakfast

- Ask learners to look at the picture and describe what food and drink they see. Ask: *How many eggs can you see? How many glasses of orange juice?*
- Ask learners to read the rules about the food we count and the food we don't count. Then, they read the rest of the text.
- As a class, ask learners to talk about what they have for breakfast.

> **Answers**
> Learners' own answers.

2 The food shop

- Ask learners to look at the picture and find food they can count and food they can't count.
- Both orange juice (uncountable) and oranges (countable) are included, so encourage learners to notice that we can count one and not the other.
- Also point out to learners that bread is usually uncountable in English, they can say 'a loaf of bread' but not 'breads'.
- Encourage them to find the similarities and differences between English and their language.

> **Answers**
> You can count: apples, bananas, carrots, oranges, cake.
> You can't count: milk, rice, cereal, soup, orange juice, bread.

72 Cambridge Global English Stage 2 Teacher's Resource

3 Play *I went to the shop*

- Tell learners that they are going to play a memory game. Ask learners to sit in a circle and explain the rules.
- Continue round the circle, each player repeating previous items and adding one more.
- Depending on the class's ability, you could let learners make up their own items or use just the ones in the shop picture.

Answers
Learners' own answers.

4 A maths story from India 50

- Tell learners that they are going to listen to a story from India. Help them find India on a map of the world. Is it far from their country?
- Read the introduction. Elicit the meaning of *tricky problem*. Tell them to listen and follow in their books.
- Play the audio at least twice. Discuss the questions as a class. Encourage learners to give reasons for their answers.
- In pairs, learners act out the story. They draw the lines on paper and put them on the floor.

Audioscript: Track 50
Clever Birbal

One day, King Akbar picked up a piece of chalk and drew a line on the floor. 'Birbal,' he said to his friend, 'I want you to make this line shorter. But you mustn't rub out the ends of the line.'

Birbal looked at the line and thought. Then he drew a long line under King Akbar's line. 'Look,' said Birbal. 'My line is longer than your line. So your line is shorter!'

King Akbar laughed. 'You are right, Birbal,' he said. 'You made my line shorter. What a clever answer!'

Answers
Suggested answer: Birbal has to make a line which King Akbar drew shorter without rubbing any of the line out.
He solves the problem by drawing a longer second line which makes the first line look shorter.

5 Verbs in the story

- Focus on the verbs. Ask learners to look for the past forms in the story.
- When they have found them, ask them to write them in their notebooks.
- Then, tell them to choose four of the words and use them to write about what they or their family did in the morning.
- When they have finished, ask them to share their sentences with the class.

- **Home–school link:** Learners read the story about clever Birbal to the family.

Answers
look	looked
think	thought
draw	drew
laugh	laughed
make	made
say	said

For further practice, see Activities 1, 2, 3 and 4 in the Activity Book.

Wrap up

- Learners circulate, asking each other what they did in the morning. You may wish to set a limit to the number of learners they can ask questions to, e.g. five.
- When they have finished, they report their answers back to the class and see what activity has been the most popular.
- **Portfolio opportunity:** Learners write a few sentences as a summary of the survey, adding their name and the date. File the summaries in learners' portfolio.

Answers
Learners' own answers.

Activity Book

1 Find the past simple verb

- Tell learners to look at the pictures and read the verb. Then, learners follow the line to find the past tense of each verb and write it.

Answers
drink	drank
see	saw
eat	ate
say	said

2 What did you do this morning?

- Ask learners to write their answer to the questions using the past tense verbs in **Activity 1**.
- Tell them to use the **Picture dictionary** in the Learner's Book for more vocabulary.

Answers
Learners' own answers.

3 Birbal and the King

- Learners read and answer the questions using a past tense verb from the **Word box**.
- They circle the best answer.

> **Answers**
> What did Birbal draw? He **drew** a **line**.
> What did Birbal say to the King? He **said**, 'My line is longer than your line. So your line is **shorter**.'
> What did the King think about Birbal's answer? He **thought** Birbal was very **clever**.
> Did the King feel cross? No, he **felt** happy. The King **laughed**.

4 Look again!

- Learners look at the lines and decide which is longer.

> **Answer**
> Line A and Line B are the same length.

I can say and write what I did this morning.

- Direct learners' attention to the self-evaluation question at the top of page 58. Ask them to think and answer. Emphasise the importance of giving an honest answer.

> **Answers**
> Learners' own answers.

> **Differentiated instruction**
>
> **Additional support and practice**
> - Make two lists. In List A, write the words in the past which learners have found in the Unit so far. Next to each one, build List B, the infinitive forms of the verbs.
> - Learners write sentences with the past form of these verbs.
>
> **Extend and challenge**
> - If appropriate, learners search the Internet and find more information about India, the country where the story was set. They make a small poster and display it in the classroom.

Lesson 5: Read and respond

Learner's Book pages: 70–72
Activity Book pages: 60–61

> **Lesson objectives**
>
> **Listening:** Listen to a story.
> **Speaking:** Discuss and act out a story.
> **Reading:** Read a story and answer questions.
> **Sight words:** *was, said, first, new*
> **Writing:** Complete sentences, make a summary.
> **Critical thinking:** Predicting, making inferences, speculating, finding patterns.

> **Language focus:** Past simple verbs, regular and irregular forms; adverbs: *loudly, quickly, quietly*
> **Vocabulary:** *leopard, contest, elephant, water ox, chimpanzee, antelope, king, spear*

> **Materials:** Map of the world.

Learner's Book

↪ Warm up

- Do the warm-up routine.
- In groups, ask learners to recite the poems they learnt in **Lesson 3**.

1 Before you read 51

- Tell learners to look at the map and find Africa and Liberia. If learners are not familiar with the area, ask questions to elicit more information. *Is Africa a country or a continent? Is Liberia far from your country? What do you know about Africa?*
- Ask learners to look at the pictures and describe what they see. Elicit the names of the animals.
- What do they think the story is going to be about? Elicit suggestions.
- Tell learners they are going to listen to the story and follow in their books. Play the audio a few times up to the point when the chimpanzee fails the contest.
- **Critical thinking:** Ask learners to predict what will happen next. Which animal do they think will win the contest and how? Encourage them to justify their answers.
- Ask learners to find verbs in the past. They write them on the board. Elicit the infinitives.
- Discuss the meaning of new vocabulary.

> **Audioscript:** Track 51. See Learner's Book pages 70–72.

> **Answers**
> Learners' own answers.

2 💬 Talk about it

- Focus on the questions. Discuss them as a class. Encourage learners to explain their answers and give reasons.
- Ask the learners questions about how animals and people do actions, e.g. *Can elephants run quickly? Which animal runs quickly, the antelope or the turtle? Does a turtle run quickly or slowly? Do you speak quietly or loudly?* Mime as you ask to make the meaning clear to the class.
- Elicit examples and invite learners to say full sentences, e.g. *A horse runs quickly. Antelopes jump high.*
- Elicit the meaning of the six adjectives listed in the activity and ask learners to decide which describes the antelope. You may extend this question by asking them to choose an adjective for each animal.

> **Answers**
> 1 **Who are the characters in this story?**
>   King Leopard, the elephant, the water ox, the chimpanzee and the little antelope.
> 2 **Where does the story take place?** In a forest in Liberia.
> 3 **Why did King Leopard want to choose a new king?** He said he was getting old and tired.
> 4 **Which animals speak loudly?** The elephant and the water ox speak loudly.
> 5 **Which animal speaks quickly?** The chimpanzee speaks quickly.
> 6 **Which of these words describe the antelope?** tiny, clever, quiet
> 7 **What was the antelope's clever idea?** He counted in twos.
> 8 **Do you think Little Antelope will be a good king?** Why or why not? (Various possible answers. Encourage learners to justify their answer.)

[AB] For further practice, see Activities 1, 2 and 3 in the Activity Book.

3 Who says it?

- Ask learners to look at the **Language tip**. Explain the use of speech marks.
- Ask learners to match the words to the character. First they look for and find the words in the story. Then they match them with the correct character.

> **Answers**
> 1 'I'm getting old and tired.' King Leopard
> 2 'I can count very quickly.' Chimpanzee
> 3 'I'm very big.' Elephant
> 4 'I'm very strong.' Water Ox
> 5 '2, 4, 6, 8, 10!' Little Antelope

4 Read the characters' words

- Read the story with the class. Help learners use the correct intonation.

Words to remember

- Write the words *was, said, first* and *new* on the board.
- Learners look for these sight words in the story. How many times do they see each word?
- Ask them to take it in turns to practise spelling them.

> **Answers**
> Learners' own answers.

Wrap up

- Assign the characters and have learners act out the story in groups.

Activity Book

1 Which character?

- Ask learners to read the clues and write the names of the animals.

> **Answers**
> 1 Water Ox
> 2 Chimpanzee
> 3 Elephant
> 4 King Leopard
> 5 Little Antelope

2 Missing words

- Ask learners to write the missing words. They use words from the **Word box** to make a summary of part of the story.

> **Answers**
> There **was** a contest in the forest.
> All the animals **came.**
> The King **said,** 'Thank you for coming.
> You **must** throw this spear and quickly count to ten.
> You must say 'ten' before the spear hits the ground.
> The winner of the contest will be the **new** king.'
> The elephant was the **first** to try.
> 'I'm **very** big,' he said. 'I think I can do it.'

3 Counting patterns

- Tell learners that counting in twos and counting in tens are counting patterns.
- Ask them to look at the incomplete patterns and write the missing numbers in each.

> **Answers**
> two   four   six   **eight**   ten   twelve
> ten   twenty   **thirty**   forty   **fifty**

Challenge

- Ask learners to look at the numbers and find the patterns. They fill in the missing numbers.
- **Critical thinking:** Learners find the patterns in the number sequences. You may wish to challenge them to find other number patterns.

> **Answers**
> twelve   ten   eight   **six**   **four**   two
> one hundred   ninety   eighty   **seventy**   **sixty**   fifty

I can read, discuss and act out a story.

- Direct learners' attention to the self-evaluation question at the top of page 60. Ask them to think and answer. Emphasise the importance of giving an honest answer.

> **Answers**
> Learners' own answers.

Differentiated instruction

Additional support and practice

- If learners are not familiar with the areas, ask them to search the Internet and look for information about Liberia. They prepare a factsheet about the country.

Extend and challenge

- Ask learners to work in groups. They write a different end to the story, e.g. the antelope fails. Which animal tries next?

Lesson 6: Choose a project

How do we use numbers?
Learner's Book pages: 74–75
Activity Book pages: 62–63

Lesson objectives
Listening: Listen and follow instructions, Listening comprehension items in the Activity Book quiz.
Speaking: Present your project to the class, have a contest.
Reading: Read instructions, quiz items.
Writing: Write contest results, write questions, make a book, write answers in the Activity Book quiz.

Language focus: Unit 5 Review

Materials
A Make a picture with 100 objects: coloured paper, scissors, glue, poster paper or large sheet of card or stiff paper.
B Have a contest: clock or stopwatch, poster.
C Make a measuring book: writing supplies, sheets of paper, staples.

Learner's Book

Warm up
- Do the warm-up routine.
- Ask learners to choose a song or a poem they have learnt so far. They recite it or sing it for the class.

Choose a project
- Learners choose an end-of-unit project to work on. Look at the examples in the pictures and help them choose. Provide materials. All the projects are done in groups.

A Make a picture with 100 objects
- Read the directions in the Learner's Book. Give out drawing and writing supplies.
- Learners cut out the sets of shapes and make the picture. They glue the shapes onto a sheet of card or poster paper.
- They write questions about the picture.
- They show their picture to the class and describe it.
- Extend this by activity by asking learners to write some sums, e.g. red triangles + yellow squares = ... ; squares + hearts = ...

B Have a contest
- Read and explain the instructions.
- Learners start the competition and record the results on a piece of paper.
- Then, they make a poster highlighting the winner.

- They present the results to the class.
- You could add alternatives, e.g. *How many numbers can you write from 1–100?*

C Make a measuring book
- Read the instructions. Learners read the questions and answer them.
- They write the questions on the book pages as instructed. Then they write the actual answer and make an openable paper flap to cover it on the book page.
- The class will try to estimate each answer. Then, they lift the flap to see if they were right.
- Circulate as learners work. Informally assess their receptive and productive language skills. Ask questions. You may want to take notes on their responses.

Look what I can do!
- Review the *I can ...* statements. Learners demonstrate what they can do.
- Revise with learners what they have learnt in this unit. Remind them of the Big question and elicit from them the different ways in which we use numbers they have read about. What facts did they find the most interesting?
- **Portfolio opportunity:** If possible, leave the student projects on display for a short while, then consider filing the projects, photos or scans of the work, in students' portfolios. Write the date on the work. Ask learners to write a few sentences about what they have found the most interesting or what they have liked most in this unit. Then they can make a picture to accompany their sentences.

Activity Book

Unit 5 quiz: Look what I can do!

Listen 94 [CD2 Track 43]
- Do the first item as a class. Play the audio several times.

Listen and write
- Learners read the question then listen and write the answer.

Read and write
- Learners complete the sentence by choosing the correct word.

Draw and write
- Learners read the instruction and draw an animal then answer the question.

Audioscript: Track 94

1 **Speaker 1:** How many shapes are there on this chart?
Speaker 2: There are fifty shapes. There are 10 circles, 20 squares and 20 stars.
Speaker 1: Are there any triangles?
Speaker 2: No, there are no triangles.

2 **Speaker 1:** What number can you see?
Speaker 2: 62.
Speaker 1: Did you say 62?
Speaker 2: Yes, 62.

3 **Speaker 1:** This animal is the biggest animal on Earth. It is as long as two buses parked end to end.
Speaker 2: What a big animal! Does it live on the land or in the water?
Speaker 1: It lives in the water.

4 **Speaker 1:** Tony went to the shop this morning. He bought some eggs, some milk, some bread and three bananas.
Speaker 2: Can you say that again please?
Speaker 1: He bought some eggs, some milk, some bread and three bananas.

5 **Speaker 1:** Yesterday Sarah went to the pet shop.
Speaker 2: What did she see there?
Speaker 1: She saw dogs and cats and birds and fish.
Speaker 2: Did she buy a dog?
Speaker 1: No, she bought a beautiful fish.

6 **Speaker 1:** Jack's pencil is 17 centimetres long.
Speaker 2: 17 centimetres?
Speaker 1: Yes, that's right. 17 centimetres.

7 **Speaker 1:** Listen to the elephant!
Speaker 2: Wow! Is that an elephant?
Speaker 1: Yes, it is.
Speaker 2: What a loud elephant!

Answers
1 b
2 c
3 a (the blue whale is the biggest animal)
4 b
5 c
6 17 cm
7 loud
8 for
9 one
10 Learners' own answer.

6 Bugs: Fact and fiction

Big question How are bugs special?

Unit overview

In this unit learners will:
- speak about insects
- compare and contrast different insects
- read and write words with a long e sound
- find rhyming words
- ask and answer questions
- read and talk about an information text.

Learners will build communication and literacy skills as they read and listen to poems and a song, read information texts and stories, compare and contrast different insects, identify words with long **e** sound, learn and use prepositions and determiners, speak about characters in a story, make a story map.

At the end of the unit, they will apply and personalise what they have learned by working in small groups to complete a project of their choice: writing bug riddles, performing a poem and creating a cartoon story.

Language focus
Questions: *Where …?, What … eat?, What can … do?, How many…?, What … look like?, How much…?, Do/Does … ?*

Prepositions: *on, under, near*

Determiners: *all, some, most*

Review of: parts of the body, spelling, past simple: regular and irregular forms

Vocabulary topics: insects, insect body parts

Critical thinking
- memorise poems and stories
- awareness of nature
- comparing and contrasting
- making inferences.

Self-assessment
- I can name and describe bugs.
- I can say how spiders and insects are similar and different.
- I can read and write words with the long **e** sound.
- I can write questions and answer them.
- I can read, discuss and act out a story.

Teaching tips

When they are working in pairs, encourage learners to correct each other's work. This will develop their awareness of mistakes and develop cooperation.

Review learners' work on the quiz, noting areas where they demonstrate strength and areas where they need additional instruction and practice. Use this information to customise your teaching as you continue to **Unit 7**.

Lesson 1: Think about it

How are bugs special?
Learner's Book pages: 76–77
Activity Book pages: 64–65

Lesson objectives

Listening: Listen to a poem, listen for specific information, listen and answer.
Speaking: Speak about insects, describe insects.
Reading: Read a poem, read and identify key vocabulary.
Writing: Write about insects.
Critical thinking: Observe nature and make conclusions, compare and contrast insects.

Language focus: Prepositions: *on, under, near*; determiners: *all, some, most*
Vocabulary: *ant, bee, butterfly, cricket, spider, web, buzz, quiet, wings, antennae, legs*

Materials: File cards, writing and drawing supplies, A3 sheets of paper for the posters.

Learner's Book

Warm up
- Do the warm-up routine.
- Ask learners about animals they like. Ask: *What's your favourite animal? Animals* is used on this page to refer to insects, mammals and spiders.
- Focus on the big question. Explain that *bugs* is a more informal word for insects. Sometimes it is used to refer to other small creatures that are not actually insects, e.g. spiders.
- Ask learners if they like insects. Elicit a few insect names and write them on the board.
- Ask them if they think bugs are special. Encourage them to explain their answers.

Answers
Learners' own answers.

1 Read and listen 52 [CD2 Track 1]
- Focus on the picture and ask learners if they know the names of the bugs. Write the names on the board.
- Tell learners they are going to listen to a poem. Play the audio and mime the poem: (line 2: brush off the bug; line 3: hand above eye, search for the bug; line 4 shrug 'I don't know'). Learners listen and read.
- Play the audio again a few times. Ask learners to listen and act out the poem.
- Play the audio again. Learners recite and join in the actions.

Audioscript: Track 52. See Learner's Book page 76.

2 What lives in your garden? 53 [CD2 Track 2]
- Tell learners they are going to listen to a description of the bugs in the picture.
- Play the audio at least twice. Learners look at the picture, listen and point to the correct insect.
- Discuss with the class which insects there are in their country. Are they the same or are they different from the ones in the picture? If they are different, ask learners to describe them, e.g. size, colour.
- **Critical thinking:** Encourage learners to compare and contrast the insects in the picture and in their region or country and find similarities and differences.

Audioscript: Track 53

Listen. What's that? It's a bee. The bee is buzzing near the flowers. Can you see it?

There are some other insects flying above the flowers. These insects are quiet—they don't make any sound. Do you know what they are? They're butterflies.

Under the ground, you can see the home of some other busy insects. Who lives in that underground home? They're ants.

Listen to the sound of another insect. Where is that insect? What is that insect? It's a cricket.

Answers
Which ones are not talked about? The spider, the frog and the bird.

3 Topic vocabulary 54 [CD2 Track 3]
- Focus on the pictures. Tell learners that they are going to listen to an audio recording. They point to the animal and say where it is.
- Play the audio up to the pause.
- Play it again. Pause after each question and answer for learners to repeat.
- Play the rest of the audio recording. Play each question and pause to allow learners time to answer.

Audioscript: Track 54

Ant. Where are the ants? The ants are under the ground.

Bee. Where is the bee? The bee is near the flowers.

Butterfly. Where are the butterflies? The butterflies are flying above the flowers.

Cricket. Where is the cricket? The cricket is on a leaf.

Spider. Where is the spider? The spider is on its web.

Web. Where is the web? The web is on the tree.

[*PAUSE*]

Which insect lives under the ground?

Which one makes this sound?

Which one is yellow and black?

Which one has wings of different colours?

Which animal has eight legs?

> **Answers**
> Which insect lives under the ground? ant
> Which one makes this sound? cricket
> Which one is yellow and black? bee
> Which one has wings of different colours? butterfly
> Which animal has eight legs? spider

[AB] For further practice, see Activity 1 in the Activity Book.

4 What do you know about insects? 55

[CD2 Track 4]

- Focus on the questions. Elicit answers from learners. You may wish to write their answers on the board.
- Tell them they are going to listen to an audio recording. Play the audio recording at least twice.
- They listen and compare the information they hear with their answers.

> **Audioscript:** Track 55
>
> Listen to the sound of the cricket. A cricket is an insect.
>
> How many legs does an insect have? Let's count the legs. 1, 2, 3, 4, 5, 6.
>
> All insects have six legs. All insects have antennae, too. Some insects, like the cricket, have long antennae. Some, like the bee, have shorter antennae. Look for the antennae on the butterflies, the bee and the ants.
>
> Some insects have wings. A cricket has four wings. It makes a sound with its wings.
>
> But some insects don't have wings. How many insects in the picture have wings?
>
> Did you find three insects? The bee, the cricket and the butterfly are all insects with wings. Now find an insect that doesn't have wings.
>
> The ant is an insect that doesn't have wings.

> **Answers**
> How many legs does an insect have? six
> Do all insects have wings? no
> Is a spider an insect? no (it has more than six legs and doesn't have antennae)

5 Write about it

- Tell learners to write the new information in their notebooks.

> **Answers**
> All insects have … six legs and antennae.
> Some insects have … wings.
> All **insects have antennae**.

[AB] For further practice, see Activity 2 in the Activity Book.

6 Find the animal

- This is a guessing game. In pairs, learners take it in turns to describe an animal and find it in the picture.

> **Answers**
> Learners' own answers.

Wrap up

- If possible, take learners to the school garden or a park and try to find insects and speak about them. They could draw the insects they find.
- **Home–school link:** Learners show the pictures to their family and teach them the names in English.

Activity Book

1 Where is the spider? Where are the ants?

- Learners draw a spider, some ants, a butterfly and some bees in the picture.
- Then, they write about the picture using *on, under* or *near.*

> **Answers**
> Learners' own answers.

2 How to draw a cricket

- Tell learners to read and follow the instructions and draw their cricket.

> **Answers**
> Learners' own answers.

I can name and describe bugs.

- Direct learners' attention to the self-evaluation question at the top of page 64. Ask them to think and answer. Emphasise the importance of giving an honest answer.

> **Answers**
> Learners' own answers.

Differentiated instruction

Additional support and practice

- Learners play a matching game, i.e pelmanism, in pairs. They make word cards and cards with pictures of insects and the parts of their bodies. They put them face down on their tables and take it in turns to turn two cards. If it is a match of picture and word, they keep both cards; if not, they put them face down again.

Extend and challenge

- Ask learners to look for information about common insects in their area or country. In groups, they make a small poster with images of the insects and a short description.

Lesson 2: Find out more

Ants and spiders

Learner's Book pages: 78–79
Activity Book pages: 66–67

Lesson objectives

Listening: Listen for information.
Speaking: Talk about ants and spiders, compare and contrast.
Reading: Read for information, read about ants and spiders.
Writing: Guided writing.
Critical thinking: Apply information, make a Venn diagram, compare and contrast.

Vocabulary: *feel, smell, taste, communicate, build, seed, trail, web, silk, light, strong, mice*

Materials: File cards, writing supplies, **Photocopiable activity 12**.

Learner's Book

Warm up

- Learners do the warm-up routine.
- Recite and act out the poem in **Lesson 1**.

1 Before you read 56 [CD2 Track 5]

- Ask learners to look at the headings in the texts on pages 78 and 79 and discuss how they are similar. Ask them to predict what they are going to learn about. Elicit some answers.
- Tell learners that they are going to listen to an audio recording about ants. They listen and follow in their books. Play the audio recording at least twice.
- Review the texts and elicit from learners the meaning of the new words. Encourage them to guess the meaning of the words using the illustrations and the context to help them.

Audioscript: Track 56. See Learner's Book page 78.

Answers
How are the headings similar? The headings are questions. The questions are the same for Ants and Spiders, but the word *ant* or *ants* has changed to *spider* or *spiders*.
What do you think you will learn about? Learners' own answers.

2 What can you remember?

- In pairs learners tell each other about ants. They can go back to their books to look for more information.
- **Critical thinking:** Learners will have to remember the information they have read. Tell them to cover the texts and use the photos as a memory aid.

Answers
Learners' own answers.

3 Interesting facts 57 [CD2 Track 6]

- Tell learners that they are going to listen to an audio recording about spiders. They listen and follow in their books. Play the audio recording at least twice.
- Review the texts and elicit from learners the meaning of the new words. Encourage them to guess the meaning of the words using the illustrations and the context to help them.
- Ask them what the most interesting fact about spiders is.

Audioscript: Track 57. See Learner's Book page 79.

Answers
Learners' own answers.

4 Compare insects and spiders

- Discuss with learners how spiders and ants are similar or different.

For further practice, see Activities 1, 2 and 3 in the Activity Book.

5 My very own bug: Draw, write and share

- Tell learners they are going to make up a bug and draw a picture of it. They will also give it a name. Encourage them to be creative.
- When they have finished the picture, learners write sentences about their bug. Tell them to use the questions as a guide.
- When they are finished, they show their bug to the class and describe it.
- **Portfolio opportunity:** You may wish to ask learners to do this activity on a separate sheet of paper and then file it in the learners' portfolios.

Answers
Learners' own answers.

Wrap up

- After presenting their bugs to the class, learners vote for their favourite, e.g. the most original, the funniest, the scariest.

Answers
Learners' own answers.

Activity Book

1 How are spiders and ants the same?

- Focus on the sentences and ask learners to circle those that are true for both spiders and insects.

Answers
They have more than four legs.
They can climb.

2 Venn diagram

- **Critical thinking:** Focus on the Venn diagram. Elicit from learners how to use it and what they use it for, i.e. to compare and contrast two or more items, in this case ants and spiders.
- Ask learners to write two facts from **Activity 1** in each section of the Venn diagram.
- When they have finished, ask them to compare their answers with a partner. Check as a class.

> **Answers**
> (other answers are possible based on learners' own observation)
> **Only true for ants:** They have antennae. They carry their food home.
> **True for ants and spiders:** They have more than four legs. They can climb.
> **Only true for spiders:** They have more than four eyes. They make webs.

3 Learn about crickets

- Tell learners to look at the three headings in the text about crickets. There is a sentence missing under each heading.
- Learners find each missing sentence at the bottom of the page and write it in the space.

> **Answers**
> … Crickets are different colours and sizes.
> … Crickets jump. Their back legs are very strong.
> … Other crickets understand their songs.

I can say how spiders and insects are similar and different.

- Direct learners' attention to the self-evaluation question at the top of page 66. Ask them to think and answer. Emphasise the importance of giving an honest answer.

> **Answers**
> Learners' own answers.

Differentiated instruction

Additional support and practice

- Give learners a copy of **Photocopiable activity 12**. Help them check their written production using the **Writer's Checklist**. They can produce more questions using these models.

Extend and challenge

- Ask learners to work in pairs or small groups and search the Internet for information about the species of ants and spiders that are more common in their country or region, e.g. the biggest/deadliest spiders, interesting facts about insects. Learners prepare a small poster and presentation about their choice.

Lesson 3: Word and sounds
Rhyming words, long *e*
Learner's Book pages: 80–81
Activity Book pages: 68–69

Lesson objectives

Listening: Listen to a song and a poem, identify rhyming words and long **e** spellings.

Speaking: Read and sing a song, read and recite a poem, do a spelling quiz.

Reading: Read a poem.

Writing: Complete sentence, answer questions about crickets, make a chart, do a crossword puzzle.

Critical thinking: Memorise a poem, find rhyming words.

Language focus: review spelling

Vocabulary: *pest, toe, knee, chest, head, flea, leaf, bump*
Review: parts of the body

Materials: Pieces of paper, file cards, writing supplies.

Learner's Book

Warm up

- Learners do the warm-up routine.
- Remind learners of the words they learnt in **Lesson 3** of **Units 1–5**.
- Ask them to find words that rhyme. Collect some rhyming words on the board.

1 Find the rhyming word

- Ask learners to read the pairs of sentences. Each missing word rhymes with the word in red. Tell them to look at the picture to find the word.
- When they have finished, ask them to compare their findings with another learners.

> **Answers**
> 1 Oh no, oh no!
>   There's a cricket on my **toe**.
> 2 Oh poor, poor me!
>   There's a cricket on my **knee**.
> 3 Oh this cricket's such a pest!
>   Now it's sitting on my **chest**.
> 4 Did you hear what I said?
>   There's a cricket on my **head**.

2 Listen and sing 58 [CD2 Track 7]

- Review parts of the body. You could play a round of 'Simon says' or simply give a few instructions: *Touch your head, shake your arms,* etc.
- Tell learners to listen to the song and point to where the cricket is while you play the audio recording.
- Play the recording at least twice. Learners listen, mime and join in.

82 Cambridge Global English Stage 2 Teacher's Resource

Audioscript: Track 58
A cricket on the floor

There's a cricket on the floor, on the floor.
There's a cricket on the floor, on the floor.
Now it's coming through the door,
That cricket on the floor.
There's a cricket on the floor, on the floor.

Now the cricket's on my toe, on my toe!
Now the cricket's on my toe, on my toe!
Oh no, oh no!
There's a cricket on my toe!
There's a cricket on my toe, on my toe!

Now the cricket's on my knee, on my knee.
Now the cricket's on my knee, on my knee.
Oh poor, poor me!
There's a cricket on my knee!
There's a cricket on my knee, on my knee.

Now the cricket's on my chest, on my chest!
Now the cricket's on my chest, on my chest!
Oh this cricket's such a pest!
Now it's sitting on my chest.
There's a cricket on my chest, on my chest!

Now the cricket's on my head, on my head!
Now the cricket's on my head, on my head!
Did you hear what I said?
There's a cricket on my head!
There's a cricket on my head, on my head!

But he jumped off ...

Now there's a cricket on the floor, on the floor.
There's a cricket on the floor, on the floor.
Look! That cricket on the floor
Is hopping out the door...
Goodbye my friend, the cricket on the floor!

Answers
Learners' own answers.

3 Long e spellings *ea* and *ee*

- Ask learners to work in pairs. They read the words and decide what vowel sound they have.
- They write the words in their notebooks and underline the letters that stand for the long **e** sound.
- Then, they play a spelling quiz taking it in turns to spell three words and guess which they are.

Answers
They all have the long **e** sound.

4 Same letters, different sound! 59

[CD2 Track 8]

- Focus on the words and ask learners to read them aloud. Compare these words with others with the same vowel sequence **ea**.
- Tell learners that they are going to listen to a poem and identify the words with the long **e** sound and those with the short **e** sound. Play the audio at least twice.

- Learners make a chart and classify the words.
- When they have finished, ask them to help you copy the chart on the board and fill it in.
- Invite learners to add further words that they know, e.g. *bread, ice-cream, peach, teacher, read* (past and present)*, feather, heading, speak.*

Audioscript: Track 59. See Learner's Book page 81.

Answers
Long: bee, flea, tea
Short: breakfast, head, went, bed

For further practice, see Activities 1 and 2 in the Activity Book.

Wrap up

- When learners have finished writing their poems in the Activity Book, they share them with the class.
- Ask learners to teach the poems to the class.
- **Home–school link:** Learners take their poem home and share it with the family.

Activity Book

1 Crossword puzzle

- Learners look at the picture clues and solve the crossword puzzle.

Answers
Across:
1 flea
5 leaf
6 three
7 bee
Down:
1 feet
2 sleep
3 eat
4 tree

Challenge

- Ask learners to write some rhyming poems.
- **Portfolio opportunity:** Write the learner's name and the date on the sheet of paper and file it in the learner's portfolio.

Answers
Learners' own answers.

2 Colour the butterfly

- Tell learners to read the instructions. They read the words and colour the butterfly.
- Tell them to say the words aloud to make sure they are making the right decisions.

Answers
green = eat, clean, teacher, please, flea, leaf, leaves
red = bread, head, heavy, measure, ready, feather, breakfast

I can read and write words with the long e sound.

- Direct learners' attention to the self-evaluation question at the top of page 68. Ask them to think and answer. Emphasise the importance of giving an honest answer.

Answers
Learners' own answers.

Differentiated instruction

Additional support and practice

- Ask learners to work in small groups. They create a song similar to the song in **Activity 2** of the Learner's Book. Then, they teach it to the class.

Extend and challenge

- Learners look for information about bees, crickets and flies and prepare a short text using the texts about spiders and ants in **Lesson 2** as models.

Lesson 4: Use of English

Writing questions

Learner's Book pages: 82–83
Activity Book pages: 70–71

Lesson objectives

Speaking: Speak about insects, ask and answer questions, play a game.
Reading: Read for information.
Writing: Complete sentences, answer questions.
Critical thinking: Develop study skills.
Language focus: Questions: *How, What, How much, Do/Does …?;* subject–verb agreement
Vocabulary: *helpful, honey, silkworm, silk, spot*

Materials: Photocopiable activity 12, writing supplies, file cards.

Learner's Book

Warm up

- Do the warm-up routine.
- Review the poems and songs about bugs the learners wrote in **Lesson 3**.

1 Ask and answer

- Ask learners to work in pairs and read the information about bees. Help them with new vocabulary, e.g. *honey*.
- Focus on the question. Tell learners to answer it.
- Now ask them to continue with the following texts and questions. They complete the questions with the missing words and answer them.
- Check as a class.

- **Critical thinking:** Tell learners to use the pictures as an aid to understanding the words they don't know. These questions will require learners to understand and apply how questions are formed in English. These questions will also require the learners to process the information as they can't just copy the answers.

Answers
Question: How **do** silkworms help people? They produce silk for people to make clothes with.
Question: How does a cricket **hear sounds**? It hears sounds through special spots on its legs.
Question: How does **a butterfly taste food**? It tastes food with its feet.

For further practice, see Activities 1 and 2 in the Activity Book.

2 Prepare a game: All about bugs

- Tell learners that they are going to prepare a game. They work in pairs. Learner A looks at the information about Ants and Learner B looks at the information about spiders in **Lesson 3**.
- They write four questions starting as shown in the activity.
- Focus on the **Language tip** box and remind learners of the correct use of the present simple in questions.
- They write their questions on a card. On the back of the card they draw one or two stars to show the difficulty of the question.
- Tell learners to use **Photocopiable activity 12**, the **Writer's checklist**, to check their work. They can also exchange their cards to check spelling and correct use of capital letters.

Answers
Learners' own answers.

3 Play 'All about bugs'

- Tell learners that they are going to play the bug game. They get together in groups and play in two teams.
- Read the rules of the games together. Learners play the game.

Wrap up

- As a grand finale, ask the winning teams to play another round to see who are the champions.

Activity Book

1 Does it fly? Do they bite?

- Tell learners to write a question about each bug using verbs from the **Word box**.

Answers
Learners' own questions and answers.

2 What's the question?

- As preparation for writing the questions for the bug game independently, tell learners to look at the questions and answers about bugs in this activity.
- Explain that part of each question is missing, the ants are carrying the missing words. They read and write the correct words in the spaces.

> **Answers**
> What do **crickets eat**?
> How does **a cricket 'sing'**?
> How many **wings does a bee have**?
> How many **wings do flies have**?
> What does a butterfly do at night?
> How do **insects smell**?

I can write questions and answer them.

- Direct learners' attention to the self-evaluation question at the top of page 70. Ask them to think and answer. Emphasise the importance of giving an honest answer.

> **Differentiated instruction**
>
> **Additional support and practice**
>
> - Learners work in pairs or small groups. They write sentences about insects on file cards but they don't write the name of the insect. They shuffle the cards and take it in turns to pick one. They read the sentence and say what insect the sentence is about.
>
> **Extend and challenge**
>
> - Learners look for information about other insects. They prepare an extension of the game using this information.

Lesson 5: Read and respond

Learner's Book pages: 84–87
Activity Book pages: 72–73

> **Lesson objectives**
>
> **Listening:** Listen to an information text.
> **Speaking:** Discuss and act out a story.
> **Reading:** Read a story and answer questions.
> **Writing:** Complete sentences, complete a story map, write the end of a story.
> **Critical thinking:** Predicting, finding the structure of a story.
> **Values:** Families and friends help each other.
> **Language focus:** Past simple verbs, regular and irregular forms
> **Vocabulary**: *beetle, worm, blow, shiver, mouse, lift up, busy, chase, scare, bite, yelp*

Materials: Map of the world, writing supplies and drawing supplies, card for the puppets.

Learner's Book

Warm up

- Do the warm-up routine.
- In groups, ask learners to think about the stories they have read so far and say which they like best and why. Do they have a favourite character?

> **Answers**
> Learners' own answers.

1 Before you read [CD2 Track 9]

- If learners are unfamiliar with the area, tell learners to look at the map and find Mexico. Ask: *Is Mexico a country or a continent? Is it far from your country? Have you read anything about Mexico in the book?* (**Unit 4 Lesson 5**) Elicit some answers.
- Ask learners to look at the pictures and describe what they see. Who do they think are the characters in the story. Ask them to give reasons. What do they think the story is going to be about? Elicit suggestions.
- **Critical thinking:** Ask learners to use the title and the pictures to predict what will happen. Encourage them to justify their answers.
- Tell learners they are going to listen to the story. They listen and follow in their books.
- **Critical thinking:** Play the audio up to certain key points in the story, e.g. when Little Ant starts to walk back home or every time Little Ant asks a new character for help. Encourage learners to predict what will happen next. Ask some questions to help them, e.g *Will Little Ant get home? Why can't Little Ant move the leaf? Why didn't the leaf move?*
- Discuss the meaning of new vocabulary. Encourage learners to use the context and the pictures to work out the meaning of new words.

Audioscript: Track 60. See Learner's Book pages 84–86.

> **Answers**
> Little Ant, Little Ant's mother, a beetle, a worm, a mouse, a cat, a dog and a flea.

2 Story map

- Focus on the explanation of what a story map is.
- Ask learners to read the story again and decide what the problem is. Elicit the answer from the class.
- Establish the chronology of the events in the story. Tell learners that stories are usually told in chronological order. They may number the events in the story and then answer.
- Encourage them to find the solution to the problem. Discuss as a class.
- Learners copy the story map structure in their notebooks.

UNIT 6 Bugs: Fact and fiction Lesson 5   85

> **Answers**
> **Problem:** A leaf falls on Little Ant.
> **What happens:**
> 1 She says to the leaf, 'Please get off me.'
> 2 She says to the mouse, 'Please lift up the leaf.'
> 3 She says to the cat, 'Please chase the mouse.'
> 4 She says to the dog, 'Please scare the cat.'
> 5 A flea hears Little Ant.
> **Solution:**
> 1 The flea bites the dog.
> 2 The dog scares the cat.
> 3 The cat chases the mouse.
> 4 The mouse lifts up the leaf.

[AB] For further practice, see Activity 1 in the Activity Book.

3 Verbs in the story

- Focus on the words and ask learners to find them in the story. They identity them and try to work out the meaning from the context.
- Then, they check their meaning in the **Picture dictionary**.
- In pairs, they take turns acting out one of the words for their partner to guess.
- When they have finished, they look for the simple past form of each verb in the story and copy the words in their notebooks making two lists, the infinitive or base form and the past simple form.

> **Answers**
> blow   blew
> shiver   shivered
> lift up   lifted up
> chase   chased
> scare   scared
> bite   bit

[AB] For further practice, see Activity 2 in the Activity Book.

4 Puppet play

- Divide the class into groups and assign a character to each group member.
- Learners make puppets for their character. Then they act out the story with their puppet.

[AB] For further practice, see Activity 3 in the Activity Book.

Wrap up

- Ask learners to show their pictures from their Activity Book and tell the class how the story ended.
- **Portfolio opportunity:** Learners copy their picture and the sentences on a sheet of paper. They write their name at the top of the paper. Collect, write the date on the back, and save in learner's portfolio.
- **Home–school link:** Learners retell the story to the family and show them the picture. They tell them what happened after Little Ant returned.

Activity Book

1 Little Ant's problem

- Ask learners to think about the story of Little Ant. They read the questions and answer them.

> **Answers**
> **What fell on Little Ant?** A leaf fell on Little Ant./a leaf
> **Did they help Little Ant?** No, they didn't./no

2 The solution

- Tell learners to read and finish the sentences. Then, they write the past tense of a verb from the **Word box**.

> **Answers**
> 1 Cousin Flea **bit** the dog.
> 2 The dog **scared** the cat.
> 3 The cat **chased** the mouse.
> 4 The mouse **lifted** the leaf.
> 5 Little Ant **ran** home to her mother.

3 What happened next?

- Ask learners to imagine what happened after Little Ant came home to her mother. What do they think they did after this? Learners draw a picture.

Challenge

- Ask learners to write sentences to go with their picture.

> **Answers**
> Learners' own answers.

I can read, discuss and act out a story.

- Direct learners' attention to the self-evaluation question at the top of page 72. Ask them to think and answer. Emphasise the importance of giving an honest answer.

> **Answers**
> Learners' own answers.

Differentiated instruction
Additional support and practice

- Ask learners to point out their favorite picture in the story to their partner. They tell their partner what is happening in the picture and/or what they like about the picture

Extend and challenge

- Ask learners to look for a story in the Learner's Book, e.g. **Unit 5 Lesson 5**. They read it again and make a story map following the model of **Activity 2** on page 87.

Lesson 6: Choose a project

How are bugs special?

Learner's Book pages: 88–89
Activity Book pages: 74–75

Lesson objectives

Listening: Listen and follow instructions, listening comprehension items in the Activity Book quiz.
Speaking: Present your project to the class, perform a poem.
Reading: Read instructions, quiz items.
Writing: Write riddles, create a cartoon story, write answers in the Activity Book quiz.
Language focus: Unit 6 Review

Materials

A Write bug riddles: writing and drawing supplies, sheets of card or paper, glue, pictures from magazines or from the Internet.
B Perform a poem: drawing supplies, sheets of paper.
C Create a cartoon story: writing and drawing supplies, sheets of paper, **Photocopiable activity 13.**

Learner's Book

Warm up

- Do the warm-up routine.
- Ask learners to choose a song or a poem they have learnt so far. They recite it or sing it for the class.

Choose a project

- Learners choose an end-of-unit project to work on. Look at the examples in the pictures and help them choose. Provide materials. All the projects are done in groups.

A Write bug riddles
- Read the directions in the Learner's Book. Give out drawing and writing supplies.
- Learners write riddles about bugs on file cards.
- They draw or find pictures and prepare picture cards.
- They ask the class to match the riddles to the pictures.

B Perform a poem
- Read and explain the instructions.
- Learners read and learn the poem and draw pictures to illustrate it.
- They perform their poem for the class.

C Create a cartoon story
- Read the instructions and give learners a copy of **Photocopiable activity 13**.
- Learners choose a bug. They write the words in the speech bubbles for the boy and the bug.

- They show their cartoon to the class.
- Circulate as learners work. Informally assess their receptive and productive language skills. Ask questions. You may want to take notes on their responses.

Look what I can do!

- Review the *I can …* statements. Learners demonstrate what they can do.
- Discuss with learners what they have learnt in this unit. Remind them of the Big question and ask them what they have learnt about bugs that they didn't know before.
- **Portfolio opportunity:** If possible, leave the student projects on display for a short while, then consider filing the projects, photos or scans of the work, in students' portfolios. Write the date on the work. You may also ask them to reflect on the difficulties they had and discuss ways to overcome them. They may write this down and revisit their notes when they have finished **Unit 7** to see if they have made progress.

Activity Book

Unit 6 quiz: Look what I can do!

Listen 95 [CD2 Track 44]

- Do the first item as a class. Play the audio several times.

Listen and write

- Learners look at the photos, listen and answer the questions.

Read and write

- Learners follow the instructions.

Audioscript: Track 95

1 **Child 1:** I am thinking of an insect. Can you find it?
   Child 2: Hmm. How many legs does it have?
   Child 1: It has six legs. All insects have six legs.
   Child 2: Does it have wings?
   Child 1: Yes, it does. This insect has wings.
   Child 2: I can see it!
   Child 1: Good! Tick the picture.

2 **Child:** Where's the bee?
   Adult: The bee is on a flower.
   Child: Where are the butterflies?
   Adult: The butterflies are flying near the flowers.
   Child: What is the frog doing?
   Adult: The frog is sitting under the flowers.

3 Ants eat leaves, seeds, bugs and other things. These ants are carrying their food home. Ants are very strong!

4 **Child:** Can a bee hear sounds?
   Adult: Yes. A bee hasn't got ears, but it can hear sounds. It hears sounds through its antennae.

5 Child: Do butterflies fly in the rain?
Adult: No they don't. When it rains, a butterfly goes under a leaf. The leaf is like an umbrella! The butterfly stays safe and dry.

6 Child 1: All spiders have a head, a body and eight legs. Some spiders have six eyes and some spiders have eight eyes. This spider has eight eyes.
Child 2: Eight eyes! That's a lot of eyes.
Child 1: Yes it is.

7 Only one insect makes food that people eat. That insect is the bee. Bees make honey. People like eating honey. It is sweet and good. Thank you, bees!

Answers
1 a
2 c
3 c
4 a
5 c
6 eight
7 a bee
8 tea, she, tree (and *the* in US pronunciation)
9 a spider
10 It has eight legs.

7 Our green earth

Big question How can we care for the earth?

Unit overview

In this unit learners will:
- speak about trees and their importance
- make rules and promises
- write *haikus*
- read and write words with a long **o** sound
- write and act out a dialogue
- read and talk about a biography.

Learners will build communication and literacy skills as they read and listen to poems, read information texts and stories, read and write haikus, identify words with the long **o** sound, learn to use *must* for rules and *will* for intentions and promises, speak about characters in a dialogue, ask for things in the market, write an autobiography.

At the end of the unit, they will apply and personalise what they have learned by working in small groups to complete a project of their choice: making a poster about our planet, making a book about their heroes or learning a poem.

Language focus
Impersonal *you*

Must/Mustn't with rules

No + -ing form

Can for permission

Will for future intentions and promises

Review of: parts of the body, spelling, past simple: regular and irregular forms.

Vocabulary topics: the earth, the park, trees, rules, the market.

Critical thinking
- Memorise poems and stories
- awareness of nature
- comparing and contrasting
- making inferences.

Self-assessment
- I can talk about rules.
- I can talk about trees and say why they are important.
- I can read words with the long **o** sound and the spelling **ow**.
- I can go shopping for plants and fruit.
- I can read and discuss a biography.

Teaching tip

When they are working in pairs, encourage learners to correct each other's work. This will develop their awareness of mistakes and develop cooperation.

Review learners' work on the quiz at the end of the Activity Book unit, noting areas where they demonstrate strength and areas where they need additional instruction and practice. Use this information to customise your teaching as you continue to **Unit 8**.

Lesson 1: Think about it

How can we care for the earth?

Learner's Book pages: 90–91
Activity Book pages: 76–77

Lesson objectives

Listening: Listen to a poem, listen for specific information, listen and follow rules.

Speaking: Recite a poem.

Reading: Read a poem, read and identify key vocabulary.

Writing: Write a poem.

Critical thinking: Make inferences; interpret, memorise and recite a poem; understand and state rules.

Language focus: Impersonal *you*; *must / mustn't* with rules; *no + -ing* form; *can* for permission

Vocabulary: *sign, rules, grass, bin, litter, cycling, fishing, sandwich, pond, haiku*

Materials: Globe, photos of Planet Earth, writing and drawing supplies, sheets of paper, a copy of **Photocopiable activity 14** for each learner.

Learner's Book

Warm up

- Do the warm-up routine.
- Show some photos of the earth, e.g. satellite photos, photos of different regions. The following sites may be useful for reference: http://www.spaceimages.com/earth.html; http://science.nationalgeographic.com/science/earth/.
- Ask learners what colours they can see, e.g. blue, white, brown, green. Ask them what the colours show, e.g. water, clouds, forests, mountains.
- Ask them what they do, if anything, to look after the earth, e.g. turn off lights after leaving the room, saving water, turning off taps while brushing their teeth. Elicit answers and supply any additional vocabulary as necessary.

1 Read and listen 61 [CD2 Track 10]

- Focus on the picture. Ask learners about all the things they see in the park: the people, signs, animals in the pond. Ask them if there is a park near their home or near the school and, if so, if they ever play in it.
- **Critical thinking:** Focus on the picture again and talk about *sandwich*. Can learners see one in the picture? Ask: *What does it mean in the poem? What are the two slices of bread?*
- Tell learners they are going to listen to the poem. Play the audio. Learners listen and read.
- Play the audio again. Ask learners to listen and act out the poem with you: paint the sky with a brush, then the earth, then make a sandwich with the palms of your two hands.

Audioscript: Track 61. See Learner's Book page 90.

2 Rules in the park 62 [CD2 Track 11]

- Elicit from learners the meaning of *rules*. Talk about school rules and rules at home. Elicit things they *can do* and *mustn't do*.
- Tell learners that they are going to listen to an audio recording. They listen for things they *can do* in the park and things they *mustn't do*.
- Play the audio several times. As a class, elicit answers. Write *Can/Mustn't* on the board and ask learners to write them in the correct category.

Audioscript: Track 62

Dad: Hi, we're new to the town. This park looks great.

Park keeper: Yes, it *is* a great park.

Girl: What can you do here?

Park keeper: Oh, lots of things! You can run and play. You can sit on the grass and eat a sandwich. Or you can watch the animals in the pond.

Girl: Can we ride our bikes in the park?

Park keeper: No, sorry, you can't. We have a rule — no cycling in the park. Look, there's a sign over there. You must leave your bikes here.

Girl: Can I fly a kite?

Park keeper: Yes, of course! Look, those people over there are flying kites.

Dad: Are there any other rules? What else mustn't we do in the park?

Park keeper: The signs tell you the rules. You must put your litter in the bin — you mustn't leave it on the grass. We want to keep the park clean. You mustn't fish in the pond — look, the sign says 'No fishing'. And you mustn't swim in the pond.

Girl: OK, thank you.

Park keeper: Oh, there's one more rule — you must have a good time at the park!

Dad: OK, we will! Thanks for the information.

Answers
What can you do in the park? You can run and play. You can sit on the grass and eat a sandwich. You can watch the animals in the pond. You can fly a kite.
What mustn't you do? You mustn't ride your bike. You mustn't drop litter. You mustn't fish in the pond. You mustn't swim in the pond.

3 Topic vocabulary 63 [CD2 Track 12]

- Focus on the pictures. Tell learners to listen, point to the pictures and say the words.
- Play the audio. Pause after each question and allow time for learners to answer.

Audioscript: Track 63

sign – How many signs can you see in the park?

rules – What is the rule about bicycles?

grass – How many children are running on the grass?

bin – How many bins are there?

litter – Where must you put your litter?

cycling – Cycling means riding a bike. Can you see anyone riding a bike?

fishing – Fishing means catching fish. Can you catch fish in the pond?

sandwich – Who is eating a sandwich?

Answers
How many signs can you see in the park? Four.
What is the rule about bicycles? You mustn't cycle in the park. You must leave your bike near the gate.
How many children are running on the grass? Four.
How many bins are there? One.
Where must you put your litter? You must put it in a bin.
Can you see anyone riding a bike? No.
Can you catch fish in the pond? No, you mustn't. The sign says 'No fishing'.
Who is eating a sandwich? A woman and a boy.

[AB] For further practice, see Activity 1 in the Activity Book.

4 Follow the rules!

- Tell learners to focus on the pictures and the question.
- They look for the matching sign in the big picture.

Answers
a (No swimming) You mustn't swim here.
b (No fishing) You mustn't fish here.
c (Don't drop litter) You mustn't drop litter here.
d (No cycling) You mustn't cycle here.

[AB] For further practice, see Activity 2 in the Activity Book.

5 Write a poem

- Focus on the poem. Explain that this kind of poem is called *haiku*. *Haiku* is a traditional form of Japanese poetry consisting of 17 syllables, in three phrases of 5, 7 and 5 respectively. This *haiku* is by Matsuo Basho (1644–1694), one of the most famous Japanese poets.
- Ask learners to read the poem out to their partner, then swap. Ask: *How does it make you feel? Do you like it?*
- Give learners a copy of **Photocopiable activity 14**. Tell them that they are going to write a poem.
- Go through the instructions with the class. Allow plenty of time for learners to work on their poem.
- This may be a difficult task for less able learners. If they find counting the syllables difficult, they can just try to write a simple poem. More able learners could try to get the syllable count right.

Wrap up

- When learners have finished writing their poems, ask them to illustrate them. Then, they read the poems to the class.
- **Portfolio opportunity:** If possible, leave the student poems on display for a short while, then consider filing the poems in students' portfolios. Write the date on the work.
- **Home–school link:** Learners teach parents and siblings the *haiku* and draw a picture together to illustrate it.

Answers
Learners' own answers.

Activity Book

1 Word puzzle

- Tell learners to find and circle the words in the puzzle. Explain that some words go from left to right and others from top to bottom.

Answers
Top to bottom: rules, grass, sign, cycling, fishing
Left to right: bin, run, sandwich, litter

2 No, no, no!

- Tell learners to look at the pictures and circle the animals who are breaking rules.
- Then, they draw a line to the rule that they are breaking.

Answers
1 No cycling: fox
2 Don't drop litter: parrot
3 No swimming: elephant
4 No fishing: chicken
5 No running: tiger
6 Don't pick flowers: dog
7 No ball games: duck and sheep

Challenge

- Tell learners they are going to think of rules that they need to follow in the classroom.
- Think of ideas together and write some rules on the board, e.g. *No shouting*.
- Tell learners to draw a sign to go with the rule in their Activity Books.

I can talk about rules.

- Direct learners' attention to the self-evaluation question at the top of page 76. Ask them to think and answer. Emphasise the importance of giving an honest answer.

Answers
Learners' own answers.

Differentiated instruction

Additional support and practice

- Make a list with learners of things they must and mustn't do at home, e.g. clean their room, tidy up, run in the living room. Ask them to choose a rule and make a picture for it.

Extend and challenge

- Ask learners to work in groups and create a set of rules for the class or the school. They make a small poster and draw the corresponding signs.

Lesson 2: Find out more

Why are trees important?

Learner's Book pages: 92–93
Activity Book pages: 78–79

Lesson objectives

Listening: Listen for information.
Speaking: Talk about trees, discuss and apply information.
Reading: Read for information, read about trees.
Writing: Guided writing.
Critical thinking: Apply information, make connections and inferences.
Values: Looking after the planet, responsibility and respect.
Language focus: *will* for future intentions and promises; *What does ... mean?*
Vocabulary: *leaves, fresh, breathe, fruit, wood, fires, furniture, roots, soil, cut down, recycle, factory*

Materials: Sheets of paper, writing supplies.

Learner's Book

Warm up

- Learners do the warm-up routine.
- Ask learners to choose a poem or a haiku and recite it.

1 Before you read 64 [CD2 Track 13]

- Ask learners what they know about trees. Elicit five facts, e.g. parts of a tree, species, the importance of trees.
- Ask them to look at the headings and the picture and predict what kind of information they can find in the text. Elicit some answers.
- Tell learners that they are going to listen to the audio recording about trees. They listen and follow in their books. Play the audio recording at least twice.
- What new information have they found? Talk about recycling and what it means, what kind of things are recycled, how popular recycling is in their city or in their country.

- **Critical thinking:** Write the word *recycling* on the board and ask learners if they notice anything special in this word, i.e. that it contains the word *cycling* from **Lesson 1**. Can they make any connection? (things going round, being used a second time, etc.) Ask learners to look for the international symbol for recycling (three arrows going round). What do they think it represents?

Audioscript: Track 64. See Learner's Book page 92.

Answers
Learners' own answers.

For further practice, see Activity 1 in the Activity Book.

2 Talk about it

- Discuss with learners what new information they have learnt about trees from the texts. Elicit ideas from them.
- Ask learners what objects they can see in the classroom that are made of wood, e.g. *pencils*.

Answers
Learners' own answers.

For further practice, see Activities 2 and 3 in the Activity Book.

3 What does it mean?

- Have learners found words they don't know? Review the texts and elicit from learners the meaning of the new words. Encourage them to guess the meaning of the words using the illustrations and the context to help them.

Answers
Learners' own answers. (*Factory* means a building where goods are made using machines.)

4 What will you do to save trees?

- Focus on the different ways in which trees can be saved.
- In pairs, learners discuss what they will do to help.
- Then, ask them to draw a picture and write their promise on a sheet of paper.

Answers
Learners' own answers.

For further practice, see Activity 4 in the Activity Book.

Wrap up

- Ask learners to read their promise to the class and show their picture.
- **Portfolio opportunity:** File the poems in learners' portfolios. Write the date on the work.

92　Cambridge Global English Stage 2 Teacher's Resource

Activity Book

1 Read and draw
- Read the instructions and tell learners to draw a picture according to the instructions.

Answers
Learners' own answers.

2 Wood from trees
- Discuss with learners how people use wood.
- They complete the sentences.

Answers
Learners' own answers.

3 Food from trees
- Learners look at the pictures and circle four foods that come from trees.

Answers
apple, pear, orange juice, nuts

4 How can we save trees?
- Ask learners to read the ideas and circle three ideas that can help.

Answers
Recycle paper. Write on both sides of the paper.
Plant new trees.

Challenge
- Learners write one new fact they learned about trees.

Answers
Learners' own answers.

I can talk about trees and why they are important.
- Direct learners' attention to the self-evaluation question at the top of page 78. Ask them to think and answer. Emphasise the importance of giving an honest answer.

Differentiated instruction

Additional support and practice
- Remind learners of the school, home and park rules in **Lesson 1**. Ask them to write a few promises using *will*, e.g. *I will help my mother at home*.

Extend and challenge
- Ask learners to work in pairs or small groups and search the Internet for information about the species of trees that are most common in their country or region and prepare a small poster and presentation about their choice.

Lesson 3: Words and sounds

Long *o* sounds
Learner's Book pages: 94–95
Activity Book pages: 80–81

Lesson objectives

Listening: Listen to a song and a poem, identify long **o** spellings, variant sounds of **ow/ou**.
Speaking: Read and sing a song, read and recite a poem.
Reading: Read a song and a poem.
Writing: Complete sentences.
Critical thinking: Memorise a poem.

Language focus: Review spelling
Vocabulary: *ground, hole, grass, tree, branch, nest, bird, feathers, seeds, flower, shower, snow*

Materials: Pieces of paper, file cards, writing supplies.

Warm up
- Learners do the warm-up routine.
- Remind learners of the words they learnt in **Unit 6, Lesson 3**. In pairs, ask them to make a tongue twister.
- They teach the tongue twister to the class.

1 Missing words
- Ask learners to look at the picture and describe what they see. They read the labels and identify the vocabulary.
- Focus on the sentences. Ask learners to complete them. Tell them to look at the picture to find the word.
- When they have finished, they say the sentences.

Answers
1 hole   4 nest
2 tree   5 bird
3 branch 6 feathers

2 Listen and sing 65 [CD2 Track 14]
- Tell learners to listen to the song and follow in their books. Play the recording at least twice.
- Play the recording again and invite learners to join in.

Audioscript: Track 65. See Learner's Book page 94.

3 Long *o* spellings *o* and *ow*
- Ask learners to work in pairs. Focus on the question and elicit answers from pairs.
- Discuss with learners why the **o** makes that sound: i.e. influence of silent **e** and **a**.
- Ask learners to write the words in their notebooks and underline the letters that stand for the long **o** sound, then write two sentences in their notebooks. Each sentence must have two or more words with a long **o** sound.

UNIT 7 Our green earth Lesson 3   93

> **Answers**
> gr<u>ow</u>　　　r<u>o</u>pe
> n<u>o</u>　　　g<u>oe</u>s
> sl<u>ow</u>ly　　　h<u>o</u>me
> b<u>oa</u>t　　　g<u>oa</u>t
> r<u>oa</u>d　　　t<u>oe</u>s

[AB] For further practice, see Activity 1 in the Activity Book.

4 The sounds of *ow* 🔊 66 [CD2 Track 15]

- Focus on the picture and ask learners to describe what they see.
- Turn to the sentences and ask learners to say both words *slow* and *cow* aloud. Do they sound the same?
- Tell learners that they are going to listen to and read a poem. As they listen and read, ask them to point with their left hand at words that rhyme with *slow* and point with their right hand at those that rhyme with *cow*.
- Play the recording a few times. Allow learners time to identify the words. Check as a class.

Audioscript: Track 66. See Learner's Book page 95.

> **Answers**
> **In which words do the letters *ow* rhyme with *slow*?** snow, grow
> **In which words do they rhyme with *cow*?** shower, flowers

Language detective

- Elicit from learners which letters make the *ow* sound like *cow* in the middle of the words.

Answer
the letters **ou**

[AB] For further practice, see Activity 2 in the Activity Book.

👉 Wrap up

- Read *Five little seeds* from **Activity 4** in the Learner's Book, or read the story of the crow from **Activity 2** in the Activity Book, as a class and encourage learners to mime as they read.
- **Home–school link:** Learners teach the family the song from **Activity 2** or poem from **Activity 4** in the lesson.

Activity Book

1 Mystery picture

- This is like a 'colour by numbers' picture, but instead of a number, each colouring space has a word. When coloured, the picture scene will reveal an image.
- Learners follow the instructions and complete the sentences.

> **Answers**
> The mystery picture is a brown **goat**.

2 Find the long *o* sounds

- Ask learners to read the story of the crow and circle all the words with a long **o** sound.

> **Answers**
> An <u>old</u> <u>crow</u> is looking for water to drink.
> He sees a <u>hole</u> in the ground.
> At the bottom of the <u>hole</u>, there is some water!
> The <u>crow</u> can't reach the water.
>
> The <u>crow</u> thinks and thinks. 'I <u>know</u> what to do!' he says.
> There are lots of little <u>stones</u> on the ground.
> The <u>crow</u> <u>throws</u> a <u>stone</u> in the <u>hole</u>.
> He <u>throws</u> lots of <u>stones</u> in the <u>hole</u>.
>
> <u>Slowly</u>, the <u>hole</u> fills with <u>stones</u>.
> The water in the <u>hole</u> gets higher and higher.
> Finally the <u>crow</u> can reach the water.
> He drinks and drinks.

Challenge

- Tell learners to read the words and make a sentence. When they have finished, ask them to read it aloud and draw a picture to go with it.

> **Answers**
> The old crow was very clever.

I can read words with the long *o* sound and the spelling *ow*.

- Direct learners' attention to the self-evaluation question at the top of page 80. Ask them to think and answer. Emphasise the importance of giving an honest answer.

> **Answers**
> Learners' own answers.

Differentiated instruction

Additional support and practice

- 💬 Ask learners to work in pairs and write two sentences that contain words from this lesson. The sentences have to be related in some way. Then they draw a picture to illustrate them.

Extend and challenge

- **Portfolio opportunity:** Ask learners to work in small groups. They use the words from the lesson to try to make a poem. File the poem in learners' portfolios.

Lesson 4: Use of English

At the market

Learner's Book pages: 96–97
Activity Book pages: 82–83

Lesson objectives

Listening: Listen for information, listen to a dialogue and complete sentences.
Speaking: Speak about plants, fruit and vegetables, ask and answer questions, act out a dialogue.
Reading: Read for information.
Writing: Complete sentences.

Language focus: *must* with instructions; *Would you like … ? I'd like …*; *this one / that one*; Revision of: *this / these, that / those*; Subject–verb agreement

Vocabulary: *vegetable, bean, carrot, tomato, water* (vb.), *dig, fill, mango, pineapple, pear*

Materials: Writing supplies, file cards.

Warm up

- Do the warm-up routine.
- Review the poem in **Lesson 3**, **Activity 4** and ask learners to recite it together.
- Ask learners if they ever go to the market. Ask: *What sorts of things can you buy there? How is it different from a supermarket?*

1 Choosing a plant 67 [CD2 Track 16]

- Ask learners if they like vegetables. What vegetables do they like? Work together to make a list of names of plants/vegetables.
- Focus on the picture and ask learners to predict what the father and the child are going to do.
- Tell them that they are now going to listen to the conversation between them. They have to find out which vegetable the child likes.
- Play the audio at least twice and elicit the answer.
- Then ask learners which vegetable they prefer.

Audioscript: Track 67
Little boy: What is this?
Dad: This is a bean plant.
Little boy: What are these?
Dad: These are carrot plants. Which do you like better, beans or carrots?
Little boy: Errr … beans.
Dad: OK. We'll get the bean plant.

Answer
beans

2 What is this? What are these?

- Review with learners the use of *this/these, that/those*.
- In pairs, tell learners to pretend they are the little boy in the picture and ask and answer questions following the model.

Answers
Learners' own answers.

For further practice, see Activity 1 in the Activity Book.

3 What must you do?

- Ask learners if they have ever planted or looked after a plant. What do they have to do? Elicit some ideas.
- Focus on the pictures and sentences. Explain that they have to read the sentences and put the pictures in order.
- Then they say the instructions to their partner. They shut the book and remember what they must do.
- Encourage learners to use *You must* rather than simply repeating the instructions with imperatives.

Answers
b Dig a hole.
d Put the plant in the hole.
c Fill the hole with soil.
a Water the plant.

For further practice, see Activity 2 in the Activity Book.

4 Would you like some? 68 [CD2 Track 17]

- Focus on the picture and ask learners to find fruits. Can they name them? Elicit the names of fruits and write them on the board.
- Tell learners that they are going to listen to the woman in the picture buying some fruit. They listen and identify the fruit she buys.
- Play the audio recording once. Elicit the answers from the learners.
- Now tell them to read the conversation and fill in the missing words from the **Word box**.
- Play the audio a few more times. Learners listen and complete the dialogue.

Audioscript: Track 68
Woman: What **nice** fruit!
Fruit seller: Thank you. Would you like **some**?
Woman: Yes, I'd like two **mangoes**, please.
Fruit seller: Are **these** OK?
Woman: Yes, those look great.
Fruit seller: Anything else?
Woman: Yes. A pineapple, **please**.
Fruit seller: How about **this** one?
Woman: Yes, that one looks nice. Thank you.
Fruit seller: You're welcome.

Answers
What fruit does she buy? Two mangoes and a pineapple.

5 Act it out

- In pairs, learners take it in turns to play the buyer and the seller.
- They ask for their favourite fruits.

> **Answers**
> Learners' own answers.

Wrap up

- Ask some of the pairs to act the dialogue out in front of the class.

Activity Book

1 Buying plants

- Ask learners to read the conversations and write the missing words. Tell them to use words from the **Word box**.

> **Answers**
> **Conversation 1**
> Boy: What's this?
> Dad: **This** is a bean plant.
> Boy: **What** are these?
> Dad: **These** are carrot plants. **Which** do you like better, beans **or** carrots?
>
> **Conversation 2**
> Boy: Look at that tree in the square pot!
> Dad: Yes. **That** is a lemon tree.
> Boy: **What** are those trees in the round pots?
> Dad: **Those** are orange trees.

2 What must you do?

- Ask learners to look at the pictures then use the words in each box to complete the sentences.
- Look at the **Writing tip** together before they begin to write.

> **Answers**
> 1 You must dig a hole.
> 2 You must put the plant in the hole.
> 3 You must fill the hole with soil.
> 4 You must water the plant.

I can go shopping for plants and fruit.

- Direct learners' attention to the self-evaluation question at the top of page 82. Ask them to think and answer. Emphasise the importance of giving an honest answer.

Differentiated instruction

Additional support and practice

- In pairs, learners write a dialogue using the dialogue in **Activity 1**, **Lesson 4** of the Activity Book as a model. They change the dialogue to include their favourite fruits and vegetables. They draw a picture of the vegetables and fruits mentioned in their dialogue and write labels for them.

Extend and challenge

- Learners work in pairs and write a dialogue using **Activity 4**, **Lesson 4** of the Learner's Book as a model. They leave some blank spaces and put the missing words in a **Word box**.
- They exchange their dialogue with other pairs and complete it.

Lesson 5: Read and respond

Learner's Book pages: 98–100
Activity Book pages: 84–85

> **Lesson objectives**
> **Listening:** Listen to a biography.
> **Speaking:** Discuss a biography.
> **Reading:** Read a biography and answer questions.
> **Sight words:** *grew, were, gone, little.*
> **Writing:** Complete sentences, write a biography.
> **Critical thinking:** Judge effects.
> **Values:** Looking after the planet, responsibility and respect.
>
> **Language focus:** Past simple verbs, regular and irregular forms, *When* clauses
>
> **Vocabulary:** *biography, village, fig, dry* (vb.), *blow away, tea, firewood, autobiography*
>
> **Materials:** Map of the world, writing supplies and drawing supplies, pictures of places with plenty of vegetation and dry places, enough copies of the sentences from **Activity 3** of the Learner's Book written on strips of paper for pairs or small groups.

Warm up

- Do the warm-up routine.
- Show learners photos of places with plenty of vegetation and dry places. Ask which they prefer and if there are places in their country like the ones in the pictures.
- Elicit from learners what a biography is. Ask: *What's the difference between a biography and a story?*

1 Before you read [AB] 69 [CD2 Track 18]

- Focus on the explanation of what a biography is. Were learners right? Ask them if they have ever read one. What kind of information can they find in a biography?
- Tell learners they are going to read about Wangari Maathai. She lived in Kenya. If learners are not familiar with the area, ask them to look at the map and find Kenya. Ask: *Which continent is it in? Is it far from your/this country?*
- Read the introduction. How do learners think she saved trees in Kenya? Elicit suggestions.
- Tell learners they are going to listen to her story. They listen and follow in their books.

- Play the audio recording at least twice. Were their predictions correct? Elicit answers from the class.
- Discuss the meaning of new vocabulary. Encourage learners to use the context and the pictures to work out the meaning of new words.
- **Critical thinking:** Discuss with learners why Wangari's village had changed so much. What happened when they planted tea? Encourage them to think what happens when we change the environment in a place, e.g. cutting down trees, introducing new plants or animals.
- **Values:** ask learners to reflect on Wangari's actions and on the importance of being respectful and responsible with our environment.

Audioscript: Track 69. See Learner's Book pages 98–100.

> **Answers**
> Learners' own answers.

[AB] For further practice, see Activity 1 in the Activity Book.

2 True or false?

- Tell learners to read the sentences and decide if they are true or false. Ask them to re-read the text before answering.

> **Answers**
> 1 false   2 true   3 true   4 false   5 true

3 What happened first? What happened next?

- Focus on the sentences. Tell learners that they aren't in order and they will have to order them.
- Divide the class into pairs and give each pair a set of the sentences written on strips of paper. They discuss, then move them around and put them in order.
- When they have finished, they read them to the class then copy them in their notebooks.

> **Answers**
> 2 Wangari planted the seeds and watered them.
> 1 Wangari took seeds from the trees.
> 5 The trees grew big. Fruit grew on the trees.
> 3 Wangari gave the little trees to women and children in her village.
> 4 Together they planted many rows of trees.

[AB] For further practice, see Activity 2 in the Activity Book.

Words to remember

- Write the words *grew, were, gone, little* on the board.
- Learners look for these sight words in the lesson. How many times do they see the words?
- Ask them to take it in turns to practise spelling them.
- Ask them to make sentences using them.
- Can they find these words in previous lessons in this unit? Ask them to read the sentences where they appear.

> **Answers**
> Learners' own answers.

4 Write your autobiography

- Ask learners what they think an autobiography is and elicit the difference between a biography and an autobiography.
- Focus on the explanation. Learners check if they were right.
- Tell them they are going to write their autobiography. Elicit ideas of what they might include.
- Read the instructions and turn to the Activity Book or the learners' notebooks.

[AB] For further practice, see Activity 3 in the Activity Book.

Wrap up

- Ask learners to read their autobiographies to the class.
- **Portfolio opportunity:** Learners copy their autobiography on a sheet of paper and display it with their pictures in the classroom. After some time, collect, write the date on the back, and save in learners' portfolios.
- **Home–school link:** Learners show their autobiography to the family. They could ask for a family photo to include in it.

Activity Book

1 Map study

- Ask learners to find the names of the countries mentioned in the biography.
- Ask them to locate them on a globe. Are they in the same continents?
- Ask them to find the countries on the map and write the names. Then, they draw arrows to show where Wangari travelled.

> **Answers**
> **Shaded countires:** top left – the United States, top right – Germany,   bottom right – Kenya.
> **Where she travelled:** Kenya to the US, then to Germany, then back to Kenya.

2 Planting a little tree

- Ask learners to put the letters in the correct order and write the words on the lines. Then label the picture 1–4.

> **Answers**
> 1 tree   2 soil   3 hole   4 water

3 Your autobiography

- Ask learners to read the questions and answer them, giving as much information as possible.
- Circulate, giving help as necessary.
- When they have finished writing, learners draw a picture of how they imagine they will look when they are older.

> **Answers**
> Learners' own answers.

I can read and discuss a biography.

- Direct learners' attention to the self-evaluation question at the top of page 84. Ask them to think and answer. Emphasise the importance of giving an honest answer.

> **Answers**
> Learners' own answers.

Differentiated instruction

Additional support and practice

- Ask learners to look for some information about the countries mentioned in the lesson: Kenya, Germany and the US, e.g. capital city, language, weather, most important natural attractions. (forests, rivers, mountains, etc.)

Extend and challenge

- Ask learners to search the Internet and look for simple ideas to protect the environment. What can they do to help in their city? Can they take action like Wangari? In groups they can make a poster with some pictures and suggestions.

Lesson 6: Choose a project

How can we care for the earth?

Learner's Book pages: 102–103
Activity Book pages: 86–87

> **Lesson objectives**
>
> **Listening:** Listen and follow instructions, listening comprehension items in the Activity Book quiz.
> **Speaking:** Present your project to the class, perform a poem.
> **Reading:** Read instructions, quiz items.
> **Writing:** Write a book. Write answers in the Activity Book quiz.
>
> **Language focus:** Unit 7 Review
>
> **Materials:**
>
> **A Make a poster:** writing and drawing supplies, sheets of card or paper, glue, pictures from magazines or from the Internet.
>
> **B Make a book about your heroes:** drawing supplies, sheets of paper, glue, pictures from magazines or from the Internet.
>
> **C Learn a poem:** writing and drawing supplies, sheets of paper.

Learner's Book

Warm up

- Do the warm-up routine.
- Recap with learners what they have learnt in this unit. What things have they liked most? What new things have they learnt? What promises have they made?
- Revise the school/home rules they wrote. Can they add some more now that they have finished the unit?

Choose a project

- Learners choose an end-of-unit project to work on. Look at the examples in the pictures and help them choose. Provide materials. All the projects are done in groups.
- **Informal assessment opportunity:** Circulate as learners work. Informally assess their receptive and productive language skills.
- Ask questions. You may want to take notes on their responses. Provide help with vocabulary and grammar, if requested.

A Make a poster

- Read the directions in the Learner's Book. Give out drawing and writing supplies.
- Discuss ideas, especially of things closely related to the learners' immediate environment.
- Learners draw their posters and write a caption for their pictures.
- They display their posters around the class and explain what they have done.

B Make a book about your heroes

- Read the instructions and give learners writing and drawing materials for the book.
- In their groups, learners talk about people that have made the world a better place. It can be someone famous, e.g. Diane Fossey, community figures such as firefighters, a doctor, a vet, or someone they know personally.
- Each group member makes a page for the book. When they have finished, they prepare a cover for the book and show it to the class.

C Learn a poem

- Read and explain the instructions.
- Learners read and learn the poem. They act it out.
- They draw the pictures and, finally, perform the poem for the class.

Look what I can do!

- Review the I can statements. Learners demonstrate what they can do.
- Discuss with learners what they have learned in this unit. Remind them of the Big question and ask them what they have learned about caring for the earth.
- **Portfolio opportunity:** If possible, leave the student projects on display for a short while, then consider filing the projects, photos or scans of the work, in learners' portfolios. Write the date on the work. You may wish to invite parents or another class to see the children present their projects.

Activity Book

Unit 7 quiz: Look what I can do!

Listen/Listen and write 96 [CD2 Track 45]

- Do the first item as a class. Play the audio several times.
- Learners read the question then listen and write the answer.

Audioscript: Track 96

1 Park keeper: Hello, welcome to our park.

Dad: Thank you! This looks like a great park. Can we eat our sandwiches here?

Park keeper: Yes, of course. On sunny days, lots of families come here to eat their sandwiches.

Girl: And can I fly my kite here?

Park keeper: Yes, you can. This is a good place for flying kites.

Girl: Can we fish in the pond?

Park keeper: No, I'm sorry. We have a rule: No fishing. You mustn't fish in the pond.

2 Young child: Excuse me. What does that sign mean?

Older child: It means: Don't drop litter.

Young child: I don't understand.

Older child: It means you must put your litter in the bin. You mustn't drop it on the ground.

Young child: OK. Thanks! I understand now.

3 Girl: Some trees grow fruit that we can eat. Some trees grow nuts that we can eat. This tree is a cherry tree. It grows wonderful cherries. I love cherries. The birds love them, too!

4 Boy: Dad, what are these?

Dad: These are little bean plants. Look! There are flowers and little beans growing.

Boy: Let's buy some bean plants.

Dad: OK!

5 Wangari Maathai wanted to help her country.

She worked with the women and children in her village.

Together, they planted rows and rows of little trees.

6 Trees have green leaves. The leaves reach into the air. They help clean the dirty air. They give us fresh air to breathe.

7 The roots of a tree reach down into the ground. The roots drink water from the ground. Trees need water to grow. Tree roots hold the soil in place for other plants and grass.

Answers
1 a You mustn't fish in the pond.
2 b The 'Don't drop litter' sign.
3 c The cherry tree.
4 a The bean plants nearby.
5 c Women and children planting trees.
6 leaves
7 roots
8 hole, go, road, crow

Look and write

- Learners read the questions and write the answers.

Answers
9 She is recycling./recycling
10 They are planting trees./planting trees

8 Home, sweet home

Big question What kinds of homes do people and animals build?

Unit overview

In this unit learners will:
- speak about parts of a house and different types of houses
- speak about intentions
- write poems and descriptions
- read and write words with a long **u** sound
- make choices and suggestions
- read and talk about animal homes.

Learners will build communication and literacy skills as they read and listen to a poem and a song, read information texts and stories, read and write poems, identify words with long **u** sound, learn to make suggestions and choices, use *will* for intentions, speak about animals and their homes and do a crossword puzzle.

At the end of the unit, they will apply and personalise what they have learned by working in small groups to complete a project of their choice: writing about animal homes, designing a play room for children or writing a poem.

Language focus

Present perfect: *Have you ever ...?*

Have + object + infinitive

Made of + common materials

Let's ...; How about ... + -ing? for suggestions

Would you like ... or ...? I'd like ...

Too to add information

Will for future intentions

Past simple questions and answers

Vocabulary topics: parts of a house, rooms in a house, types of houses, materials,

Critical thinking
- memorise poems and stories
- make connections and inferences
- compare and contrast
- using context to find the meaning of words
- share information to answer questions
- collecting information in a table.

Self-assessment
- I can talk about parts of a house.
- I can talk about different kinds of homes.
- I can read words with the long **u** sound.
- I can ask about and make choices: *Would you like ... or ...?*
- I can read and talk about an information text.

Teaching tips

As far as possible, bring books to the class suitable for extended reading. They might be related to the topic of the unit or similar to a piece of literature learners have read in a lesson. Encourage them to explore the books and devote some time every week to silent reading.

Review learners' work on the quiz, noting areas where they demonstrate strength and areas where they need additional instruction and practice. Use this information to customise your teaching as you continue to **Unit 9**.

Lesson 1: Think about it

What kinds of homes do people and animals build?

Learner's Book pages: 104–105
Activity Book pages: 88–89

Lesson objectives

Listening: Listen to a poem, listen for specific information, listen and answer questions.

Speaking: Recite a poem, explain things, talk about homes and animals.

Reading: Read a poem, read and identify key vocabulary.

Writing: Write sentences, answer questions, label a picture.

Critical thinking: Make inferences; explain, memorise and recite a poem.

Language focus: Present perfect; *have you ever … ?*; *have* + object + infinitive

Vocabulary: *nest, hive, hole, tree house, roof, wall, stairs, ladder, railing, juice, crisps, magazines*

Materials: Pictures of animals, e.g. bear, birds, rabbits, squirrels, of different types of houses and of animal homes.

Learner's Book

Warm up

- Do the warm-up routine.
- Ask learners to draw a house. They can be as imaginative as they wish. They show it to the class. Ask questions, e.g. *Is it big/small? Where is it? In the city, near the sea, in the mountains?*
- Display pictures of different types of houses and ask learners to choose the ones they like.
- Show pictures of different animals and ask learners if they know where each animal lives. Elicit some ideas.
- Introduce vocabulary using the pictures, e.g. *cave, nest, hole, house, hive, tree house*. You can add more words if learners require them.

Answers
Learners' own answers.

1 Read and listen 70 [CD2 Track 19]

- Focus on the picture. Ask learners to describe what they see. Can they find any animals in the picture?
- Tell learners they are going to listen to the poem. Play the audio. Learners listen and read. Then, they point to the animal homes.
- Play the audio again. Pause after each line for learners to repeat the line.
- **Critical thinking:** Ask learners to practise reciting the poem to memorise it.

Audioscript: Track 70. See Learner's Book page 104.

Answers
nest – on the roof of the tree house
hive – to the left, in the background
hole – bottom left of the picture
house – the tree house

2 A tree house 71 [CD2 Track 20]

- Focus on the picture again, what kind of house is that? Ask learners if they have ever been in one and if they would like to have one. Why?
- Tell learners that they are going to listen to a girl talking about the tree house. They listen and answer the two questions.
- Play the audio several times. As a class, elicit answers.
- **Critical thinking:** Ask learners to explain their answers as fully as possible. Ask them to explain why they think small children can't go up into the tree house (it's dangerous, they may fall).

Audioscript: Track 71

Mia: Have you ever been in a tree house? Our tree house is really cool! It has two floors. To get to the first floor, you walk up some stairs. There's a railing around the first floor so children don't fall off. There are lots of children on the first floor now. Look! They're walking in a big circle around the trunk of the tree.

The second floor of the tree house is only for big children. You must be seven years old to go to the second floor. To get to the second floor, you climb up a ladder. On the second level there is a room with four walls, a roof, a door and three windows. My friend Jenna is up there now. Can you see her? She's at the window. She's pulling up a basket on a rope. Look what I put in the basket – some magazines to read, some water to drink, and some crisps to eat! Now I'm going to climb up the ladder and go up to our tree house!

Jenna: Hey Mia! Come up here!

Mia: I'm coming!

Answers
How do you get to the second floor? You climb up a ladder.
Can all children go there? No, you must be seven or older.

3 Topic vocabulary 72 [CD2 Track 21]

- Focus on the pictures. Tell learners that they are going to listen to the audio recording.
- Play the audio at least twice. Learners listen, point to the pictures and say the words.
- Play the audio again and ask learners to listen to the questions.
- Pause after each question and allow time for learners to answer.

Audioscript: Track 72

Roof. What is on the roof of the tree house?

Wall. How many walls has the tree house got?

Stairs. The stairs go up to the first floor of the tree house. What colour are the stairs?

Ladder. Where does the ladder go to?

Railing. Why is there a railing around the first floor?

Hole. Can you find a rabbit hole? Where is it?

Answers
What is on the roof of the tree house? a nest
How many walls has the tree house got? four
What colour are the stairs? blue (and red)
Where does the ladder go to? It goes to the second floor.
Can you find a rabbit hole? Where is it? next to the tree
Why is there a railing around the first floor? So that the little children don't fall off.

[AB] For further practice, see Activities 1 and 2 in the Activity Book.

4 Talk about it

- Tell learners to work in pairs and talk about the questions.
- Encourage them to make notes of their partner's answers. Then they report back to the class.
- **Informal assessment opportunity:** Circulate, listening to the learners' conversations. Take notes of good performance and of mistakes for remedial work.

Answers
Learners' own answers.

5 What's in the basket?

- Focus on the picture and elicit from learners what the girls have got in the basket.
- Write the answer on the board and underline the structure *Have* + object + infinitive. Ask learners to complete the sentence in their notebooks.
- Focus learners' attention on the words and pictures in the box. Ask them to discuss in pairs what they would put in the basket.
- **Critical thinking:** Encourage learners to use words from the box and their own ideas. Encourage them to explain why they would choose a certain item.
- **Informal assessment opportunity:** Circulate, checking for correct pronunciation and use of the target structure. Keep a record of learners' performance.

Answers
They've got some magazines to read, some crisps to eat and some water to drink.

[AB] For further practice, see Activity 3 in the Activity Book.

Wrap up

- When learners have finished writing about what they would take to the tree house, they compare with other learners. With their help, collect the results on the board and see what items have been the most popular.
- **Home school opportunity:** Learners teach parents and siblings the poem and then draw a picture of their ideal house.

Activity Book

1 A tree house

- Tell learners to look at the picture and write the words on the lines to label the picture.

Answers
Labels for: stairs, railing, ladder, roof, wall, door, window, basket, rope.

2 Questions and answers

- Ask learners to read the questions and write the answers on the lines.
- Check as a class.

Answers
How do I get to the second floor of the tree house? Climb the ladder.
What is on the roof of the tree house? a nest.
Which part of the tree house do you like best? Learners' own answers.

3 What's in the basket?

- Ask learners to choose what they would put in a basket to read, to eat and to drink in the treehouse.
- They draw three things in the basket and then write about it.
- **Portfolio opportunity:** When learners have finished, ask them to write their names and the date and file the work in their portfolios.

Answers
Learners' own answers.

I can talk about parts of a house.

- Direct learners' attention to the self-evaluation question at the top of page 88. Ask them to think and answer. Emphasise the importance of giving an honest answer.

Answers
Learners' own answers.

Differentiated instruction

Additional support and practice
- In small groups or as a class divided into two teams, learners play a spelling game to review new vocabulary.

Extend and challenge
- Play *I Spy*. You say: *I spy with my little eye something beginning with 'N'*. Students try to guess the object (e.g. nest). Use the vocabulary from this lesson.

Lesson 2: Find out more

Homes around the world
Learner's Book pages: 106–107
Activity Book pages: 90–91

Lesson objectives
Listening: Listen for information.
Speaking: Talk about homes, discuss and apply information.
Reading: Read for information, read about homes.
Writing: Guided writing.
Critical thinking: Apply information; make connections and inferences; compare and contrast.
Values: People live in many different kinds of homes; home is a place where families live and take care of each other.

Language focus: *made of* + common materials
Vocabulary: *beehive, stilt, cave, skyscraper, mud, concrete, wood, glass, metal, rock*

Materials: Map of the world, sheets of paper, file cards, writing supplies.

Warm up
- Learners do the warm-up routine.
- Ask learners to recite the poem in **Lesson 1**.
- Elicit from them information they remember from **Lesson 1**, e.g. *What was the lesson about? What new things did you learn?*

1 Before you read 73 [CD2 Track 22]
- Focus on the pictures and ask learners if there are houses like these in the pictures in their city or country.
- **Critical thinking:** Learners compare and contrast the houses in the pictures with houses in their country. Ask: *How similar or different are they?*
- Ask learners to look at the headings and predict what kind of information they can find in the text. Elicit some answers.
- Tell learners that they are going to listen to the audio recording about houses. They listen and follow in their books. Play the audio recording at least twice.
- What new information have they found? Are there any words they don't know? Remind learners to use the photos and the context to understand them.
- Focus on the materials used in the buildings and ask learners to find examples in their classroom.

Audioscript: Track 73. See Learner's Book pages 106–7.

Answers
Learners' own answers.

For further practice, see Activity 1 in the Activity Book.

2 True or false?
- Ask learners to re-read the text and decide if the statements are true or false.
- You may ask them to correct the false ones.
- Check as a class.

Answers
1 A beehive house has lots of windows. **false**
2 A skyscraper has lots of windows. **true**
3 A cave home keeps you warm in winter. **true**
4 Stilt houses are built only in cold, dry places. **false**

For further practice, see Activity 2 in the Activity Book.

3 Where do they live?
- Learners look at the pictures and discuss where each person lives. In order to do this, they need to read the clues carefully. Encourage them to go back to the text for help.
- **Informal assessment opportunity:** Circulate, checking for correct pronunciation and use of language. Make notes of mistakes for remedial work.
- When they have decided on the answers, check as a class. Encourage learners to justify their answers.

Answers
Layla – a skyscraper
Mohammed – a stilt house
Ahmed – a beehive house
Harika – a cave house

For further practice, see Activity 3 in the Activity Book.

Wrap up
- Ask learners to show their house from **Activity 3** in the Activity Book and describe it using vocabulary from this lesson, e.g. *This is my house. It's a … it's made of … the walls are … .*

UNIT 8 Home, sweet home Lesson 2 103

Activity Book

1 Where can you find these homes?
- Ask learners what countries are mentioned in the text. Write them on the board.
- Focus on the photos. Ask learners to read the country name under each photo and find the country on the map in the Learner's Book. **Picture dictionary** on page 128.
- They then answer the questions.

> **Answers**
> **Which two countries are next to each other?** Syria and Turkey
> **Which country is nearest to where you live?** Learners' own answers.

2 Which one?
- Focus on the questions. Learners look for the information in the text and answer them.

> **Answers**
> 1 Which home is only built in hot, dry places? beehive house
> 2 Which home is only built in hot, wet places? stilt house
> 3 Which home is made of wood? stilt house
> 4 Which home is made of mud? beehive house
> 5 Which home is made of rock? cave house

3 Join the dots
- Tell learners to draw lines to join the dots 1–60. Then they colour the house. Remind them to think about what their house is made from before they start to colour.

> **Answers**
> Learners' own answers.

I can talk about different kinds of homes.
- Direct learners' attention to the self-evaluation question at the top of page 90. Ask them to think and answer. Emphasise the importance of giving an honest answer.

> **Answers**
> Learners' own answers.

Differentiated instruction

Additional support and practice
- Ask learners to write a description of their house on a separate sheet of paper using vocabulary and language they have learnt.
- **Portfolio opportunity:** Learners write their names and the date on their work. File the sheets in the learners' portfolios.

Extend and challenge
- Ask learners to work in pairs or small groups and choose one of the places mentioned in the lesson. They search the Internet for information about the places and prepare a small poster. They then make a short presentation.

Lesson 3: Words and sounds

Long *u*
Learner's Book pages: 108–109
Activity Book pages: 92–93

Lesson objectives
Listening: Identify long **u** spellings, variant sounds of **oo**, listen to instructions.
Speaking: Describe rooms and houses, discuss where to put things in a house.
Reading: Read instructions.
Writing: Guided writing, solve a crossword puzzle.
Critical thinking skills: Memorise a poem, understand how a crossword puzzle works and solve it.

Language focus: *Let's ...; how about ... + -ing* for suggestions
Vocabulary: *bedroom, bathroom, kitchen, living room, bed, sink, TV, shower, toilet, table, cooker, chair, cupboard, bookcase*

Materials: Photocopiable activities **15** and **16**, drawing supplies, cardboard toilet rolls, watercolours, small cardboard boxes, scissors, sticky tape, clay, sticks, stones, plastic bits of packaging.

Warm up
- Learners do the warm-up routine.
- Remind learners of the types of houses they read about in **Lesson 2**. Encourage them to describe the houses to revise vocabulary and the structure *made of* + material.

1 Let's build a cool house! 74 [CD2 Track 23]
- Ask learners to look at the picture and describe what they see. What do they call that building? (*castle*) Write the word on the board.
- Elicit what materials a castle is made of. Ask: *Are those materials the same as the ones in the picture?*
- Tell learners that they are going to listen to the instructions to make this castle. They look at the words in blue and identify the sound they hear.
- Play the audio at least twice and elicit the answer.
- Ask them to find words that rhyme with *zoo* and words where the vowel has the same spelling as the examples.

Audioscript: Track 74. See Learner's Book page 108.

> **Answers**
> a long **u** sound
> **Find words that rhyme with *zoo*.** you, glue, too, few
> **Find words where the vowel has the same spelling as:**
> **zoo** – cool, too, room
> **blue** – glue
> **new** – few

2 The sounds of *oo* 75 [CD2 Track 24]

- Write the words *too* and *zoo* on the board and ask learners to say them. How is the vowel sound spelt? Elicit the answer **oo**.
- Focus on the exercise. Tell learners to listen to the words. Play the audio. Ask them to repeat.
- Then ask them to describe the picture using the words.
- Point out that the letters **oo** sometimes stand for a different sound. Focus on the words and ask learners to say them. Do they notice any difference?
- Ask learners to use the words to talk about the picture.

> **Audioscript:** Track 75
> goose   moon   roof   food
> wood   foot   book   look

> **Answers**
> Suggested answers
> The goose is on the roof. He's looking at the moon. There's some food in the basket.
> The goose's friend is reading a book. There's a bug on his foot.
> The house is made of wood.

- For further practice, see Activities 1 and 2 in the Activity Book.

3 What will you put in your house? 76

[CD2 Track 25]

- Ask learners to work in pairs. Ask learners to look at the rooms in the picture. Do they have the same rooms in their homes? Ask them about the number of rooms, bedrooms, etc. they have.
- Focus on the list of things to put in the home. Where would they put the sink, the bed and the TV? Elicit answers from the class.
- Tell them they are going to listen to the audio recording of children talking about where they will put the different items. They listen and compare with their own suggestions.
- Play the audio at least twice. Elicit answers.
- Give learners copies of **Photocopiable activities 15** and **16** and tell them to cut out the furniture items.
- Play the recording again. Learners move the cut-outs and put them in the correct place in the rooms.
- In pairs, learners play with the cut-out furniture items and decide where to put them using the dialogue as a model.
- **Informal assessment opportunity:** Circulate, checking for correct pronunciation and use of target structures. Praise good work and set up remedial work if necessary.

> **Audioscript:** Track 76
> **Child A:** This house has a bedroom, a bathroom, a kitchen and a living room. Let's put the bed in the bedroom.
> **Child B:** OK. How about the sink?
> **Child A:** Let's put the sink in the kitchen.
> **Child B:** OK … . How about putting the TV in the living room?
> **Child A:** That's a good idea.

> **Answers**
> bed – in the bedroom
> sink – in the kitchen
> TV – in the living room
> Learners' own answers.

4 Make and write

- Display the materials for making the houses. Tell learners to use whichever materials they like.
- Allow plenty of time for them to make the house. When they have finished, they write some sentences about the house on a file card.
- **Informal assessment opportunity:** Circulate, asking questions and encouraging learners to describe what they are doing.
- **Portfolio opportunity:** Ask learners to write their names and the date on the cards and file them in learners' portfolios.

- For further practice, see Activity 3 in the Activity Book.

Wrap up

- When learners have finished making the houses, set up a display zone in the classroom and ask learners to describe their work. They could vote for the prettiest house, the most original, etc.
- Invite another class or parents to see the display.
- **Home–school link:** Learners take their houses home and show them to the family.

Activity Book

1 Crossword puzzle

- Focus on the crossword puzzle. Ask learners to look at the clues and write the words.
- **Critical thinking:** Remind learners of other crossword puzzles they have done before. Ask: *How did you solve it? What are the clues for?*

> **Answers**
> **Across**
> 3 goose
> 6 wood
> 7 moon
> 8 glue
>
> **Down**
> 1 tube
> 2 food
> 4 school
> 5 foot

Challenge

- Most of the words have a long **u** sound like in *you*. Two words have a short sound like in *look*. Write the words.

> **Answers**
> wood, foot

UNIT 8 Home, sweet home Lesson 3

2 Words with the long *u* sound

- Tell learners to draw a line under each word that has the long **u** sound. Then they circle the letters that make the long **u** sound.

> **Answers**
> The huge blue goose flew to the moon.

3 My favourite room

- Ask learners what their favourite room in their home is. Tell them to draw a picture of the room.
- Tell them to label the furniture items in the room. They can look for more vocabulary in the **Picture dictionary** in the Learner's Book.

> **Answers**
> Learners' own answers.

I can read words with a long *u* sound.

- Direct learners' attention to the self-evaluation question at the top of page 92. Ask them to think and answer. Emphasise the importance of giving an honest answer.

> **Answers**
> Learners' own answers.

> **Differentiated instruction**
>
> **Additional support and practice**
> - Ask learners to look at **Activity 2** of the Learner's Book again and write the sentences to match the picture.
> - Tell them to write another sentence of their own using some of the words.
>
> **Extend and challenge**
> - After learners have finished **Activity 3** of the Learner's Book, they glue the cut-out furniture on **Photocopiable activity 15** and write a description of what there is in each room.
> - **Portfolio opportunity:** Learners write their name and the date on the description. File it in their portfolios.

Lesson 4: Use of English

Making choices

Learner's Book pages: 110–111
Activity Book pages: 94–95

> **Lesson objectives**
> **Listening:** Listen for information, listen to a dialogue and complete sentences.
> **Speaking:** Role play, sing a song.
> **Reading:** Read for information.
> **Writing:** Complete sentences, write sentences.

> **Language focus:** *Would you like … or …?*; *I'd like…*; *too* to add information; *will* for future intention; past simple questions and answers
> **Vocabulary:** *playground, bridge, straight, curvy, slide, rope, wooden, ladder, swing, tower, princess, fairy, wand, forest, prince, sword, rope web, roundabout, jumping mat, climbing wall, spinner, seesaw*

> **Materials:** Writing and drawing supplies, file cards, sheets of paper.

Learner's Book

⇨ Warm up

- Do the warm-up routine.
- Ask learners if they ever go to the playground. What do they do there? What are some of the things they can see and play with there? Elicit ideas and supply new vocabulary as necessary.
- Focus on the picture. Is there anything like that in their playground? Would they like to have one? Why?

> **Answers**
> Learners' own answers.

1 What would you like in your playground? 77
[CD2 Track 26]

- Tell learners that the children in class 2 are having a playground designed for them. They are going to listen to the conversation between the playground designer and the children in class 2.
- Tell them to point to the things the children choose. Play the audio at least twice and elicit the answers.
- Draw learners' attention to use of *too*. Point out that it doesn't mean *two*. We use it to add something else.

> **Audioscript:** Track 77
> **Playground designer:** OK, everyone. You are going to have a lovely new playground. Your playground will have two towers. What would you like between the two towers – a bridge or a tube?
>
> **Children:** We'd like a bridge!
>
> **Playground designer:** OK, we'll have a bridge. Would you like a straight slide or a curvy slide?
>
> **Children:** A straight slide, please.
>
> **Playground designer:** OK, we'll have two towers, a bridge, and a straight slide too. How about a ladder? Would you like a rope ladder made of rope, or a ladder made of wood?
>
> **Children:** A ladder made of rope, please.
>
> **Playground designer:** Fine, a rope ladder. And the last thing, would you like rings or swings?
>
> **Children:** We'd like swings, please.
>
> **Playground designer:** Wonderful. We'll have swings. I'll be back next week and we'll build you a playground!
>
> **Children:** Hooray! Thank you!

> **Answers**
> towers, bridge, the straight slide, the rope ladder and the swings

[AB] For further practice, see Activity 1 in the Activity Book.

2 Design your own playground!

- In pairs, tell learners to choose what they would like for their playground.
- Ask them to take notes of what they decide.

> **Answers**
> Learners' own answers.

[AB] For further practice, see Activity 2 in the Activity Book.

3 Draw and write

- When learners have finished deciding what to put in their playground, tell them to draw the picture and write a description.
- They do this in the Activity Book.

> **Answers**
> Learners' own answers.

[AB] For further practice, see Activity 3 in the Activity Book.

4 The princess in the tower 78 [CD2 Track 27]

- Tell learners that they are going to listen to a song. Ask them to look at the picture and predict what it will be about.
- Ask them to find words they don't know. Encourage them to work out the meaning using the picture as an aid. They may ask for other words using the question as a model.
- Play the audio recording a few times and encourage learners to join in as they grow more confident.
- Encourage them to mime as they sing.

Audioscript: Track 78. See Learner's Book page 111.

> **Answers**
> Learners' own answers.

5 Ask and answer questions

- In pairs, learners take it in turns to ask and answer questions about the story in the song.
- Focus on the question forms with *did*. Model how the infinitive form is used in the question and the simple past form in the answer.

> **Answers**
> 1 She lived in a big high tower.
> 2 She fell asleep because a fairy waved her magic wand.
> 3 She slept for a hundred years.
> 4 He chopped down the trees with his sword.
> 5 He kissed her hand.

6 Tell the story with pictures

- Ask learners to read the story again and draw pictures to show what happened.
- Ask them to write sentences to go with the pictures.
- **Portfolio opportunity:** Collect learners' work and file it in their portfolios.
- **Home–school link:** Learners take their work home and tell the story to their family.

> **Answers**
> Learners' own answers.

Wrap up

- Ask learners to show their work and tell the story using their pictures to help them.

> **Answers**
> Learners' own answers.

Activity Book

1 Find the differences

- Tell learners to look at the two playgrounds. They compare them and put a cross **x** next to the things that are different.
- Then, they write the things that are different on the lines below the pictures.

> **Answers**
> differences:
> railing — no railing
> curvy slide — straight slide
> tunnel — bridge
> rope ladder — wood ladder
> two swings — one swing and a pair of rings

2 More playground choices

- Direct learners' attention to the activity and tell them that there are some other things they can have in a playground.
- Ask them to tick three they would like.
- **Informal assessment opportunity:** Circulate, listening to the learners' interaction and take notes of mistakes for remedial work.

> **Answers**
> Learners' own answers.

3 Draw and write

- Learners draw their playground and write the description.
- **Portfolio opportunity:** You could ask learners to do this activity on a separate sheet of paper and then file it in their portfolios.

> **Answers**
> Learners' own answers.

I can ask about and make choices: *Would you like … or …?*

- Direct learners' attention to the self-evaluation question at the top of page 94. Ask them to think and answer. Emphasise the importance of giving an honest answer.

> **Answers**
> Learners' own answers.

Differentiated instruction

Additional support and practice

- Look for a similar story about a princess, e.g. *Rapunzel* or a local story, and tell it to the class.
- In pairs, learners write some questions in the past simple using **Activity 5** in the Learner's Book as a model. They exchange questions with another pair and answer them.

Extend and challenge

- Learners search the Internet for similar stories or look for them in the school library, e.g. *Cinderella, Snow White* or local stories. They bring the stories to the class and retell them to their classmates.

Lesson 5: Read and respond

Learner's Book pages: 112–115
Activity Book pages: 96–97

Lesson objectives

Listening: Listen to information about animal homes.
Speaking: Discuss an information text.
Reading: Read an information text and answer questions, jigsaw reading, look up the meaning of new words, recognise sight words: *their, down, middle, with*, read a poem.
Writing: Answer questions.
Study skills: Use a dictionary.
Critical thinking: Use context to find the meaning of words; share information to answer questions; collect information in a table.

Vocabulary: *beaver, termite, tunnel, rabbit hole, fox, stamp, enemy, branch, rock, pond, cut down, sharp, huge, above, underwater, wolf, lay eggs, queen, mushroom, air hole*

Materials: Dictionaries.

⮕ Warm up

- Do the warm-up routine.
- Focus on the pictures and ask learners if they know the names of the animals. Elicit some answers.
- Ask them to look at the headings and check if they were right.
- Ask learners to predict what the text is going to be about.

> **Answers**
> Learners' own answers.

1 Before you read 79 [CD2 Track 28]

- Tell learners they are going to work in groups of three. Each group member is going to read one of the texts, e.g. learners are divided A, B and C. All the As read the rabbit text, all the Bs the beaver text, etc.
- Ideally, they should listen to their part of the audio as they read for the first time. Then, they come together in threes, i.e. an A, a B and a C, to pool their information after reading. Learners could then read the other texts for homework, or listen to all three on audio.
- If this is not possible, ask them to read their part, they do **Activities 2** and **3** together and then listen to the recording as a class.

Audioscript: Track 79. See Learner's Book pages 112–114.

> **Answers**
> Learners' own answers.

2 New words

- Ask learners to find two words in the text that they didn't know. They look up the meaning in a dictionary.
- Then, they teach the new words to the class.
- **Critical thinking skills:** Before looking the words up in the dictionary, encourage learners to discover the meaning using the context. Then they can check with the dictionary.
- **Study skills:** Model the activity first. Choose a word at random and show learners how to look up words in a dictionary.

> **Answers**
> Learners' own answers.

3 Share your information

- Tell learners to get together in groups of three. Each group member must have read a different text.
- They read the questions and share the information about the animals.
- Tell them to take notes of the other group members' information.
- **Critical thinking:** Learners have to process the information before sharing it. Then, as they share they have a complete picture of all the texts. You may wish to ask them to collect the information in a table as shown in the example. Then ask them to share it with the class.
- **Informal assessment opportunity:** Circulate, listening to learners' questions and answers. Take notes for remedial work.

Answers

	Rabbits	Beavers	Termites
Where does your animal build its home?	Under the ground	In the middle of a pond	In huge towers and in the ground below
What is the home made of?	Mud	Branches, rocks and mud	Mud
Does it have rooms? Who lives in the rooms?	Yes – baby rabbits and their mother	Yes – the beavers and their babies	Yes – the queen lives there
Why is it a good home?	It keeps the rabbits warm, dry and safe.	It keeps the beavers safe, dry and warm.	It keeps them cool when the weather is hot.

4 Which animal home?

- Focus on the questions. In their groups, learners pool information to answer them.
- They write the answers in their notebooks.

Answers
1 Which animal home has a garden inside? termites' home
2 Which animal home is made of wood? beavers' home
3 Which animal home has doors under the water? beavers' home
4 Which animal stamps its foot when it sees an enemy? rabbit
5 Which animal home looks like a beehive house? termites' home
6 Which animal's enemy is a fox? rabbit

[AB] For further practice, see Activities 1, 2, 3 and 4 in the Activity Book.

Words to remember

- Write the word *their, down, middle, with* on the board.
- Learners look for these sight words in the lesson. How many times do they see each word?
- Ask them to take it in turns to practise spelling them.
- They could make sentences using them.
- Can they find these words in previous lessons in this unit? Ask them to read the sentences where they appear.

Answers
Learners' own answers.

Wrap up

- Ask learners to recite and act out the poem from the Activity Book.
- **Home–school link:** Learners tell the family about the animals and teach them the rabbit poem.

Activity Book

1 Comparing animal homes

- Tell learners to read the questions and look at the pictures.
- Tell them to use the words and pictures in the Learner's Book to find the information.

Answers
1 Whose home is under the ground? rabbit
2 Whose home is under and above the ground? termite
3 Whose home is in a pond? beaver
4 Whose home has special rooms for babies or eggs? rabbit and termite
5 Whose home is made of branches? beaver
6 Whose home is made of mud? termite

2 Animal enemies

- Ask learners to read the questions and decide who the animals' enemies are.
- They look for the answers in the text and complete the sentences.
- Circulate, giving help as necessary.

Answers
b an animal that eats rabbits
Name an animal that is an enemy of a beaver. wolf (or other reasonable answer)
Name an animal that is an enemy of a mouse. cat (or other reasonable answer)

3 Picture quiz

- Tell learners to look at the pictures in the Learner's Book and answer the questions.

Answers
1 How many rabbit holes can you see in the picture of the rabbit home? one
2 How many underwater doors can you see in the picture of the beaver home? two
3 Which animal home looks most like a beehive house? termite house

4 A rabbit poem

- Tell learners to read the poem and write the missing words using words from the **Word box**.
- When they have finished, they recite the poem together as a class.

Answers
1 bunny
2 hole
3 sound
4 jumps
5 ground

I can read and talk about an information text.
- Direct learners' attention to the self-evaluation question at the top of page 96. Ask them to think and answer. Emphasise the importance of giving an honest answer.

> **Answers**
> Learners' own answers.

> **Differentiated instruction**
>
> **Additional support and practice**
> - Play a quiz game. Each learner writes two or more questions about the text they read. They give them to the rest of their group to answer.
>
> **Extend and challenge**
> - Ask learners to search the Internet and look for information about the fox and the wolf. They prepare a small poster with information and pictures.

Lesson 6: Choose a project
What kinds of homes do people and animals build?
Learner's Book pages: 116–117
Activity Book pages: 98–99

> **Lesson objectives**
>
> **Listening:** Listen and follow instructions, listening comprehension items in the Activity Book quiz.
> **Speaking:** Present your project to the class, recite a poem.
> **Reading:** Read instructions, Activity Book quiz items.
> **Writing:** Write factual information, write a poem, write answers in the Activity Book quiz.
>
> **Language focus: Unit 8** Review
>
> **Materials**
> **A Write about an animal home:** writing and drawing supplies, sheets of card or paper, glue, pictures from magazines or from the Internet, Internet access or reference books.
> **B Design a play room for children:** drawing supplies, sheets of paper, glue, pictures from magazines.
> **C Write a poem:** writing and drawing supplies, sheets of paper.

⇨ Warm up
- Do the warm-up routine.
- Recap with learners what they have learnt in this unit. What things have they liked most? What new things have they learnt? What kinds of homes do they like most? What is their favorite word in this unit?

> **Answers**
> Learners' own answers.

Choose a project
- Learners choose an end-of-unit project to work on. Look at the examples in the pictures and help them choose. Provide materials. All the projects are done in groups.

A Write about an animal home
- Read the directions in the Learner's Book. Give out drawing and writing supplies.
- Learners choose an animal and look for information in the Internet or in reference books.
- Learners draw their posters and write a caption for their pictures.
- They display their posters around the class and explain what they have done.

B Design a play room for children
- Read the instructions and give learners writing and drawing materials.
- They discuss what they will put in the room.
- They make a poster and write words on the picture.
- More proficient learners can write a full description.

C Write a poem
- Read and explain the instructions.
- Learners write two new verses for the poem '*Homes*' on page 104 of the Learner's Book.
- They draw pictures.
- Encourage them to be creative – they can write about homes for animals and homes for things.
- Circulate as learners work. Informally assess their receptive and productive language skills. Ask questions. You may want to take notes on their responses. Provide help with vocabulary and grammar if requested.
- **Portfolio opportunity:** If possible, leave the student projects on display for a short while, then consider filing the projects, photos or scans of the work in learners' portfolios. Write the date on the work. You may wish to invite parents or another class to see the children present their projects.

Look what I can do!
- Review the *I can …* statements. Learners demonstrate what they can do.
- Discuss with learners what they have learned in this unit. Remind them of the Big question and ask them what they have learned about homes for people and animals.

Activity Book

Unit 8 quiz: Look what I can do!

Listen 97 [CD2 Track 46]
- Do the first item as a class. Play the audio several times.

Listen and write
- Learners listen and write the name of the animal.

Read and write

- Items 7–9: Learners look at the pictures and put the letters in the right order to make the word.
- Item 10: Learners complete the sentences.

Audioscript: Track 97

1. **Boy:** Look up in that tree!
   Girl: What can you see?
   Boy: I think I can see two baby birds.
   Girl: Here comes a bird flying to the nest.
   Boy: I think that's the mum or the dad.
   Girl: Cool!

2. **Girl:** Hi. My name is Jill. To get to my tree house, you climb up a ladder. There is a railing around the tree house so you don't fall off. My tree house has a roof, but there are no walls!

3. **Boy 1:** Let's go up to our tree house.
   Boy 2: OK. Let's get something to eat and drink when we are there.
   Boy 1: I'd like some grapes.
   Boy 2: I'd like some crisps.
   Boy 1: Do you want something to drink?
   Boy 2: Yes, I'd like some water.
   Boy 1: Let's put the grapes, the crisps, and the water in the basket. Then we can pull it up to the tree house.
   Boy 2: Good idea!

4. My name is Ahmed. I live in a city. We live in a very tall building. My family lives on the 10th floor.

5. My name is Nina. My house is built above the water. It is built on stilts. To get to my house, I ride in a boat. The wind blows under the floor of my house and around the walls. It is hot where I live. The wind keeps us cool. I love my home on stilts.

6. This animal's home is under the ground. There are lots of tunnels and rooms in this home. When this animal hears an enemy, it runs and jumps down a hole into its home.

Answers
1. b
2. c
3. c
4. a
5. b
6. rabbit
7. roof
8. tubes
9. moon
10. Learners' own answers.

9 Inside and outside cities

Big question What can we do in the town and the countryside?

Unit overview

In this unit learners will:
- speak about places in the city
- speak about likes and preferences
- write poems and descriptions
- identify opposites
- make choices and suggestions
- read and talk about a fable.

Learners will build communication and literacy skills as they read and listen to a poem and a song, read a fable, read and write poems and *haikus*, identify opposites, count syllables, learn to make suggestions and choices, use *so do I*, speak about places and holidays, and compare and contrast life in the country and in the city.

At the end of the unit, they will apply and personalise what they have learned by working in small groups to complete a project of their choice: making a book of poems, making their own café or making a travel poster.

Language focus
So do I/I don't
Questions: *How many …?; What…?; Is …?*
Would you like … or …? I'd like …
What would you like…? how about …?
Can I have …?
Comparatives: *-er; more + adjective; better*

Vocabulary topics: places in a city, food and drink, opposites, holiday places.

Sight words: *something, want, great, come*

Critical thinking
- memorise poems and stories
- make connections and inferences
- compare and contrast
- use context to find the meaning of words.

Self-assessment
- I can talk about places I like.
- I can say what I would like to eat and drink.
- I can count syllables.
- I can compare places.
- I can read, talk about and act out a story.

Teaching tip

As far as possible, bring books to the class suitable for extended reading. They might be related to the topic of the unit or similar to a piece of literature learners have read in a lesson. Encourage them to explore the books and devote some time every week to silent reading.

Lesson 1: Think about it

What can we do in the town and the countryside?

Learner's Book pages: 118–119
Activity Book pages: 100–101

Lesson objectives

Listening: Listen to a haiku, listen for specific information, listen and answer questions.
Speaking: Recite a poem, ask questions, talk about city and country.
Reading: Read a poem, read and identify key vocabulary.
Writing: Write sentences, answer questions.
Critical thinking: Explain, memorise and recite a poem
Values: Different people have different taste and opinions (respecting diversity).

Language focus: Questions: *What …? How many …? Is …?; So do I*

Vocabulary: *helicopter, safety belt, hospital, ambulance, entrance, zoo, library, shopping centre, museum*

Review: places in town (see Unit 2), colours.

Learner's Book

Warm up

- Do the warm-up routine.
- Ask learners what buildings they can see in a town or city. Remind them of the words they learnt in **Unit 2 Lesson 4**. Work together to make a list of names of shops and other places.

Answers
Learners' own answers.

1 Read and listen 80 [CD2 Track 29]

- Ask learners if they live in a city. Have they ever seen a rainbow? What colour is the rainbow? Elicit the answer.
- **Critical thinking:** If learners live in a city, especially in a big one, it's quite likely they have never seen a rainbow. Ask them why they think this is so, e.g. too many tall buildings, difficult to see the sky. Encourage them to think where it is easier to see a rainbow.
- Focus on the picture. Ask learners to describe what they see. What buildings are there?
- Tell learners they are going to listen to a *haiku*. Elicit from learners what a *haiku* is. Do they remember any *haikus*? Remind them of the *haikus* they learnt and wrote in **Unit 7**.
- Play the audio. Learners listen and read. Then, they read the *haiku* aloud.
- Elicit the meaning of *peeking*. Ask: *Why does the rainbow 'peek' through skyscrapers?*
- **Critical thinking:** Ask learners to practise reciting the poem and memorise it. Then they recite it to the class.

Audioscript: Track 80. See Learner's Book page 118.

Answers
Learners' own answers.

2 A helicopter ride 81 [CD2 Track 30]

- Focus on the picture again. Ask learners if they have ever flown in a helicopter? Would they like to? Why?
- Tell learners that they are going to listen to Malik and his father. They are going for a ride in the helicopter. What do learners think they have to do first? Elicit suggestions.
- Play the audio several times. As a class, elicit answers.
- **Critical thinking:** Ask learners to explain why they must fasten their seat belts (*it's dangerous, they may fall*). In what other circumstances do they have to do the same? (*when they go somewhere by car*)

Audioscript: Track 81

Pilot: Hello, Malik, have you ever been in a helicopter before?
Malik: No, I haven't! It'll be great!
Dad: No, he hasn't. He's really looking forward to it.
Pilot: Would you like to sit by the window, next to your dad? OK. One important thing. We must wear our safety belts. Get ready … let's take off!
Malik: Wow! I can see everything!
Dad: What a fantastic view!
Pilot: This is the best way to see a city. Can you see all the animals in the zoo? Can you see the elephant?
Malik: What's that?
Pilot: Where? Oh, that! That's the Sunshine Shopping Centre. It's one of the biggest shopping centres in the world.
Malik: I don't like shopping.
Pilot: And next to the shopping centre, that's the library.
Dad: The library! I like reading.
Malik: So do I! What's that other tall building, over there?
Pilot: That's the hospital.
Malik: Look, Dad, can you see the ambulance driving to the hospital?
Dad: Oh, yes! And what's that building next to the market?
Pilot: That's the museum.
Malik: I really like that museum.
Pilot: So do I! … Those are the mountains over there. Look, Malik!
Dad: I love this helicopter ride!
Malik + Pilot: So do I!

Answers
They must put on their safety belts.

3 Topic vocabulary [82] [CD2 Track 31]

- Focus on the pictures. Tell learners that they are going to listen to the audio recording.
- Play the audio at least twice. Learners listen, point to the pictures and say the words.
- Play the audio again and ask learners to listen to the questions.
- Pause after each question and allow time for learners to answer.

> **Audioscript:** Track 82
> Helicopter. How many people are flying in the helicopter?
> Safety belt. Is the Dad wearing his safety belt?
> Hospital. Is the hospital opposite the market or opposite the shopping centre?
> Ambulance. What colour is the light on the ambulance?
> Shopping centre. Is the shopping centre small or tall?

> **Answers**
> How many people are flying in the helicopter? three
> Is the Dad wearing his safety belt? Yes, he is.
> Is the hospital opposite the market or opposite the shopping centre? opposite the shopping centre.
> What colour is the light on the ambulance? blue
> Is the shopping centre small or tall? It's tall.

[AB] For further practice, see Activities 1 and 2 in the Activity Book.

4 Who says it? [81] [CD2 Track 30]

- Focus on the activity. Ask learners to read the sentences and decide who says what. Encourage them to explain their answers.
- When they have finished, play the audio (same track as for **Activity 2** – see script above) and ask them to check their answers.

> **Answers**
> 1 Would you like to sit by the window? the pilot
> 2 We must wear our safety belts. the pilot
> 3 Wow! I can see everything! Malik
> 4 I don't like shopping. Malik
> 5 I love this helicopter ride! Dad

5 So do I! [83] [CD2 Track 32]

- Ask learners to look at the table and see what Dad and Malik like. Do they like the same things? Elicit some answers.
- Tell them to listen to the dialogue. Play it at least twice. Elicit from learners how Malik agrees with his father.
- In pairs or small groups, ask learners to look at the pictures, say what things they like and find out if the other learners like the same things.
- Model first with a learner.

- **Values:** Take advantage of this activity to highlight the fact that different people have different tastes and opinions and it is important to respect diversity.

> **Audioscript:** Track 83
> **Dad:** I like going to the library.
> **Malik:** So do I.
> **Dad:** I love helicopters.
> **Malik:** So do I.
> **Dad:** And I really like shopping.
> **Malik:** Euh, I don't.

[AB] For further practice, see Activities 3 and 4 in the Activity Book.

Wrap up

- When learners have finished **Activity 3** in the Activity Book, they compare with other learners, asking them if they like the same activities. With their help, collect the results on the board and see which activities are the most popular. Extend this by adding more activities, e.g. riding a bicycle, fishing.
- **Home–school link:** Learners make a chart like the one on page 119 of the Learner's Book to ask their family about which activities they like or dislike.

Activity Book

1 Word puzzle

- Tell learners to find and circle the words in the puzzle. All the words go from left to right.

> **Answers**
> D F H O S P I T A L C F L M I J R
> M U S E U M H G F R B N P O P
> T Y S H O P P I N G C E N T R E
> M A R K E T N C E U X O X Z O O
> C C H E S W I M M I N G P O O L
> S P S S U D F R L I B R A R Y C U

Challenge

- Learners read and answer the questions about their favourite place in the city.

> **Answers**
> Learners' own answers.

2 Safety belts

- Ask learners to look at the picture in the Learner's Book, read the questions and answer *yes* or *no*.
- Then, check as a class.

114 Cambridge Global English Stage 2 Teacher's Resource

> **Answers**
> **Is the pilot wearing a safety belt?** yes
> **Are Malik and his dad wearing safety belts?** yes
> **Do you wear a safety belt when you travel by car?** learners' own answers.

3 So do I!
- Ask learners to look at what Malik likes and say if they like the same things or not.
- Check as a class.

> **Answers**
> Learners' own answers.

4 Maze
- Ask learners to follow the lines to find out where Malik and his friends are going.
- They write where each person is going.

> **Answers**
> Malik is going to the swimming pool.
> Zak is going to the library.
> Anil is going to the park.
> Eva is going to the shop.

I can talk about places I like.
- Direct learners' attention to the self-evaluation question at the top of page 100. Ask them to think and answer. Emphasise the importance of giving an honest answer.

> **Answers**
> Learners' own answers.

> **Differentiated instruction**
> **Additional support and practice**
> - In small groups or as a class divided into two teams, learners play a spelling game to review new vocabulary.
>
> **Extend and challenge**
> - Learners write down the conversations they had with their friends in **Activity 5** of the Learner's Book.
> - **Portfolio opportunity:** When learners have finished, ask them to write their names and the date, and file the work in their portfolios.

Lesson 2: Find out more

Cafés in different places
Learner's Book pages: 120–121
Activity Book pages: 102–103

Lesson objectives
Listening: Listen for information.
Speaking: Talk about unusual cafés, talk about food, role play.
Reading: Read for information, read about unusual cafés.
Writing: Guided writing.
Critical thinking: Apply information, make connections and inferences, compare and contrast.

Language focus: *Would you like something to drink? How about …? I'd like some …, please Can I have some …?*
Vocabulary: *menu, drinks, pizza, cake, banana, orange juice, apple juice, lemonade, strawberry milkshake, chocolate, tomato, cheese, olives, pepper, honey, lemon*

Materials: Sheets of paper, file cards, writing supplies.

Warm up
- Learners do the warm-up routine.
- Ask learners to recite the haiku from **Lesson 1**.
- Elicit from them information they remember from **Lesson 1**, e.g. *What was the lesson about? What places in town do you like most?*

1 Before you read 84 [CD2 Track 33]
- As a class discuss the question with learners. Encourage them to describe the cafés they have been to.
- Focus on the pictures and ask learners if there are places like these in their city.
- **Critical thinking:** Learners compare and contrast the cafés in the pictures with cafés in their city. How similar or different are they? Can children go to these places?
- Tell learners that they are going to listen to the audio recording about these places. They listen and follow in their books. Play the audio recording at least twice.
- What new information have they found about the cafés? Ask them to choose which one they would like to go to and explain why.
- Are there any words they don't know? Remind learners to use the photos and the context to understand them.
- Elicit from learners the difference between a *city* and a *town*, e.g. a city is bigger.

> **Audioscript:** Track 84. See Learner's Book page 120.

> **Answers**
> Learners' own answers.

For further practice, see Activity 1 in the Activity Book.

2 Which café?

- Ask learners to re-read the text and decide which café each sentence is about.

> **Answers**
> 1 the jungle café
> 2 the tree house café
> 3 the tree house café
> 4 the tree house café
> 5 both cafés
> 6 the jungle café

3 What would you like to eat and drink? 85

[CD2 Track 34]

- Learners look at the menu. Ask them what things they like to eat and drink when they go to a café. Elicit some answers and write the words on the board.
- Tell them they are going to listen to Rosa and Josh talking to the waiter. Ask them to take notes of what Rosa and Josh order.
- Play the audio a few times. Check as a class.

> **Audioscript:** Track 85
> **Waiter:** Hello, Josh and Rosa. Welcome to our café! Would you like something to drink? Rosa?
> **Rosa:** Yes, please! I'd like some lemonade, please.
> **Waiter:** OK. A big glass or a small glass?
> **Rosa:** I'd like a big glass, please.
> **Waiter:** Great! A big glass of lemonade. And how about you, Josh?
> **Josh:** Er … I'd like a strawberry milkshake.
> **Waiter:** OK! Now … would you like something to eat, Rosa?
> **Rosa:** Let's have a pizza! How many toppings can we have?
> **Waiter:** You can have three toppings. Which would you like?
> **Rosa:** Er … I think I'll have olives and peppers.
> **Waiter:** How about some cheese, too?
> **Rosa:** Oh yes, I'll have some cheese, too.
> **Waiter:** So … that's one pizza, with cheese, olives and peppers. How about you, Josh?
> **Josh:** I don't like pizza very much.
> **Waiter:** Well … how about some cake, then? We have chocolate cake, honey cake and lemon cake. They're delicious.
> **Josh:** Oh yes, what a good idea. Can I have some chocolate cake, please?

> **Answers**
> **Rosa:** a big glass of lemonade + pizza with olives, peppers and cheese
> **Josh:** a strawberry milkshake + chocolate cake

4 Over to you!

- Play the audio recording (track 85) again. Focus on the language used by the waiter and the children. Ask learners to help you write the examples on the board.

- In pairs, ask them to role play the situation. They take it in turns to be the waiter and the customer.
- **Informal assessment opportunity:** Circulate, checking for correct pronunciation and use of language. Make notes of mistakes for remedial work.

> **Answers**
> Learners' own answers.

Wrap up

- Ask learners to show their café and the menu from **Activities 1** and **2** in the Activity Book and compare it with the rest of the class.

Activity Book

1 Read and draw

- Tell learners that they are going to finish off a drawing of a café. They have to think of a name for the café and write it on the line.
- They draw the extra items in the picture, following the instructions.
- **Portfolio opportunity:** You may ask learners to do this activity on a separate sheet of paper and answer the questions as a paragraph. Write the name and date and file it in their portfolios.

2 Make a menu

- Ask learners to make a menu for their café. They decide what food and drinks they will have and write them on the menu.
- You may wish to give learners drawing and writing supplies and make a 'real' menu on card or on a sheet of paper.

> **Answers**
> Learners' own answers.

3 What would you like to eat?

- After learners have finished **Activity 2**, they write what they say to the waiter. They choose something from their own menu and write it as a dialogue.
- **Portfolio opportunity:** Learners write their names and the date on their work. File the sheets in the learners' portfolios.
- **Home–school link:** Learners take their menus home and role play the dialogues with the family. They ask the family what their favourite food is.

> **Answers**
> Learners' own answers.

I can say what I would like to eat and drink.

- Direct learners' attention to the self-evaluation question at the top of page 102. Ask them to think and answer. Emphasise the importance of giving an honest answer.

Differentiated instruction

Additional support and practice

- Ask learners to write and illustrate sentences containing food vocabulary words. They can choose their favourite food and make the cards.

Extend and challenge

- 💬 Ask learners to work in pairs or small groups and find out information about a café in their city or region. They search the Internet for information about it and prepare a small poster.

Lesson 3: Words and sounds

Opposites and syllables

Learner's Book pages: 122–123
Activity Book pages: 104–105

Lesson objectives

Listening: Identify opposites.
Speaking: Read and sing a song, count syllables.
Reading: Read a song and a *haiku*.
Writing: Write a *haiku* following syllable rules.
Critical thinking skills: Memorise a poem.

Vocabulary: Opposites: *black/white, day/night, weak/strong, high/low, smile/frown, up/down, lost/found, sit/stand, yes/no, right/left, water/land, right/wrong, hot/cold, fast/slow, long/short, moon/sun*.

Materials: Writing supplies, copies of **Photocopiable activity 17**.

Learner's Book

🔁 Warm up

- Learners do the warm-up routine.
- Ask learners about their family's favourite food. Encourage them to use the structures *So do I/I don't*, e.g. *My father likes coffee. I don't.*

> **Answers**
> Learners' own answers.

1 🎵 Sing an opposites song 86 [CD2 Track 35]

- Tell learners they are going to listen and sing an opposites song. Ask them to read the words of the song through before they listen, taking the separate blue and green parts.
- Play the audio a few times and encourage learners to join in.

Audioscript: Track 86. See Learner's Book page 122.

2 💬 Find the opposites

- In pairs learners look at the picture on page 122 of the Learner's Book and find the opposites. Ask them to write them down.
- Check as a class. Ask learners to help you write the list on the board.

> **Answers**
> black/white; day/night; weak/strong; high/low; smile/frown; up/down; lost/found; sit/stand; yes/no; right/left; water/land; right/wrong; hot/cold; fast/slow; long/short; moon/sun

📘 For further practice, see Activities 1 and 2 in the Activity Book.

2 💬 📘 How many syllables?

- Ask learners to work in pairs. They focus on the picture and clap according to the number of syllables.
- Explain and demonstrate first with some of the words and ask learners to clap along with you.
- Circulate, checking learners have correctly understood the activity and helping if necessary.

> **Answers**
> hospital - 3 syllables
> skyscraper - 3 syllables
> school - 1 syllable
> museum - 3 syllables
> farm - 1 syllable
> mountains - 2 syllables
> market - 2 syllables
> shopping centre - 4 syllables
> river - 2 syllables
> desert - 2 syllables

📘 For further practice, see Activity 3 in the Activity Book.

3 ✏️ 💬 Write a desert *haiku* 87 [CD2 Track 36]

- Remind learners of the *haikus* they learnt in **Unit 7** and in **Lesson 1** of this unit. Invite them to recite the *haikus* they wrote.
- Tell them they are going to listen to a desert *haiku*.
- Look at the description of what a desert is. Ask them if there is a desert where they live. Do they know the names of famous deserts?
- Play the audio a few times. Ask learners to count and clap the syllables in each line.
- Ask learners to work in pairs and write a *haiku* about their playground. Each learners should have a copy of the *haiku*.
- **Informal assessment opportunity:** In **Unit 7**, the activity offered the option of following the syllable count rules as a challenge. Here, after their work on syllables, learners should be able to attempt writing a proper *haiku* with the correct number of syllables.
- **Portfolio opportunity:** Ask learners to write their names and the date on the *haikus* and file them in learners' portfolios.

Audioscript: Track 87. See Learner's Book page 123.

[AB] For further practice, see Challenge in the Activity Book.

Wrap up
- When learners have writen the *haikus*, they recite them to the class.
- **Home–school link:** Learners take their *haikus* home and show them to the family.

Activity Book

1 Opposites
- Ask learners to look at the two lists and match the opposites.

> **Answers**
> up — down
> right — wrong
> lost — found
> strong — weak
> low — high
> hot — cold

2 Change the picture
- Ask learners to read the instructions and change the picture.

> **Answers**
> Learners' own answers.

3 How many syllables?
- Ask learners to count the syllables in each word. Then, they write the number on the line.

> **Answers**
> market 2
> hospital 3
> desert 2
> shopping centre 4
> helicopter 4
> river 2
> farm 1
> swimming pool 3
> café 2

Challenge
- Ask learners to write a *haiku* about one of the places shown or about a different place that they like. They answer if their place is in the city or outside the city.
- They write their *haiku* on a separate sheet of paper or card and then they may draw a picture.
- **Portfolio opportunity:** Ask learners to write their names and the date on the *haikus* and file them in learners' portfolios.

I can count syllables.
- Direct learners' attention to the self-evaluation question at the top of page 104. Ask them to think and answer. Emphasise the importance of giving an honest answer.

> **Answers**
> Learners' own answers.

Differentiated instruction
Additional support and practice
- Give learners copies of **Photocopiable acitivity 17**. Focus on the table and count the syllables in the examples. Tell learners look at *The City* section of the **Picture dictionary** and write down words in different categories with the corresponding number of syllables.

Extend and challenge
- As an extension of the previous activity, you may ask learners to work in pairs or small groups. Ask each pair or group to focus on a different topic in the **Picture dictionary**.
- Ask them to find one or two examples for each category. There are sections in which most are short 1- or 2-syllable words, so perhaps you may ask them to look at two sections instead of one.
- After learners have done **Photocopiable activity 17**, ask them to choose a few words and write a poem, a tongue-twister or a riddle. Encourage them to re-visit previous units to find models.
- **Portfolio opportunity:** Learners write their name and the date on the poems. File them in their portfolios.

Lesson 4: Use of English
Choosing and comparing
Learner's Book pages: 124–125
Activity Book pages: 106–107

> **Lesson objectives**
> **Listening:** Listen for information.
> **Speaking:** Role play, compare places.
> **Reading:** Read for information.
> **Writing:** Guided writing, answer questions.
>
> **Language focus:** *Where/what would you like to …?;* comparative adjectives: *-er, more + adjective, better.*
> **Vocabulary**: *swim, play, climb, have fun, go to, see, mountains, beach, amusement park, city, desert*

> **Materials**: Writing and drawing supplies, file cards, sheets of paper, pictures of different holiday places.

Learner's Book

⇨ Warm up

- Do the warm-up routine.
- Ask learners if they ever go on holiday. Focus on the pictures. Have they ever been to any of those places? Where did they go the last time?
- Elicit as much information as possible, e.g. what they saw and did, what they liked most.

Answers
Learners' own answers.

1 Choosing a holiday 88 [CD2 Track 37]

- Tell learners that they are going to listen to a conversation between Josh and Rosa and their mother about the holidays.
- Tell them to find out where the children would like to go and what they would like to do there. Play the audio at least twice and elicit the answers.

Audioscript: Track 88

Mum: Let's go on holiday. Where would you like to go, Rosa? Would you like to go to the beach?

Rosa: No, I'd like to go to the mountains. The mountains are more exciting than the beach.

Mum: What would you like to do there?

Rosa: I'd like to climb a mountain.

Mum: How about you, Josh? Where would *you* like to go?

Josh: I'd like to go to the beach. The beach is nicer than the mountains.

Answers
Josh – the beach; Rosa – the mountains
Josh – because the beach is nicer than the mountains;
Rosa – because she would like to climb a mountain

2 💬 Where would you like to go?

- Focus on the photos in **Activity 1**. Elicit something you can do in each place.
- In pairs, learners talk with their partner about the places they would like to go to and what they would do there.
- **Informal assessment opportunity:** Circulate, listening to the conversations and noting down mistakes for remedial work. Make notes on good performance and file them in the learners' portfolios.

Answers
Learners' own answers.

3 ✏️ Draw and write

- When they have finished **Activity 2**, learners draw the place they would like to go to and write a sentence about it.
- More proficient learners may write more than one sentence.

- **Portfolio opportunity:** Collect the pictures, write the names and dates on them and file them in learners' portfolios.

Answers
Learners' own answers.

4 Comparing places

- Look at the list of comparative adjectives in the **Word box** and elicit the meaning.
- Focus on the rules for making comparative adjectives and provide more examples on the board. Also provide more detailed explanations of spelling of comparatives, e.g. doubling consonants as in *bigger, funnier*.
- As a class, talk about the places in the photos in **Activity 1**.
- Turn learners' attention to the **Language detective box**. Focus on the irregular comparative of *good*. You may also add the irregular comparative of *bad – worse*.

Answers
Learners' own answers.

[AB] For further practice, see Activities 1, 2 and 3 in the Activity Book.

⇨ Wrap up

- Ask learners to show their work from **Activity 3** in the Activity Book and tell the class about their ideal holiday.
- **Home–school link:** Learners take their work home and tell their family about holiday places.

Activity Book

1 Talking about places

- Ask learners to look at the pictures of two hotels and answer the questions. When they have finished, check as a class.

Answers
1 **Which hotel is bigger?** Hotel Black Cloud
2 **Which hotel is more fun?** Hotel Blue Sky
3 **Which hotel is more scary?** Hotel Black Cloud
4 **Which hotel is more beautiful?** Hotel Blue Sky
5 **Which hotel is nicer?** Hotel Blue Sky
6 **Which hotel would you like to go to for your holiday?**
Learners' own answers.

2 Comparing things

- Ask learners to write a sentence comparing the two things in the pictures. Check that they use the correct form of the word next to the pictures.

Answers
1 slower
2 more beautiful
3 taller
4 smaller

UNIT 9 Inside and outside cities Lesson 4   119

3 Draw and write

- Learners draw a picture of a place where they would like to go on holiday.
- Then, they write a short paragraph using the questions as a guide.
- **Portfolio opportunity:** You may ask learners to do this activity on a separate sheet of paper and then file it in their portfolios.

> **Answers**
> Learners' own answers.

I can compare places.

- Direct learners' attention to the self-evaluation question at the top of page 106. Ask them to think and answer. Emphasise the importance of giving an honest answer.

> **Answers**
> Learners' own answers.

> **Differentiated instruction**
>
> **Additional support and practice**
>
> - Ask learners to choose comparative forms of adjectives from the lesson and write sentences. They also draw pictures to illustrate them.
>
> **Extend and challenge**
>
> - Ask learners to look for adjectives in previous units. Then, they turn them into the comparative. They make a list with the base form and the comparative form. Then, they write sentences with some of the adjectives. You could give learners some old magazines for them to cut out pictures they like and illustrate the sentences.

Lesson 5: Read and respond

Learner's Book pages: 126–127
Activity Book pages: 108–109

> **Lesson objectives**
>
> **Listening:** Listen to a story.
> **Speaking:** Discuss and act out a story.
> **Reading:** Read a story, recognise sight words: *something, want, great, come.*
> **Writing:** Answer questions.
> **Critical thinking:** Use context to find the meaning of words, act out a story.
>
> **Vocabulary**: *change places, show, wonderful, bright lights, party, amazing, picnic, berries, nuts, hide, owl, scary*
>
> **Materials: Photocopiable activity 18**, lollipop sticks, scissors, glue, card to mount the puppets, coloured pencils.

Learner's Book

Warm up

- Do the warm-up routine.
- Focus on the pictures and ask learners to predict what the text is going to be about. Do they know this story?
- *The City Mouse and the Country Mouse* is a very old story. It first appeared as one of '*Aesop's fables.*' This is an updated version.

1 Before you read 89 [CD2 Track 38]

- Discuss with learners what they like more, the city or the countryside. Ask them to give reasons for their answers. Are they 'city mice' or 'country mice'?
- Tell learners that they are going to listen to the story. They listen and follow in their books.
- Draw attention to the difference between *scary/scared* and to the different pronunciation of hard and soft **c** in: *city, Cindy; country, Callie, Carlos, cat, picnic.*

> **Audioscript:** Track 89. See Learner's Book pages 126–129.

> **Answers**
> Learners' own answers.

2 Talk about it

- Discuss the story as a class. Focus on the questions and elicit answers from learners.
- **Informal assessment opportunity:** Circulate, listening to learners' questions and answers. Take notes for remedial work.

> **Answers**
> 1 **What did Callie like about the city?** She liked it because the streets were full of life. There were shops and cafés, bright lights and music. She said it was amazing.
> 2 **What didn't Callie like about the city?** It was too scary.
> 3 **What did Cindy like about the country?** She liked it because it was beautiful.
> 4 **What didn't Cindy like about the country?** It was too scary.

For further practice, see Activities 1 and 2 in the Activity Book.

3 Act out the story

- Ask learners to work in small groups. They decide which character they want to be and they rehearse the story.

> **Answers**
> Learners' own answers.

4 Write and draw

- Prepare the learners for this activity. Come up with some ideas through an oral discussion as some learners may be familiar only with one or other environment.
- Provide a list of things or show pictures from magazines, e.g. birds and animals, a cinema, lots of cars, a farm, mountains, an underground train. Learners decide where they would find them, town or country or both.

- You could make a graphic representation on the board through a Venn diagram and ask learners to fill it in.
- Then they write their sentences. You may wish to ask them to write them on a separate sheet of paper and then make a picture to accompany their text.
- **Informal assessment opportunity:** Circulate, asking questions and checking how they are progressing through the activity.

> **Answers**
> Learners' own answers.

Words to remember

- Write the words *something, want, great, come* on the board.
- Learners look for these sight words in the lesson. How many times do they see each word?
- Ask them to take it in turns to practise spelling them.
- They could make sentences using them.
- Can learners find these words in previous lessons in this unit? Ask them to read the sentences where they appear.

> **Answers**
> Learners' own answers.

Wrap up

- When they have finished **Activity 4**, ask learners to show their pictures and read their texts to the class.
- **Portfolio opportunity:** File the learners' work in their portfolios.
- **Home–school link:** Learners tell the family the fable.

Activity Book

1 Write the words

- Ask learners to look at the words and put the letters in the correct order.
- Then, they write the words on the lines and circle the things that they usually find in the city.

> **Answers**
> 1 shop 2 café 3 nuts 4 building 5 owl 6 bees 7 taxi

Challenge

- Tell learners that the story is a *fable*. Explain that a fable is a special kind of story where we learn something.
- Encourage them to reflect about what they learn from this story. They tick ✓ the best answer.

> **Answers**
> We like the places that we know best.

2 Cindy or Callie?

- Learners read the sentences and write Cindy or Callie next to each sentence.

> **Answers**
> 1 **A cat scared her.** Callie
> 2 **An owl scared her.** Cindy
> 3 **She liked the city better than the country.** Cindy
> 4 **She liked the country better than the city.** Callie

3 Mystery picture

- Tell learners to join the dots starting from number 1 to discover the mystery picture.
- They answer the questions.

> **Answers**
> **What animal is this?** Owl.
> **Does it live in the city or the countryside?** It lives in the countryside.

Challenge

- Ask learners to answer the question and provide reasons for their answer.

> **Answers**
> Learners' own answers.

I can read, talk about and act out a story.

- Direct learners' attention to the self-evaluation question at the top of page 108. Ask them to think and answer. Emphasise the importance of giving an honest answer.

> **Answers**
> Learners' own answers.

Differentiated instruction

Additional support and practice

- Divide the class into pairs and give each pair a copy of **Photocopiable activity 18**.
- Learners cut out the characters of the Country mouse and the City mouse and colour them. Then they mount them on card and glue them onto lollipop sticks to make puppets.
- When the puppets are ready, learners use them to act out the story.

Extend and challenge

- Ask learners to search the Internet or the school library and look for more fables. They choose one and tell or read it to the class.

Lesson 6: Choose a project

What can we do in the town and the countryside?

Learner's Book pages: 130–131
Activity Book pages: 110–111

Lesson objectives

Listening: Listen and follow instructions, listen to comprehension items in the Activity Book quiz.
Speaking: Present your project to the class, recite a poem.
Reading: Read instructions, read Activity Book quiz items.
Writing: Write factual information, write a poem, write answers in the Activity Book quiz.

Language focus: Unit 9 Review

Materials

A Make a book of poems: writing and drawing supplies, sheets of card or paper, glue.
B Make your own café: drawing supplies, sheets of paper, glue, pictures from magazines.
C Make a travel poster: writing and drawing supplies, sheets of paper.
Photocopiable activity 19.

Learner's Book

Warm up

- Do the warm-up routine.
- Recap with learners what they have learnt in this unit. What things have they liked most? What new things have they learnt? What kinds of holidays do they like most? What is their favorite word in this unit?

> **Answers**
> Learners' own answers.

Choose a project

- Learners choose an end-of-unit project to work on. Look at the examples in the pictures and help them choose. Provide materials. All the projects are done in groups.

A Make a book of poems
- Read the directions in the Learner's Book. Give out drawing and writing supplies.
- Learners write poems about places they like.
- Learners draw the pictures or collect pictures from magazines. They make the book.
- They display their books and read the poems to the class.

B Make your own café
- Read the instructions and give learners writing and drawing materials.
- They discuss the questions and the menu.
- They write the menu and roleplay the situations.

C Make a travel poster
- Read and explain the instructions.
- Learners decide where they would like to go and look for information and pictures.
- They make the poster and write their description of the holiday.
- Circulate as learners work. Informally assess their receptive and productive language skills. Ask questions. You may want to take notes on their responses. Provide help with vocabulary and grammar if requested.
- **Portfolio opportunity:** If possible, ask parents to visit the class and display the learners' work. Then file the projects, photos or scans of the work, in learners' portfolios. Write the date on the work.

Look what I can do!

- Review the *I can …* statements. Learners demonstrate what they can do.

Discuss with learners what they have learned in this unit. Remind them of the Big question and ask them what things we can do in the town and in the countryside.

Activity Book

Unit 9 quiz: Look what I can do!

Listen 98 [CD2 Track 47]

- Do the first item as a class. Play the audio several times.

Listen and write

- Learners listen and answer the questions.

Read and write

- Learners read and answer the questions.

> **Audioscript:** Track 98
> **1 Adult:** We <u>must</u> wear our safety belts in the car.
> **Child:** OK, I know.
> **2 Boy:** Excuse me. Have you got any books about life in the country?
> **Woman:** Here's a book about animals in the country. Would you like this one?
> **Boy:** Thank you. That looks interesting.
> **3 Waitress:** Hello, would you like something to eat?
> **Girl:** Er … can I have some honey cake, please?
> **Waitress:** Yes, of course. Here you are.
> **Girl:** Thank you. I love cake.

4 Waitress: How about something to drink? Some water, perhaps?

Boy: I'd like some orange juice, please.

Waitress: A big or a small glass?

Boy: Small, please.

5 Woman 1: I'd like to go to a big city for my holiday.

Woman 2: Why? Don't you like the countryside?

Woman 1: Yes, I do – but I'd like to see museums and skyscrapers and I'd like to go shopping.

Woman 2: That sounds exciting!

6 skyscraper

7 market

Answers
1. b
2. a
3. b
4. b
5. b
6. 3
7. 2
8. stand
9. (suggested answer) She's in a café. She's drinking.
10. (suggested answer) They are in the countryside. They are eating/having a picnic.

- Make up a certificate for each learner using **Photocopiable activity 19**.
  Don't forget to celebrate their achievements!

Photocopiable activities

Photocopiable activity 1: Weather symbols

cloudy	windy	rainy
sunny	snowy	cold
hot	cool	warm

124 Cambridge Global English Stage 2 Teacher's Resource © Cambridge University Press 2014

Unit 1

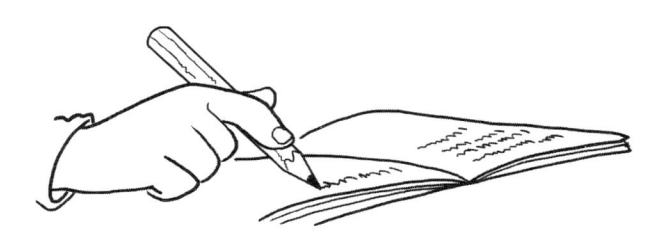

Photocopiable activity 2: Writer's checklist A

Words that begin with a capital letter

☐ The first word of a sentence begins with a capital letter.
This is a book.

☐ The word *I* is always written with a capital I.

☐ A name begins with a capital letter.
Tanya   Mr Kim

☐ The name of a city, country, or school begins with a capital letter.
Mecca   Korea   International School

☐ The days of the week begin with a capital letter.
Monday   Tuesday

☐ The names of the months begin with a capital letter.
January   February

Unit 1

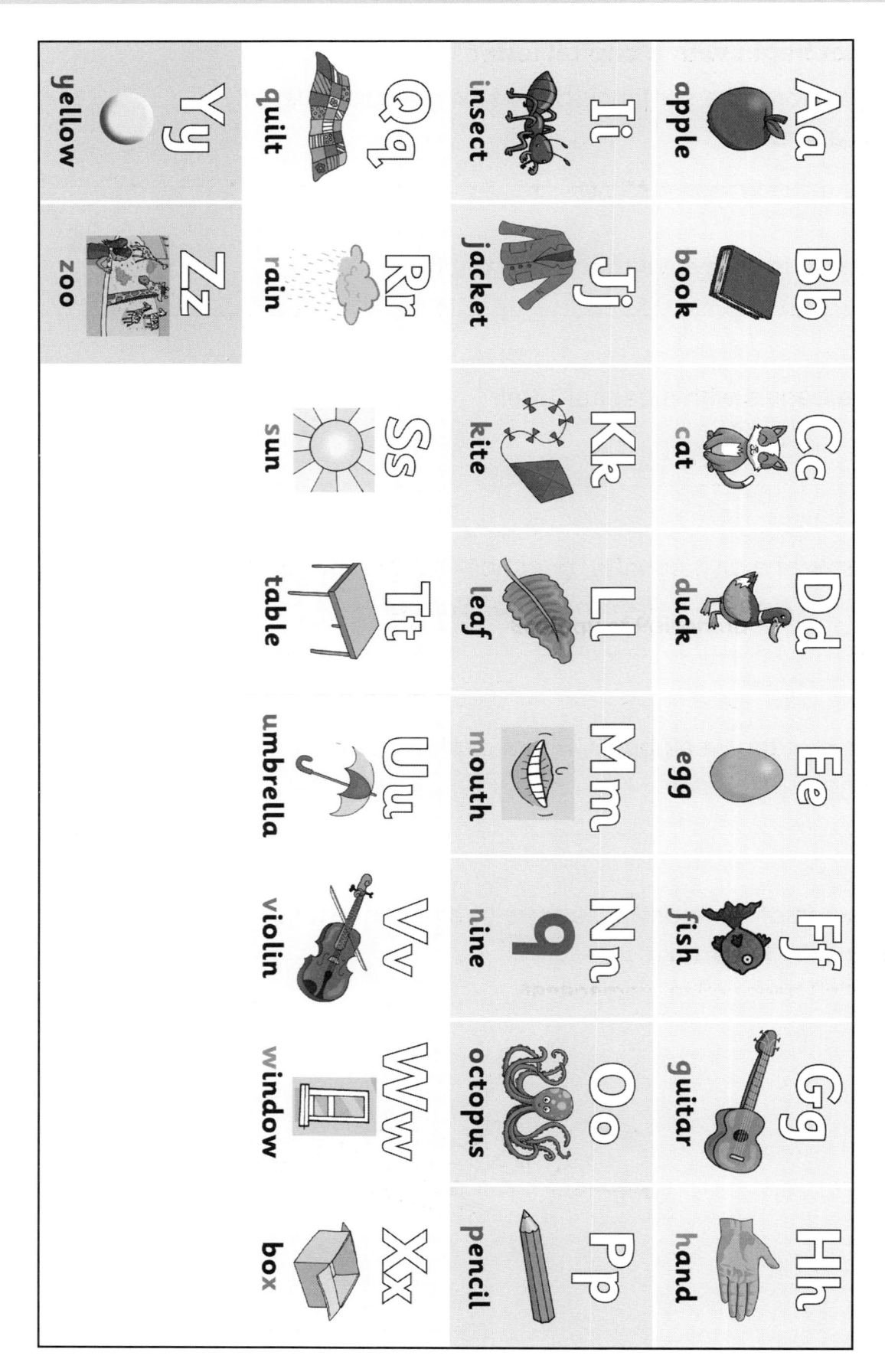

Photocopiable activity 3: The alphabet in pictures

Aa apple	Ii insect	Qq quilt	Yy yellow
Bb book	Jj jacket	Rr rain	Zz zoo
Cc cat	Kk kite	Ss sun	
Dd duck	Ll leaf	Tt table	
Ee egg	Mm mouth	Uu umbrella	
Ff fish	Nn nine	Vv violin	
Gg guitar	Oo octopus	Ww window	
Hh hand	Pp pencil	Xx box	

126 Cambridge Global English Stage 2 Teacher's Resource © Cambridge University Press 2014

Unit 1

Photocopiable activity 4: Have you got a book?

hairbrush	skipping rope	jacket
book	jumper	pencil
camera	lunchbox	sock

Cambridge Global English Stage 2 Teacher's Resource © Cambridge University Press 2014

Unit 2

Photocopiable activity 5: Writer's checklist B

Final punctuation

☐ Most sentences end with a full stop.
   My name is Tony. ←

☐ A question ends with a question mark.
   What's your name? ←

☐ A sentence that shows surprise or excitement ends with an exclamation mark.
   My name is Tony, too! ←

Check the verb form!
Present simple

We usually add 's' to a verb after one person or thing.

I sing.   *The boy sings.*   *The birds sing.*

With verbs that end in **sh, ch, ss,** or **x**, we add **'es'**.

*I wash   Amy washes   Tomas and Daniel wash
my hands.   her hands.   their hands.*

Present continuous

Use *I am …, You are …, He is … She is …, We are … They are …*

I am talking.   **We are** waving.
You are walking.   **You are** eating.
He is sitting. **She is** standing.   **They are** painting.

Unit 2

Photocopiable activity 6: Treasure hunt

	A	B	C
1			
2			
3			

Unit 3

Photocopiable activity 7: Pick a colour, pick a number

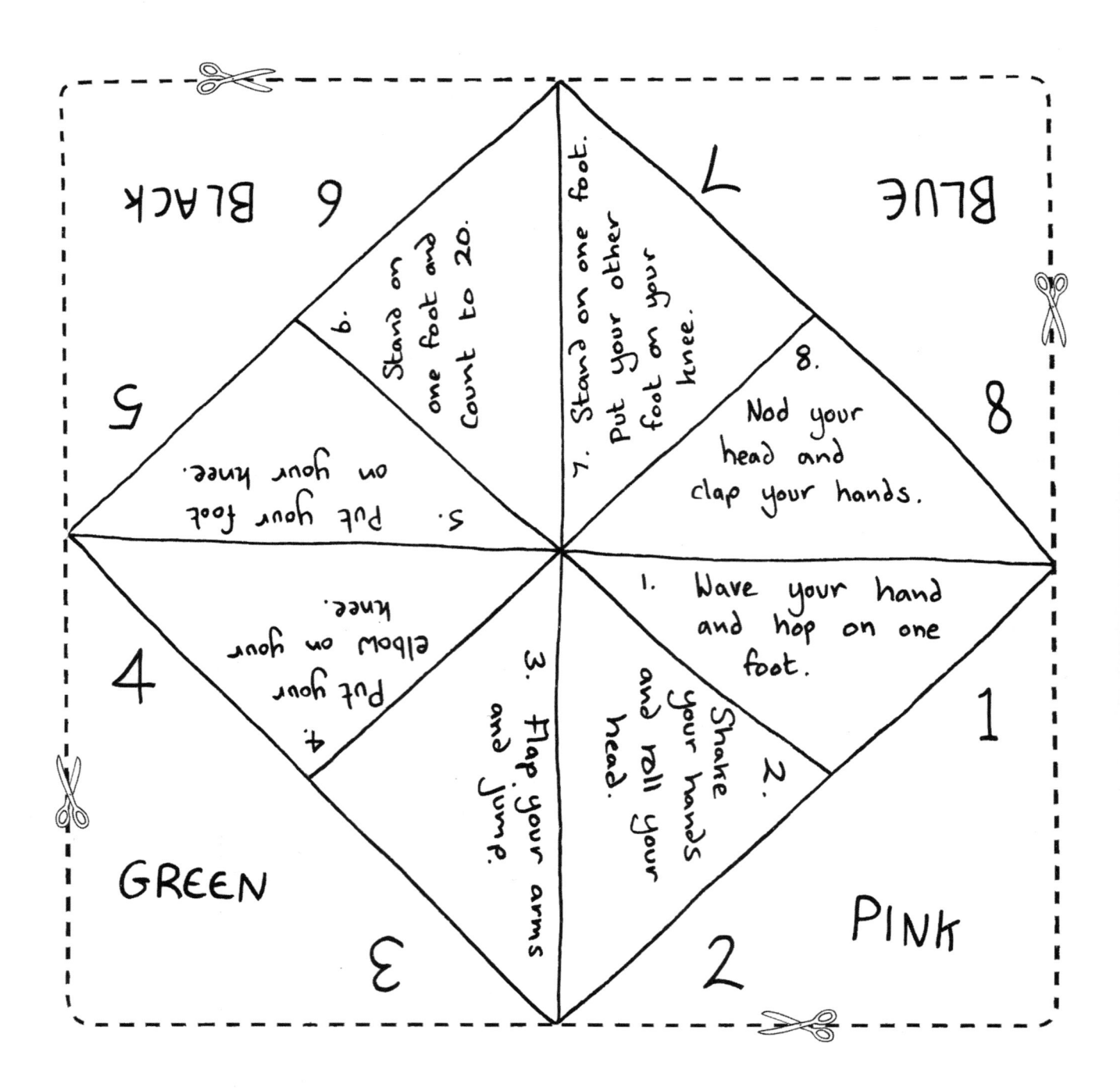

Corners (colours): BLACK, BLUE, PINK, GREEN
Numbers around edges: 6, 7, 8, 1, 2, 3, 4, 5

Flap contents:
- 6. Stand on one foot and count to 20.
- 7. Stand on one other foot. Put your other foot on your knee.
- 8. Nod your head and clap your hands.
- 1. Wave your hand and hop on one foot.
- 2. Shake your hands and roll your head.
- 3. Flap your arms and jump.
- 4. Put your elbow on your knee.
- 5. Put your foot on your knee.

1 Cut out the square. Fold the 4 corners into the centre.

2 <u>Turn the paper over.</u> Fold the 4 corners into the centre.

3 Fold the paper so it looks like this.

4 Put your thumb and pointer fingers under the colour flaps. Practise opening and closing.

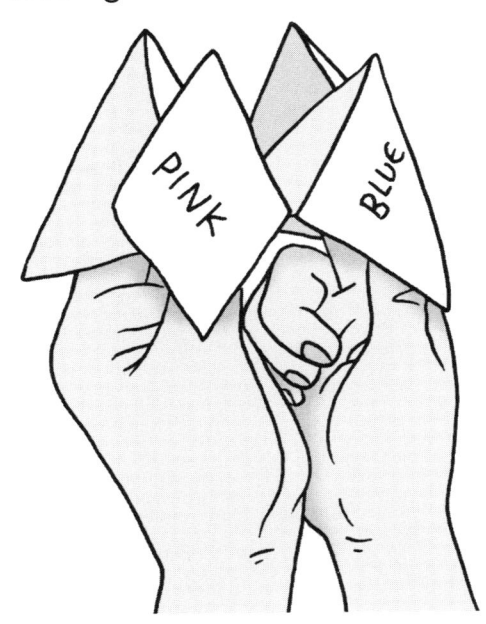

Unit 4

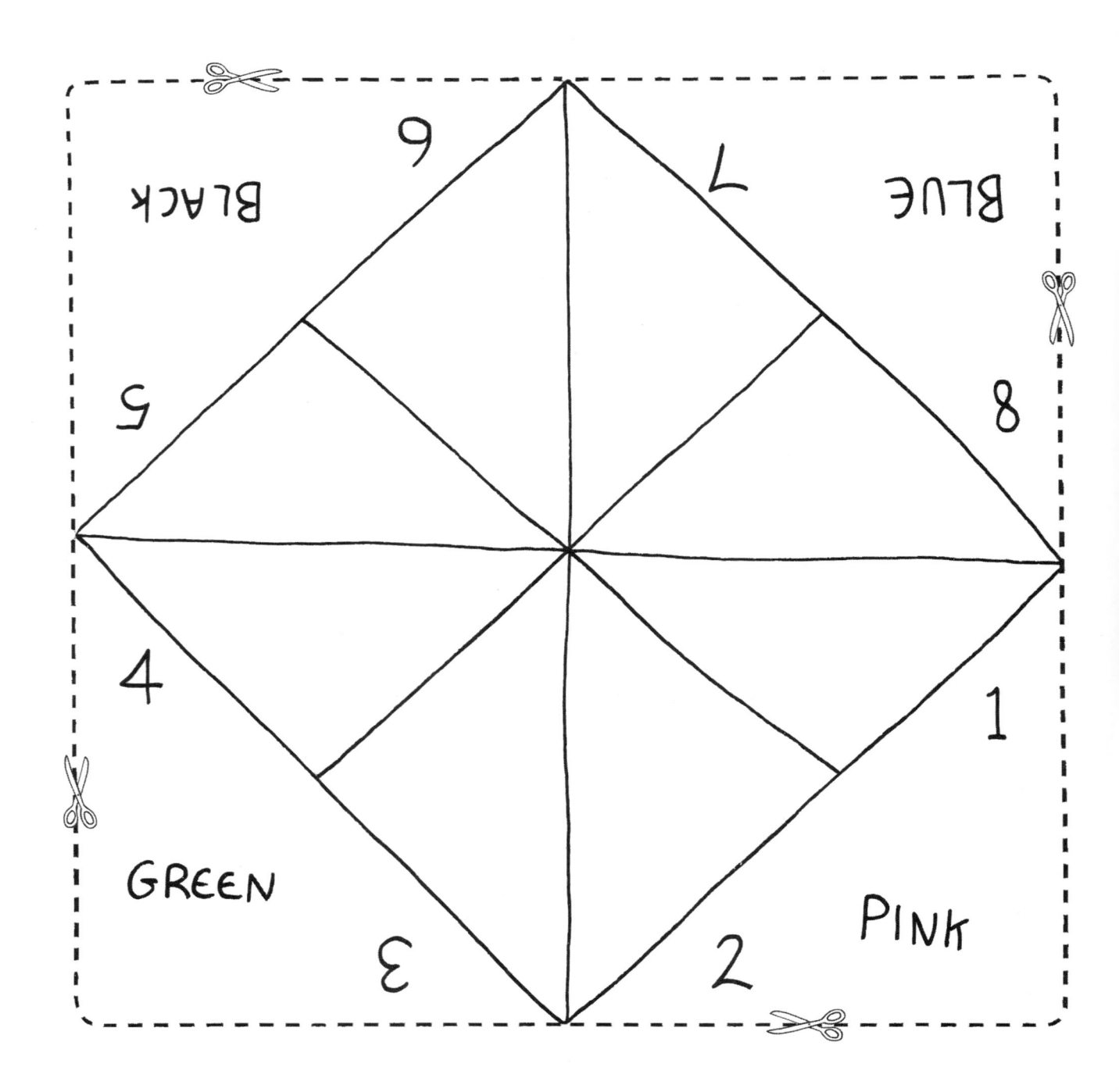

Photocopiable activity 8: Pick a colour, pick a number — Make your own game!

132 Cambridge Global English Stage 2 Teacher's Resource © Cambridge University Press 2014

Unit 4

Photocopiable activity 9: Make a hand shadow

Unit 5

Photocopiable activity 10: Group game – SMILE!

☺☺ SMILE! ☺☺				
S (numbers **50–59**)	M (numbers **60–69**)	I (numbers **70–79**)	L (numbers **80–89**)	E (numbers **90–99**)

☺☺ SMILE! ☺☺				
S (numbers 50–59)	M (numbers 60–69)	I (numbers 70–79)	L (numbers 80–89)	E (numbers 90–99)
57	61	70	86	93
51	69	72	88	96
50	66	73	84	94
58	64	77	89	95
53	62	75	80	92

Unit 5

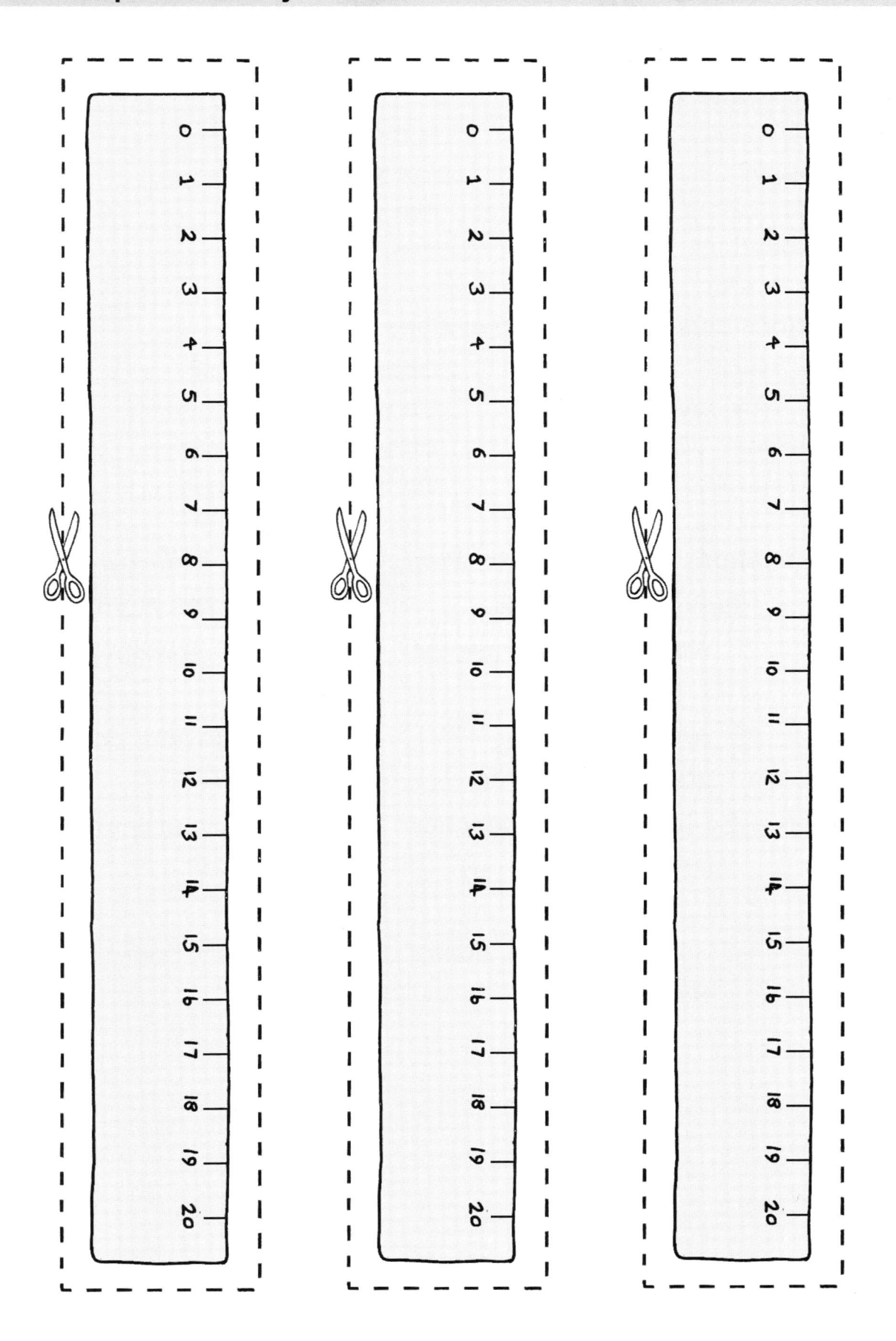

Photocopiable activity 11: Ruler

Cambridge Global English Stage 2 Teacher's Resource © Cambridge University Press 2014 135

Unit 6

Photocopiable activity 12: Writer's guide

Writing questions: Present simple

Yes/No questions with *to be*

- ☐ **Am I** late? _____
- ☐ **Are you** happy? _____
- ☐ **Is she** tired? _____
- ☐ **Is he** at home? _____

- ☐ **Is it** on the table? _____
- ☐ **Are we** ready? _____
- ☐ **Are you** wet? _____
- ☐ **Are they** big? _____

Yes/No questions beginning with *Do* or *Does*

- ☐ **Do I** have a pencil? _____
- ☐ **Do you** like rainy days? _____
- ☐ **Does she** watch TV? _____
- ☐ **Does he** ride a bike? _____

- ☐ **Does it** have wings? _____
- ☐ **Do we** know the answer? _____
- ☐ **Do you** see the birds? _____
- ☐ **Do they** play football? _____

Information questions beginning with *What, Where, How,* and *How many*?

you	1 person or animal	lots of people or animals
☐ What **do you** eat?	☐ What **does a mouse** eat?	☐ What **do spiders** eat?
☐ Where **do you** live?	☐ Where **does your grandmother** live?	☐ Where **do your cousins** live?
☐ How **do you** get to school?	☐ How **does your teacher** get to school?	☐ How **do your friends** get to school?
☐ How many books **do you** have?	☐ How many books **does she** have?	☐ How many books **do they** have?

Unit 6

Photocopiable activity 13: Project C – Cartoon story *The boy and the bug*

Draw and write a cartoon story about a boy and a bug. How are they different?
- Choose your bug. What will you write about – an ant, a cricket, or a bee?
- Write what the boy says.
- Draw your cartoon bug and write what your bug says.

I have _____

I have _____

Draw your bug here

I can _____

I can _____

Draw your bug here

Unit 7

Photocopiable activity 14: Write a poem

Haiku
An old silent pond ...
A frog jumps into the pond,
Splash! Silence again.
Matsuo Basho

A *haiku* is a short poem about nature. There are 3 lines in a *haiku*.
- The first line has 5 syllables.
- The second line has 7 syllables.
- The third line has 5 syllable.

Read the *haiku* again. Count the syllables in each line.

Now write your own 3-line poem about nature. Here are some ideas for a first line. Use one of these lines or think of a new one.

A ripe red pepper
On a small green leaf
The wind in the trees
I watch a spider
My favourite rock

CHALLENGE: As a challenge, you can follow the syllable rules for writing a *haiku*. Or you can just write a 3-line poem. Draw a picture to go with your poem.

_____ (5 syllables)

_____ (7 syllables)

_____ (5 syllables)

Unit 8

Photocopiable activity 15: Rooms in a house

Cut out the objects from **Photocopiable activity 16** and put them in these rooms.

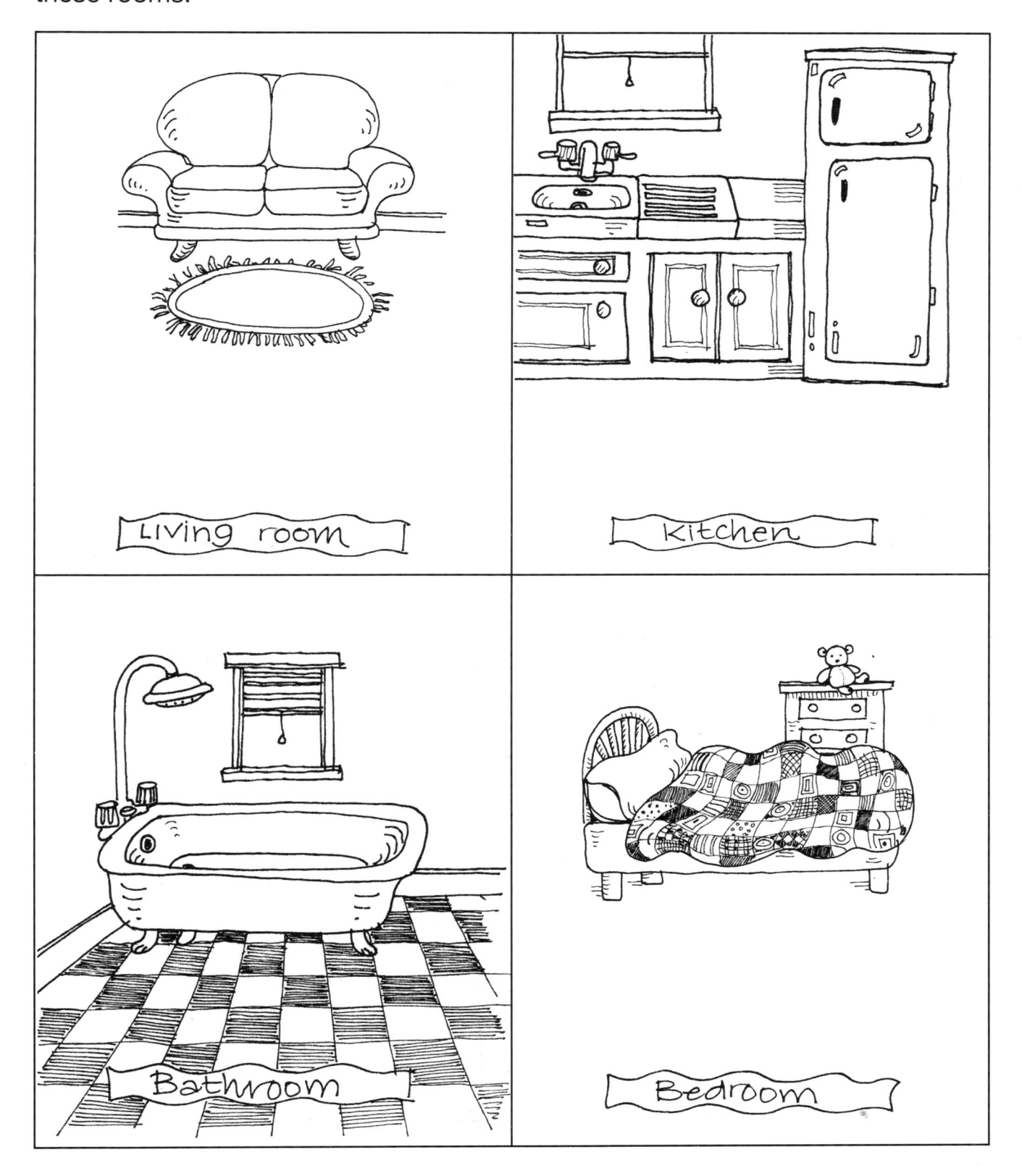

Living room

Kitchen

Bathroom

Bedroom

Unit 8

Photocopiable activity 16: Objects in a house

Cut out these objects and put them in the rooms on **Photocopiable activity 15**.

140 Cambridge Global English Stage 2 Teacher's Resource © Cambridge University Press 2014

Unit 9

Photocopiable activity 17: How many syllables?

1 syllable	2 syllables	3 syllables	4 syllables
farm	market	skyscraper	shopping centre

Unit 9

Photocopiable activity 18: Finger puppets – City mouse, Country mouse

142   Cambridge Global English Stage 2 Teacher's Resource © Cambridge University Press 2014

End of book

Photocopiable activity 19: Congratulations certificate for completing Stage 2 of *Cambridge Global English*

Congratulations!

You have completed Stage 2 of *Cambridge Global English*.

Name: _____

Class: _____

Teacher: _____

Well done!

Photocopiable word lists

Unit 1

amazing	cupboard	recipe
author	dinosaur	scary
backpack	fiction	skipping rope
bookcase	hairbrush	tablet
camera	information	volcano
chapter	jumper	whisper
character	lunchbox	

Unit 2

address	geography	toyshop
balcony	ladder	treasure
bookshop	neighbourhood	unfriendly
bridge	nurse	unhappy
clue	rescue	uniform
continent	street cleaner	world
firefighter	taxi driver	

Unit 3

clap	hungry	shopping
excited	kiwi	skipping
feathers	ostrich	swan
fingernail	penguin	swimming
foot	ridiculous	tired
hand	scared	wiggle
head	shake	

Unit 4

astronomer	measure	submarine
astronomy	moon	sun
calendar	moonlight	sunlight
camera	nightclothes	telescope
cloudy	planet	watch
daylight	rainy	windy
drop	spaceship	

Unit 5

antelope	circle	leopard
bread	cottage	racehorse
breakfast	elephant	rectangle
centimetres	fence	square
chalk	grapes	tricky
cherries	juice	wide
chimpanzee	leaf	

Unit 6

antennae	cricket	smell
beetle	feel	spider
bite	helpful	taste
blow	honey	trail
butterfly	scare	web
chase	seed	worm
communicate	silkworm	yelp

Unit 7

bean	fruit	recycle
biography	furniture	roots
breathe	hole	soil
carrot	leaves	tomato
cycling	litter	village
firewood	mango	wood
fishing	pineapple	

Unit 8

bathroom	mushroom	sword
beaver	railing	termite
beehive	roundabout	tunnel
curvy	sharp	underwater
hive	shower	wolf
huge	skyscraper	wooden
kitchen	straight	

Unit 9

ambulance	honey	olives
beach	hospital	pepper
cheese	lemonade	shopping centre
chocolate	library	strawberry
climb	milkshake	swim
entrance	mountains	tomato
helicopter	museum	